KU-167-050

MEN AND WOMEN
IN HISTORY

MEN AND WOMEN
IN HISTORY

R. J. UNSTEAD

ADAM & CHARLES BLACK

FIRST PUBLISHED IN ONE VOLUME 1967
A. & C. BLACK LTD
4, 5 & 6 SOHO SQUARE   LONDON W.1

AVAILABLE ALSO IN FOUR PARTS

Also by R. J. Unstead

LOOKING AT HISTORY
PEOPLE IN HISTORY
LOOKING AT ANCIENT HISTORY
A HISTORY OF BRITAIN
TRAVEL BY ROAD
A HISTORY OF HOUSES
MONASTERIES
EARLY TIMES
TEACHING HISTORY
IN THE JUNIOR SCHOOL

© 1967 A. & C. BLACK LTD
SBN 7136 0153 1
MADE AND PRINTED IN GREAT BRITAIN BY
MORRISON AND GIBB LTD, LONDON AND EDINBURGH

Foreword

"The history of the world is but the biography of great men."

"There is properly no history; only biography."

While we may doubt if either of these statements is wholly true, they do seem to be striking ways of saying that history is full of all kinds of remarkable people.

Here, in this book, are the stories of more than thirty men and women whose lives seemed to me to be of exceptional interest. They do not belong to a particular period of history because ever since I began to take an interest in what happened and why, these are some of the hosts of people who have kept thrusting themselves forward or nudging my elbow, with their "Find out about me!"

So I have picked out a few, starting with the first known visitor to Britain and encountering one and another down to the present day. They are, I hope, a varied crowd; not all of them were great and several were anything but good. There are cruel, foolish and over-ambitious people here but others who were brave or compassionate; quite a number of them made their mark because they were fired by a passion to *know*, to find out how the body worked or what lay over the horizon. Every one had some quality which, for good or ill, set him apart from the others of his time.

R.J.U.

CONTENTS

Part One

Part Two

CONTENTS

Part Three

Part Four

Part 1

Heroes and Saints

Pytheas

THE GREEK SEA-CAPTAIN

THERE was bustle and excitement down at the waterside of the port of Massilia. A pile of stores stood on the wharf. Slaves carried jars of wine, baskets of figs and live chickens, bundles of cloth, rope, hides and tools up a plank on to the deck of a stout merchant ship.

Seamen stowed the cargo in the hold while their captain gave orders to the men who were testing the rigging and shaking out the great sail.

A passer-by joined the crowd of citizens on the quay:

"Why is everyone watching a ship being loaded?" he asked.

"You must have been sleeping, friend," answered his neighbour, "if you do not know that the Council of Six has chosen Pytheas to sail to the north in search of tin."

"Pytheas the navigator?"

"That's the man, the bravest and most cunning of all our captains."

"But what of those cut-throats, the Carthaginians? Will they not sink his ship before it even reaches the Pillars of Hercules?"

"Friend, you must be deaf as well as stupid. Surely you know that Carthage has made war on the city of Syracuse? The fleet of Carthage has sailed to other waters and the way to the unknown Ocean is open."

The citizens of Massilia were Greeks who had made their home in what is now called the South of France. They traded along the shores of the Mediterranean Sea and they also went inland to do business with the Gauls who liked to buy the beautiful and useful goods which the Greek merchants could supply.

These Greek traders were afraid of the Carthaginians. Carthage was a splendid town on the north coast of Africa and, at this time, the Carthaginians were the best sailors in the world. They sailed through the Straits of Gibraltar, known as the Pillars of

Hercules, and brought back cargoes of tin and amber from the unknown lands of the north. They would not let any other ships pass the Pillars, so no one knew where these precious things came from.

But now the Carthaginians were at war and the Council of Massilia had decided to send a ship to discover the mysterious Tin Islands.

They chose Pytheas to be captain because he was not only brave but he was also a clever seaman who could read the stars and measure the distance of each day's sailing.

At last the ship was ready. Prayers were said and sacrifices were made to the Goddess Artemis who watched over the city. Then the graceful ship moved out to sea. Pytheas ordered the steersman to keep the bow pointing to the west.

First, the ship sailed along the coast of Spain and through the Pillars of Hercules. The sailors could see the African shore, but there was no sign of Carthaginian warships. Presently, they came out into the great ocean and turned north.

The sea was rough but the little ship rode lightly over the waves. By day, Pytheas kept within sight of the shore, for he knew that his sailors would be frightened if they could not see land. At night, they lowered the sail and rode at anchor in some quiet bay.

As they sailed northwards, the sky became cloudy and sometimes the sea was covered with a cold mist

that the Greeks had never known before. But
Pytheas told his men not to be afraid. They must be
near the Tin Islands.

*   *   *   *   *   *

A year passed and then another. Sometimes, in
the market-place of Massilia or in one of the wine-
shops along the water-front, men would talk about
Pytheas and shake their heads:

"He must have offended the goddess," they said.
"Perhaps he has been wrecked or eaten by the giants
that dwell in the North."

One evening, a ship came slowly into the harbour
of Massilia. Its sail was stained and patched, its
planks were weather-beaten, but its ragged crew
waved and shouted like men filled with a great joy.
People ran to the harbour and the sailors' cries
reached them across the water:

"Pytheas! Pytheas!" they shouted. "Pytheas has
come home!"

The elders of the city hurried to welcome their
bearded captain. When he had been bathed by slaves
and dressed in a new tunic, a feast was held in his
honour and, afterwards, while his sailors were
boasting over their wine, he told the tale of his great
voyage.

"The waters of the Ocean," he said, "are far
steeper than those of our own sea. Often we feared
for our lives as the waves rose higher than the mast
and we were sunk in a valley of green water. But our

Pytheas tells his story at the feast

ship rose like a sea-bird and at last we came to the land of the Brythons."

"Tell us," said his listeners, "what kind of people they are."

"They are like the Gauls," he replied. "They plough the land and grow wheat and barley on the hillsides, but the valleys are filled with great forests and marshes. Yet the people are not savages. Though they live in little houses made of wood, they weave cloth and they have tools of iron and ornaments of gold. They have war chariots but I saw no fighting, for they seem to be a simple kind of people not given to war. In some places, there are great stones set upright in circles, in honour of their gods."

"What of their food, Pytheas? Do they eat like us and drink wine?"

"No, friend, they have no wine. It is too cold for grapes to grow. Instead, they make a drink from barley and honey. We did not like it, for it tastes bitter.

"Nor do they thresh wheat out of doors as we do. Because of the rain that falls nearly every day, they thresh it in big barns. Then they store the corn in pits dug in the ground. As I went further north, I saw that wheat will not grow in such a cold land, so the people live by hunting and by keeping animals for their flesh and milk."

"But what of the tin you went to seek?"

"They take the tin from deep holes, creeping into

Crossing to Ictis with waggon-loads of tin

tunnels cut in the rock. They smelt the tin and hammer it into pieces shaped like knuckle-bones which they carry to an island named Ictis. They wait until the tide has drained the water between this island and the mainland and then they drive waggon-loads of tin across the sand. They say that merchants come from Gaul to buy the tin, but I think that these are Carthaginians."

Pytheas went on to tell how he sailed right round the Tin Islands which were shaped like a triangle. Afterwards, he sailed northwards for six days to find the Land of Amber where the beautiful stones could be picked up upon the seashore.

He came to a country that he called Thule, which may have been Norway, but the weather was so cold that the Greek sailors were unhappy and he had to turn southwards. But he had seen the midnight sun, had learned that the sea sometimes turned solid in the winter and he had noted that as the moon changed, so the tides changed too.

All these strange tales made people wonder if Pytheas was telling the truth. Some said that he was a liar. Others said that his wits had been taken away by the demons of the mist. No one could be sure that there really were any lands beyond the Pillars of Hercules.

Pytheas smiled. He knew that he had spoken the truth. One day, others would sail the same ocean and discover the same islands that he had seen. He had reached Britain, had gone ashore to explore parts of Cornwall and Kent, had sailed into the North Sea and had come safely home with a cargo of tin, hides and amber.

Even if some people did not believe him, he told one of his slaves to write down the story of his great voyage. When it was finished, the Greek slave looked up from his writing-tablet and said:

"Master, what shall be the title of your book?"

Pytheas looked out across the bay and answered:

"I am a sailor. My life has been with ships and all my knowledge is of the sea. Let my book be called *About the Ocean*."

The Britons speak to Caesar

Julius Caesar

A YOUNG officer entered the general's tent and saluted:

"The men from Britain are here, O Caesar," he said.

"Send them in," replied Julius Caesar.

The great man rose and welcomed the Britons, inviting them to be seated, while orderlies brought food and wine. Presently he began to question the visitors: how big was their island? How many tribes were there? Had they any harbours? Was the harvest good?

The Britons answered carefully.

"We are come, O General," they said, "to offer corn and gold. We know how great is the power of Rome and we ask peace for our island. More we cannot say."

Seeing that he could learn little from these messengers, Caesar told them that they could go home.

"I promise you peace," he said. "My friend Commius, the Gaul, will travel with you. He understands your language and when I hear from him, I myself may visit your island."

But, as soon as the Britons had gone, Caesar sent for Labienus, his most trusted officer:

"Make ready the ships and the legions, Labienus," he said. "We will sail to Britain as soon as the wind changes. These Britons pretend to be friends of Rome, but for many years they have given aid to the rebellious Gauls. We must teach them a lesson. What is more, I believe that the islands are rich in tin, gold and corn."

Julius Caesar had been commanding the Roman army in Gaul for more than three years. He was now about forty-five, rather bald, with a sharp expression and bright eyes. He led his soldiers so well that they always obeyed him, for although he was very strict, he was fair and he knew most of the men by their names.

On the march, Caesar led his troops on foot. Sometimes, he would dash off shouting, "Follow me!" and they would have to follow for miles over rough country. Sometimes, he would raise the alarm in the middle of the night and order them to march at once. He did these things to train his men to obey at all times, but he would also joke with them and let them enjoy themselves after they had won a victory.

When the fleet was ready, Caesar set sail for Britain at midnight. His force was not very big but every man was well used to hardships and fighting. By morning, the Roman ships were close to the coast of Britain. The soldiers could see high cliffs, with waves dashing against the rocks.

The army could not land there. Caesar gave the order to sail along the coast until he came to a place where a pebble beach sloped down to the sea.

From the cliffs, the Britons had watched every move. They knew that these long ships had not come on a peaceful visit and they were ready to defend their island. The warriors followed along the cliffs and, as the Roman ships came close inshore, they dashed down to the beach, hurling their javelins and driving their chariots to the water's edge.

The Romans were dismayed. Although their archers and sling-men let fly from the decks, the soldiers did not move. They were afraid to jump down into the waves. The shore was lined with yelling, painted savages, some of whom were already in the shallow water, waving their spears and daring the Romans to come on.

At this moment, the soldier who carried the Eagle of the 10th Brigade, cried out:

"Jump, lads, unless you want to lose your Eagle. I mean to do my duty. Follow me!"

Holding aloft the pole that carried the silver eagle, he jumped down into the water and the soldiers, knowing that it was a terrible disgrace to lose their Standard, leapt after him with hoarse shouts. Men from the other ships followed their example and a furious battle took place in the shallow water and all along the shore.

Gradually, the Romans got a footing on the beach. Then they formed into ranks, charged the enemy and drove them into the woods. They could not chase them any further because the ships carrying the cavalry had not arrived, so they built a strong camp and waited for the morning.

Next day, the Britons sent messengers to Caesar. They brought Commius the Gaul with them.

"We ask for peace, great Caesar," they said. "We are very sorry that some foolish persons tied the hands of your friend Commius. He is quite well now, as you see, and we ask for pardon."

Caesar sternly told them to tell their people to go back to their homes and fields. They must stop fighting and they must send their chiefs to the Roman camp.

22

Not long afterwards, a storm blew up and wrecked many of the Roman ships lying at anchor. Some of the ships that had been pulled up the beach were carried away by a high tide.

The Britons saw their chance. They made a sudden attack on a company of Roman soldiers who were out in the fields cutting corn. From the woods and marshes, a large force of Britons began to surround the camp.

As always, Caesar was ready for every danger. Ordering some of the soldiers to use the nails and planks from the wrecked ships to mend those that were less badly damaged, he led the rest of his army against the Britons and drove them off. Next day, he sailed back to Gaul.

Caesar was a great soldier. He had won many battles and he was not going back to Rome while men could say he had been beaten by the British tribesmen. He began to gather more soldiers and many ships.

Next year, all was ready. A larger force, with two thousand horses, landed on the coast of Kent but, this time, the Britons did not rush down to the beach. Their chief, Cassivellaunus, had made up his mind to fight inland.

As Caesar advanced from his camp on the shore, his troops were attacked by horsemen and by charioteers. They rode furiously at the Romans and then disappeared into the woods. This kind of fighting took place right across Kent, but Caesar pushed on steadily and crossed the River Thames at a ford where a sharp battle took place on the river bank.

Cassivellaunus could see that it was useless to fight battles against troops so steady and well-armed as the Romans. So he kept watch on their line of march, cut off any stragglers, burned the corn and drove off the cattle so the Romans became short of food. But Caesar captured the British stronghold near St. Albans and many of the tribes began to surrender.

After the men of Kent had failed in a surprise attack on the shore camp, Cassivellaunus sent envoys to Caesar to ask for peace.

"Tell Cassivellaunus," said Caesar, "that he must send corn and gold. This he shall pay to Rome every year. He shall promise not to harm Commius nor any of the chiefs who have made peace with me and, to make sure that he keeps his promise, he shall send me young men of noble birth who shall be hostages to his word."

As soon as the hostages arrived, Caesar marched back to the coast, for messengers had brought word that the Gauls were in revolt. The Romans and their prisoners went aboard the ships and within a few hours they had landed on the coast of Gaul.

Caesar never came back to Britain. After he had defeated the Gauls, he became ruler of Rome and of all the countries that border on the Mediterranean. He became so mighty that his enemies thought he wanted to be king.

One day, when Caesar was in the Senate House, a man stepped up to him to ask a question. Suddenly, he pulled out a dagger. Caesar leapt back but found himself surrounded by men with knives. They stabbed him to death and ran out into the streets, crying, "Caesar is dead! Long live the Republic!"

Hostages on the march

The Emperor Hadrian

IN about the year 120, two soldiers of the Ninth Legion were polishing their armour in the barrack-room of the great fort at York:

"They say that the Emperor Hadrian is coming to Britain," said one.

"Then it will be drill, march and dig for us poor fellows," replied Otho the Gaul.

"What do you mean?" asked his companion.

"This Hadrian is made of iron. They say that his legs are never tired, for he walks all day, prying here, inspecting there. Everywhere he goes, he puts up new buildings and, most of all, he likes walls and ditches. There will be some digging to be done when he comes here, my friend."

"Why does he do this?"

"Gallus, the horse-dealer, who was in Germany buying horses for the cavalry, told me that when

Hadrian became Emperor after his uncle Trajan, he made up his mind that the Empire was big enough. He said that there would be no more wars. He means to build a wall all round the Empire and then the legions will have to keep the barbarians out."

"That's what we are here for, eh, Otho?"

"Right enough, Marcus. We march tonight to teach these wild Picts to mind their manners. Brr— but it's cold in this island!"

Marcus and Otho never came back to York. Somewhere in Scotland, the Ninth Legion was cut to pieces. Trapped perhaps in a glen, caught by a snow-storm or led into an ambush by a false guide, the Ninth was lost. A few officers and a handful of shivering men came back but no one ever knew what really happened to the proud legion. Worst of all, its Eagle Standard had vanished.

Not long after this terrible disgrace, the Emperor Hadrian arrived in Britain. He landed in Kent, at the port called Richborough, and he brought with him from Germany the Sixth Legion.

Travelling north on a broad firm road, Hadrian noted the signs of Roman law and order. He passed through new towns, with shops, market-places, public halls and baths. He saw fields of corn and sleek cattle; he passed merchants with waggons and pack-horses laden with hides, wool, iron and salt.

At York, the Emperor summoned the Roman commander and his chief officers to tell him about the loss of the Ninth Legion. He listened carefully and then he went himself to see something of this wild country whose tribesmen refused to be conquered. Bareheaded, he went everywhere on foot, walking at great speed, climbing rocks and hills to gain a view of the countryside, while his officers panted behind, cursing the rain and the cold which Hadrian seemed not to notice.

He visited the troops at their outlying forts, made them drill and throw their javelins, watched the cooks at work and sat down to eat the same food as the soldiers.

When he had seen all that he wanted, Hadrian called his officers together again. They looked curiously at this Emperor who never took any rest. He was broad-shouldered and of middle height, with a large nose and curly hair that lay thick on his forehead. Unlike most Emperors, he wore a short beard trimmed close to his cheeks and chin. His light-blue eyes had a strange far-away look and no one knew what he was thinking.

People said that Hadrian was a Spaniard but, although his family had lived in Spain for many years, he was proud of his Roman ancestors and he had spent much of his youth in Rome and Athens. Then he had travelled widely with his uncle Trajan, had fought in the wars and had seen more of the Roman Empire than any man alive. But he was more than a general and a peace-maker.

Hadrian addresses the officers at York

Hadrian was a painter, an architect and a poet.
He put up many beautiful temples and theatres, he
wrote verses and was the friend of artists, singers
and writers. He helped the poor and the homeless,
for he wished to win the love of the people, yet he
could live as hard as any soldier on the frontier and
sometimes he was as cruel as the barbarians themselves.

So the officers at York listened fearfully to this
Emperor who was so clever and so strict:

"I have seen much in a short time," began Hadrian.
"Your forts are good, your soldiers are well trained.
I can praise their sword-work and their javelin-
throwing, but there are some things I cannot praise.
I will not speak much about the Ninth Legion. It

brought disgrace upon the name of Rome and, having lost its Eagle, it no longer exists. There is no Ninth Legion any more."

The officers gasped. A defeated legion was usually given fresh soldiers; sometimes it was moved to another part of the Empire. But this stern Emperor had wiped out the name of the Ninth.

"The Sixth Legion will take over the frontier," went on Hadrian. "Unroll the map, Florus. A wall is to be built from here to here. That is the shortest line from sea to sea. It measures seventy-six Roman miles. The wall is to be 10 feet thick and 20 feet high. In front there is to be a ditch 30 feet wide. I have given orders for the forts, signal-posts and turrets.

"From the wall, you will be able to control Caledonia. Peaceful traffic may pass freely through the gates. Your task is to protect the South from robbers and to put an end to the raids of the northern tribes. Inside my Empire, there must be peace."

Shortly afterwards, Hadrian left Britain to con-

tinue his travels, for there was much to be done in places more important than the small island on the edge of the Roman world. Men never understood him and he died near Rome, lonely and in pain, but he was perhaps the greatest of all the Emperors.

Parts of Hadrian's Wall can still be seen. It runs for mile after mile across the hills from Wallsend, near Newcastle, to Carlisle and the great ditch in front can still be traced. The wall was built of stone by the soldiers themselves. There was a walk along the top wide enough for two men to march abreast, and there were seventeen forts with "mile-castles" in between, each a mile apart and each with its gateway wide enough for a cart to pass through.

At least ten thousand soldiers dug the earth and lifted the stones into place. It took them five years. Later, the wall had to be altered and another line of forts was built farther away to the north. But, for two hundred and fifty years, Hadrian's Wall kept the Roman part of Britain safe from the fierce tribesmen of Caledonia.

31

Queen Ethelburga and
Saint Paulinus

QUEEN Bertha of Kent carefully drew a gold
thread through the cloth that lay on her lap.
The cloak was finished and now she had begun
to embroider its edges with a pattern of gold and
scarlet.

As she sewed, the Queen talked to her little
daughter Ethelburga, who was playing with her
mother's bronze work-box on the bench where they
sat together in the sunshine.

"Tell me, Mother, the story of Augustine," said the little princess.

"You know the story well, child, but I will tell it again," replied the Queen.

She told how she herself had crossed the sea from Gaul to marry Ethelbert, King of Kent. She loved her husband but she had been sad because he worshipped Thor and Woden. Bertha was a Christian, brought up in Paris, for her father was King of the Franks.

One day, Augustine had come to Kent, leading a band of forty monks who sang as they carried their silver cross over the flat fields to the place where King Ethelbert waited under an oak-tree with his nobles.

"For my sake," went on Queen Bertha, "your father said that he would listen to Augustine, though the priests of Woden were very angry. Afterwards, the King gave us the church of Saint Martin. It was in ruins then, but you know how pretty it is now, with its pink floor and the pictures of saints on the walls."

"But tell me how my father was made a Christian," said the little girl.

"Well, he pondered for a long time and then he said that he would be baptized. It was by the river. While the monks sang, Augustine blew in his face to drive away the bad spirits. Then he put salt in his mouth and led him into the river to dip him three times in the water. After that, the men of Kent were baptized too."

M.W.—3

The child smiled, for this was one of her favourite stories. But it was time to go. She helped her mother to collect up the bronze needles and the threads of silk and wool, for the bell of Augustine's church was ringing for evening service.

Princess Ethelburga grew up happily at Canterbury. The land was peaceful, for Ethelbert was a wise ruler, obeyed by many under-kings beyond the borders of Kent. He was kind to Ethelburga when her mother died and he helped the monks to teach the people about God.

Suddenly, all was changed. Ethelbert died and his son Edwald became King. Edwald, with his fair beard, his loud laugh and his skill with axe and spear, was like one of the sea-pirates who had conquered Kent long ago. But he was also weak and lazy. When his father died, Edwald turned back to Thor and Woden, the old gods of the Saxon warriors.

The Church in Kent was almost overthrown. Some of the monks fled to Gaul, others went into hiding, but Archbishop Lawrence stayed at Canterbury, with Paulinus, a young priest from Italy, who acted as teacher to Princess Ethelburga.

The priests of Woden laughed and bowed to their idols. Feasts were held in the royal Hall and poets sang the praises of the young king who had brought back the old gods. Again and again, the Chief Priest told Edwald that he must banish his sister and kill the monks.

The good-natured Edwald stops his sister

But Edwald was fond of his sister. One day, as he came in from the hunt, he caught her by the wrist as she was going to her bower to say her prayers:

"Don't cry, little one," he roared in his good-natured way. "No one is going to hurt you. I won't send you away, but tell those Christian friends of yours to go while they are still alive."

"O brother, let these good men stay," pleaded Ethelburga. "Archbishop Lawrence cannot leave his flock and Paulinus is my friend. For the sake of our dear mother, let them stay."

"No, no," cried Edwald. "They must go tomorrow or they will die!"

Ethelburga ran to the place where she knew that she would find Paulinus and the archbishop. She told them that they must leave the kingdom at once.

"If only you could speak to my brother," she cried, "you would know that he is not really wicked.

35

The High Priest and some of the elders have led him away to the heathen gods. Perhaps God will tell us what to do."

That night, Lawrence dreamed that he saw Saint Peter himself. In the morning, Lawrence went to the Great Hall and demanded to speak with the King.

With shining eyes, Lawrence told Edwald that Saint Peter had appeared to him in a vision, telling him not to leave Kent. Disaster would come upon the kingdom if he left its shores but the fate of Edwald would be far more terrible if he did not return to the faith of his father and mother. Then the archbishop turned back his robe to show the King where Saint Peter had laid marks upon his back as a sign.

The young king fell on his knees and begged to be taken back into God's family. He promised that he would live as a Christian for the rest of his days.

Edwald kept his word. The monks came back from Gaul, the churches were open again and Ethelburga was able to go on helping the poor and teaching the children with the help of Paulinus.

Some time later, a messenger arrived at Canterbury. He came, he said, from Edwin, King of Northumbria, who sent words of greeting and gifts.

The royal messenger's servants brought in rich cloaks and tunics with gold wrist-clips, a pair of boar-hounds, arm-bracelets and a lady's work-box, inlaid with gold and precious stones. This last gift,

said the messenger, was for the Princess Ethelburga.
His royal master asked for her hand in marriage.

King Edwald stroked his beard and then answered
slowly:

"Our thanks to Edwin for his noble gifts. We
know him to be a great and valiant king, but we
also know that he has not been baptized into the
faith of Jesus Christ.

"Our sister is a Christian. If King Edwin would
take her hand in marriage, he must promise not to
hurt the Christian faith."

"O King," replied the messenger. "My master
has bidden me to say that the fair princess may
worship in her own way and her priests may speak
of their God at all times. The King himself is ready
to listen to the new teaching."

When he heard this, Edwald agreed that his sister
could marry the northern King.

In the year 625, Ethelburga set out from Canterbury with Paulinus and a helper named James the
Deacon. Maids, servants and a strong bodyguard
travelled with them.

It was a long journey, across hills and rivers, along
woodland tracks where only a guide could tell the
way. The princess rode behind a servant. Often she
walked and sometimes, where the road was deep
with mud, she had to be carried.

King Edwin was overlord to the Middle Angles
and the East Angles, so their spearmen rode out to

meet the princess. Each night, they brought her to a royal manor where she dined and rested.

At last, the travellers reached the Great Hall of Edwin. The King came forward to greet his bride, taking both her hands in his and kissing her upon each cheek. Then his eyes turned to the tall, dark stranger who stood beside the fair-haired girl. He started with fear:

"Who is this man, princess?" he cried.

"He is Paulinus, my lord," answered Ethelburga. "A man of God who has travelled with me to your northern land according to your promise."

"Paulinus? I have seen his thin, dark face before. Now I remember. It was long ago, when I was homeless, a man without land or followers, and I saw in a dream this dark man. He gave me a sign and told me that I should be great one day. Was it you, stranger? Do you recall the sign?"

Paulinus looked keenly at the King but he did not answer. Slowly he raised his hand and placed it on the King's head. The nobles stared. Surely the King would be angry, but Edwin stood quite still.

"Yes, that was the sign I saw in my vision," he murmured.

King Edwin was a strong, hard man. His life had been full of adventure and fighting but now that he had won back his father's kingdom, he meant to rule well with his Kentish bride to help him.

From the moment he saw her, Edwin loved

Ethelburga travels north to marry Edwin

Ethelburga and granted all her wishes. Her gentle manner, her pity for the poor and her strange religion filled him with wonder. Her way of speaking, her dress and her skilful needlework made her different from the northern ladies and, unlike them, she could read and could sing most beautifully. Every day, she and Paulinus prayed and sang together but, so far, Edwin took no interest in their religion.

About a year after the royal wedding, a man named Eomer came to the court with a message from the King of the West Saxons. There had been a quarrel between the two rulers but, even so, Eomer was taken to the Great Hall where Edwin sat with his nobles. The messenger knelt and opened his cloak as if to present a gift or a letter.

At that moment, the thane Lilla, standing by the King's seat, flung himself forward as Eomer aimed a dagger at the King's heart. So strong was the blow that the blade passed through Lilla's body and wounded Edwin. A dozen hands struck down Eomer, but Lilla was already dead. He had saved the King's life.

That same evening, Ethelburga's first baby was born, a girl who was named Eanfled. King Edwin was filled with thankfulness and he sent for Paulinus:

"The Queen, my lady wife, says that my life was saved by your prayers to the Christian God. She wishes our new-born child to be the first Christian to be baptized in Northumbria."

Paulinus asked the King if he remembered the vision and the sign. Edwin spoke again:

"When my wound is healed, I shall march against the West Saxons. If I am given victory, I too will become a Christian."

After the baby had been baptized, the King and his warriors set out to punish the King of Wessex. The two armies met on a bare hillside where the Northumbrian axes cut through the enemy ranks and the spearmen finished the victory.

At home again, Edwin kept his promise. He called together the earls and the wise men of the kingdom and told them that he wished them to listen to Paulinus.

The tall priest told how Jesus had chosen pain and death, how He had won the battle with death and had risen gloriously to open the door of God's kingdom to all who had the courage to follow Him.

With burning words, Paulinus went on to explain why Christians believed that mercy and kindness were better than hate and cruel revenge. He also spoke about life after death.

When he had finished, the warriors and the old men looked silently at the stranger who stood unarmed in their midst, a man who had come to them from far-off Italy because he believed in a God so different from the heathen gods.

At last, the King asked a white-bearded counsellor to speak. The old man rose:

Coifi hurls his spear at the idol of Woden

"The life of a man, O King," he said, "is like the flight of a sparrow through the Hall when we sit at meat in winter time with the fire blazing. It flies in through one door and quickly out of the other. For a little while, it is safe from the storm but soon it vanishes into the winter again.

"Our life is like the sparrow. Where he came from and where he goes we know not. If Paulinus can tell us these things, we should follow his teaching."

Then Coifi, the High Priest, sprang up and cried:

"I am telling the truth, O King, when I say that our gods are useless. No one has served them better than I, but they have brought me no luck or favour. Give me, I beg, a straight spear and a horse and I will show what should be done to the old gods."

When he was mounted, Coifi rode furiously to the temple and hurled his spear at the idol of Woden. Then he called to the people to burn down the temple, for Northumbria was to be a Christian kingdom.

Paulinus and James the Deacon hurried to build a little wooden church at York and here, amid the ruins of the Roman city, Edwin and his court were baptized.

Once the King had become a Christian, the people came flocking to listen to Paulinus. He and James tramped all over Northumbria, teaching and baptizing the crowds who gathered on the banks of streams and rivers to receive the blessing of God.

Edwin was now the most powerful king in England. When he went out with his Queen to see that the land was well ruled, his banners were carried in front of him. Men said that the realm was so peaceful that a woman with her baby could walk from sea to sea in safety.

At York, King Edwin gave orders for a church of stone to be built, but before its walls were finished, he lay dead on a battlefield.

Penda, the heathen ruler of Mercia, helped by a Welsh king, attacked Northumbria, wiped out its army and carried the dead King's head on a spear into York. The victors tore across the land like a gale, killing and burning as they went.

When the terrible news of the battle reached Ethelburga, she fled with her daughter to Paulinus. For a time they were safe, but soon they had to flee to the coast.

What should Paulinus do? His churches were destroyed, the King was dead and the heathens

were killing Christians wherever they found them. The way to the South was barred by the enemy and, in any case, there were no troops to guard the royal travellers.

At last, Paulinus found a sea-captain who was sailing back to Gaul because, as he said, there was no trade when men were afraid to come out of doors. For a handful of gold, he would take the priest and his friends on board his ship.

James the Deacon bravely declared that he would stay, so Ethelburga, her daughter and Paulinus sailed away from Northumbria and, after many days, were put ashore on the coast of Kent.

King Edwald gave a kind welcome to his sister. He was not strong enough to march against the savage Penda but he thought of a plan that might bring happiness to Ethelburga.

At Lyminge, there was a royal manor with good pastures where fat sheep were raised. It was big enough to provide the food and money that were needed to support a small abbey. Edwald gave the manor of Lyminge to his sister.

Here, with her daughter, Ethelburga spent the rest of her life in the quiet countryside of Kent. She lived in a little house by herself and there were separate buildings for the nuns and for the young girls called novices. There was a chapel, a dining-room, a hospital for the sick and a house for Paulinus and for the monks who came to join him.

Ethelburga's manor at Lyminge

Ethelburga and Paulinus never went back to York. Often, when they met in the garden at Lyminge, they would talk of their journey to Northumbria, of the miracle of King Edwin's conversion, and of the five happy years before he was killed in battle. Many times they spoke of James the Deacon and wondered if he was still alive.

One day, a traveller brought the good news that James had managed to go on teaching a few Christians in secret until a prince named Oswald had driven Penda out. Then Saint Aidan had come from Iona to bring back Christianity to Northumbria.

Ethelburga was happy.

"Our work was not wasted, Paulinus," she cried. "The word of God will never again die out in Northumbria."

St. Cuthbert of Durham

"CARELESS rascals," growled the old shepherd, "throwing stones instead of minding the flock. What will the master do to ye when he knows that one of his fine sheep is trapped in a cleft on a rock-face where a fly could hardly crawl?"

"I'll fetch her down," cried the tallest of the three shepherd-boys.

"You, Cuthbert?" said the old shepherd. "Well, ye may try. But it's your neck that will be broken."

The boy laughed and began to climb the steep rock-face. Bits of rock broke away under his bare feet. Once he almost fell but he held on by his finger-nails until his toes found a tiny ledge to stand on.

He climbed until he reached the place where one of the sheep was wedged in the rocks. Then he lifted the animal out, set it on its feet and followed it up to the hillside above.

46

By an easier path, Cuthbert brought the sheep back to the flock. The old shepherd grunted and the boys grinned their thanks. They knew Cuthbert. He was as hard and whippy as a leather thong and he loved to test his strength in ways that were too difficult for them.

By nightfall, the flocks had been brought to an open space by a small river. The shepherds lit a fire and ate their bread and bacon. Then, while one kept watch, the others curled themselves to sleep in the shelter of the boulders.

When it was his turn, Cuthbert went up to a higher patch of ground from which he could see the sheep all round him. The night was cold and very still and the sky was a dark bowl filled with stars.

Cuthbert shivered. He remembered the prayers that Kenwith the Widow had taught him. She had looked after him since the time when his mother died and his father had been killed fighting the Mercians. He was on his knees praying when he saw the great light.

Far off, yet brilliantly clear, a globe of fire passed across the sky and in it the boy saw what seemed to be a company of angels rising upwards to Heaven. What could it be? Was it a sign, perhaps for him alone? He stood up. The shepherds were still asleep, the sheep were quiet, but Cuthbert knew that he had seen a vision.

A few days later, Cuthbert was telling his story to Basil, prior of the monastery at Melrose.

"Yes, my son," said the prior gravely, "on that very night, Bishop Aidan died at Lindisfarne. What you saw was that holy man's soul being carried to Heaven. It is a sign that you are called to do God's work."

The prior went to see Cuthbert's master to ask if the lad could enter the monastery. The thane shook his head:

"No, Father. Our King has called me to raise a hundred spearmen for the royal army of Northumbria. The lad Cuthbert is sixteen, tall and strong for his age. He will be doing God's work by keeping the kingdom safe from the heathen Mercians. But if he lives, I promise that he shall enter your house."

So Cuthbert, mounted on a shaggy pony, followed his lord to war. For two years, he carried his spear against the Mercians and he knew what it was to live hard, to ride all night and to go into battle at dawn.

At last, the fighting came to an end and Cuthbert went to speak to his lord:

"I made a vow to enter the Church, master," he said. "May I now leave your service?"

The thane looked at the young man:

Cuthbert goes to war against the Mercians

"You have served me well and I would not lose so good a man. But a promise was given. Go, in Christ's name. Is it to Lindisfarne you go?"

"No, master. I know that Aidan's church has many holy men. But the prior Basil has been my friend. I will go to Melrose."

When Cuthbert reached Melrose, he gave his horse and his spear to the servant who opened the gate. Basil welcomed him and said that he must go to see Eata, the abbot.

"So you would turn from war to be a monk?" asked Eata. "I have heard of the vision that God showed you. But there is much for you to learn. Can you read?"

"Not yet, Father. But I will learn."

"So you shall, my son, and I will be your teacher."

The shepherd-lad learned quickly and the other monks at Melrose came to look on him as a natural leader. He was so strong that they chose him to be the chief builder, but since he was kind and friendly, they also chose him to look after the guests and travellers who stayed at the monastery.

When Basil died, the monks asked Eata if Cuthbert could be their prior. He lived at Melrose for several years and there were many stories of his adventures.

Cuthbert was not content to stay quietly inside the monastery walls. He made many a journey northwards into the wild land of the Picts. There he would search out the tribesmen, follow them to their mountain homes and baptize them in the name of Jesus.

The fierce Picts liked the preacher who had been a soldier and was afraid of no one. He had the gift of healing sick people and a wonderful way with horses and wild creatures.

Once, he and two of the brothers from Melrose crossed the Firth of Forth in a storm. Drenched to the skin, dog-tired and hungry, they dragged their little boat out of reach of the waves and saw, waiting for them on the shore, three portions of dolphin's flesh.

On another occasion, returning from a journey to heal a sick woman, Cuthbert and his fellows lost their way and were all day without food until an

Cuthbert and his friends drag their boat ashore and find
three portions of dolphin flesh

eagle brought them a large fish. The monks told how
Cuthbert made them give half of the fish to the eagle
for its own dinner.

The monks also told of the time when Cuthbert
was praying on the sea-shore. It was bitterly cold and
they saw two little seals come up out of the sea to
lick and warm his frozen feet.

When Eata was made a bishop, he sent Cuthbert
to the famous monastery at Lindisfarne, an island
off the coast of Northumbria. After a time, Cuthbert
told the monks that he must leave them:

"I would be alone with God," he said.

"But, here on Lindisfarne, you can rest and pray,"
cried the monks.

"Truly," replied Cuthbert, "it is peaceful here in Aidan's house. There is shelter from the sea-wind and warmth in the sunshine by the wall. But I do not seek shelter and warmth. As the Saint hath said, 'Go ye bare. As Christ had nothing, so shall ye have nothing.' "

So Cuthbert went to live alone on the isle of Farne, one of a group of tiny islands, nine miles from Lindisfarne. There he dug down into the earth to make a space to dwell in and he built an outer wall, moving by himself great stones that four of the brothers could not have lifted.

At this time, people looked on hermits as holy men. On fine days, the monks of Lindisfarne would row across to Farne to visit their brother. They would find him in his cell, surrounded by a wall so that he could only see the sky. Often they found him praying and they would go away without a word, leaving some food outside his cell.

While Cuthbert was following this lonely way of life, there was no bishop of Lindisfarne. At last, the King of Northumbria called a meeting of the clergy and, with one voice, they chose Cuthbert.

Then a party set out by boat to the tiny island. They called to Cuthbert to speak with them and, when he would not answer, they drew him up gently out of his cell and asked him to be their bishop:

"Your brothers implore you with tears to come back," they cried.

Cuthbert in his cell is visited by the monks

At this, Cuthbert yielded. The monks rowed him to the mainland and led him to the meeting where, in the presence of the King, the Archbishop held the service by which the hermit of Farne became Bishop of Lindisfarne.

After many years, Cuthbert fell ill and knew that he was going to die. He asked a few of the brothers to take him for the last time to his cell on the little island:

"I wish to be buried there," he said.

But the brothers begged to be allowed to arrange his burying-place in the church at Lindisfarne. Cuthbert spoke again:

"You may do so. But, remember this: if wicked men come to rule this land, I ask you to take my bones and go to whatever place God may lead you."

Cuthbert died on the Farne island in March 687 and the monks buried him by the side of the altar at Lindisfarne.

A hundred years passed. Then, one day, a band of Danish raiders burnt the monastery and killed many of the monks. Cuthbert's tomb escaped the fire and,

after the raiders had gone, monks came out from the mainland to rebuild the monastery.

Another eighty years went by and the heathen Danes were conquering all the kingdoms of the north and east. One by one, the monasteries of Northumbria were robbed and burnt. At Lindisfarne, Bishop Erdwulf spoke sadly to the monks:

"Brothers, the time has come when we should remember Saint Cuthbert's dying words. He told us not to live under wicked masters but to take his bones from this place."

Without delay, the monks crossed to the mainland, taking with them Cuthbert's coffin and the Lindisfarne Gospels that had been written and decorated so gloriously in his honour. Seven young priests carried the coffin on their shoulders, and later it was placed on a cart drawn by a bay horse.

For seven years, the bishop and the monks and a little band of Christians wandered about trying to find a resting-place safe from the Danes. At last, in despair, they decided to take the coffin to Ireland where the Irish Christians would give it shelter.

Bishop, abbot and bearers went aboard a ship that was lying in the mouth of the River Derwent. When the sails were set, the rest of the company stood on the shore, weeping:

"Do not leave us," they wailed. "Stay with us, Cuthbert, in our time of need!"

A storm arose with waves so violent that the ship was driven back. Then the bishop ordered the coffin to be carried ashore. The Saint had made it clear that his bones were not to leave the kingdom.

The company set out on their wanderings again and came to Chester-le-Street in the county of Durham. Because his people could travel no further, the bishop said that all must settle there.

With the Danes not far away at York, the Christians had an anxious time for many years. They lived in fear and, time after time, they seemed to be doomed. But somehow they were saved and their church still stood. People felt sure that Saint Cuthbert was their protector in the North.

Indeed, everyone said that it was with Saint Cuthbert's help that King Alfred defeated the Danes in Wessex. Then Alfred's grandson, the great Athelstan, travelled to the North to visit the Saint's tomb and to make the Danes promise to be Christians.

So, in 995, the day came when it was safe to move Saint Cuthbert's coffin to Durham where it has rested ever since.

The Venerable Bede

"COME, my son," said Abbot Benedict, taking the hand of the small boy who was following him through the monastery gate, "this is your home now. Here, at St. Peter's, you can grow up in God's keeping."

The good abbot took the boy first into the church, where the child's eyes lit up with wonder at the bright pictures of saints on the walls and at the glass windows, newly brought from Gaul. Presently, the abbot paused to speak to a monk, who was carefully painting a great capital letter at the head of a page

of the book that he was copying. The boy hung back and seemed unwilling to go on to see the gardens and the kitchens where other monks were working.

"What is it?" asked the abbot. "Does the book interest you?"

"I have never seen a book before, Father," answered the boy. "Will I have one when I learn to read?"

"You shall have many books, my son, if you work hard at your lessons."

The boy's name was Bede. He was only seven years old when both his parents died and the kind-hearted abbot brought him to live at the monastery at Wearmouth in Northumbria, not far from the Roman Wall of Hadrian. In the year 680, monasteries were the only places where orphans and sick people could find peace and safety. They were the only places, too, where boys could learn to read and write.

Young Bede was happy at Wearmouth. He helped in the kitchen and the bakery, he ran errands and he learned to sing with the monks in the great church. Most of all, he enjoyed his lessons. Soon, the prior was able to tell the abbot that the little orphan was very clever:

"The boy learns so fast that there are not enough

books for him to read. Already, he reads Latin and Greek as easily as the birds fly."

"Books are precious," replied the abbot, "but I promised on the day when he came here that he should have them. I will make a journey to find books for this boy, for it is clear that God has chosen him to be a great scholar."

Abbot Benedict was as good as his word. He set out to ride from one monastery to another; he crossed to France and travelled to Italy and back to the Low Countries searching always for books which he might buy or borrow for the library of his monastery in the north of England. As he had said, books were precious. Each one had to be copied by hand on sheets of parchment and almost all of them were written in Greek or Latin and some were in the Hebrew language.

Young Bede helping in the bakery

After several years, the abbot returned to Northumbria with a wonderful collection of books strapped carefully to the pack-horses that clattered into the abbey courtyard. The monks welcomed their abbot joyfully and, in the church that evening, the voice of the boy Bede could be heard high above the others as he sang his gladness that his friend had come home bringing so many books filled with knowledge.

By this time, Bede was living at Jarrow, at the monastery of St. Paul, which Abbot Benedict had founded before he went on his travels.

When Bede was fourteen, an illness, called the plague, came to Jarrow and so many of the monks fell ill and died that there was no one left to take the services in the church, except the prior and Bede. The singing was too difficult for the monks who were being trained to take the place of those who had died, so the prior and the boy sang alone, each taking his turn, until the new monks had learned their parts.

After this, the monastery at Jarrow grew larger. Its library of books collected by the abbot became so famous that scholars came from abroad to visit it, and nobles sent their sons there to be taught by the monks. Bede himself became a monk after he had grown up and men began to say that he was not only the wisest man in England but the best scholar in Europe.

Bede teaching his pupils

In those days, clever men spent most of their time studying the Scriptures and the writings of Rome and Ancient Greece. Bede was interested in everything, in music, history and nature, as well as in the Scriptures. Soon he began to write books himself.

He wrote not only about saints and the early history of the Church, but also about science, grammar, the stars and his own two monasteries. Much of his writing was done to help the boys and the young monks who came thronging to Jarrow, for he remembered how much he had longed for books when he was a boy.

So many people wanted to send their sons to Bede that he started a school. There were six hundred pupils, many from France, Spain and Italy. They came great distances to Jarrow to be taught by the quiet monk who was always too busy himself to go on journeys, except to visit his friends at neighbouring monasteries.

One day, when he was walking in the garden, his friend Nothelm spoke lovingly of the school and of the books which Bede had written for the boys:

"There is one book, brother, above all others that I would like to write," said Bede.

"What is this book?"

"It is a book about the history of the Church in England," replied Bede. "I would tell how the Word of God came to our shores and spread over the land. I would have our boys know the stories of the saints and of great happenings long ago."

"Of all men, you can surely write such a book," cried Nothelm.

"No, brother, I have never travelled and know little of the happenings in the Kingdom of Kent or in East Anglia or Wessex. I cannot leave my school and my books to find out the history of those places."

"But there are those who will help you. You alone can write this book but others can bring you the things you need to know. I myself was a monk in Kent and there is Brother Albinus of Canterbury, a far more learned man than I. There is Bishop Daniel to send word of the West Saxons; there are Wilfred and Acca who have travelled far and John who was long in Rome.

Bede writing his history of the Church

"All these and many others will bring you books and writings from distant monasteries. You must write your history of the Church."

So it was that Bede wrote the first great history book in England. His friends helped, but it was Bede, the story-teller, who told so beautifully how Christianity came to Northumbria, how Caedmon the cowherd received the gift of poetry, how Cuthbert and many others served God. To Bede, we owe most of our knowledge of what happened in those far-off days.

The history of England took a long time to write, and when it was finished Bede was growing old. There was one more task he meant to do:

"All my books have been written in Latin," he said. "The common people cannot understand them, so I will translate the Gospel of Saint John into their tongue, so that when it is read to them, they can understand."

63

The monks were very surprised that a great scholar should think of turning the Scriptures into Anglo-Saxon, but Bede was already at work. He seemed to know that his life was nearly over for he wrote all day for as long as daylight lasted. When he became too ill to hold his pen, a young monk acted as his scribe, sitting at his bedside in his little cell. In the evenings, when it was too dark to write any more, the old man would chant the songs that he knew so well and think about the book that was almost finished.

On the Feast of the Ascension, all the monks went to take part in the procession round the church, but Bede could not leave his bed. He was alone with the scribe.

"We must begin, Wilbert," he said, "I do not want my boys to have to finish this when I am dead and I do not want them to read what is untrue."

"But, master, there is only one chapter to write. Rest now, for it is too difficult for you to speak."

"No, it is easy. Take thy pen and write quickly."

Making all haste, the young man wrote down the words of his dying master. All day they continued and as the sun began to sink, Bede paused and smiled at several of his friends who had gathered in the cell. He made a little gift to each one and then turned to his scribe:

"Where are we, my son?" he asked.

"There is one more sentence to write, dear master."

"Then write quickly what I tell you."

Presently, the monk laid down his pen and sighed happily:

"Now, it is finished."

"Thou hast spoken truly," said Bede. "All is finished."

Then he asked his friends to carry him to his usual place of prayer. They helped him to kneel down and after he had prayed, he sang a little and they carried him, still singing, back to his cell. He did not wake next morning and the monks buried him at Jarrow where he had worked so well for almost all his life.

Bede was mourned far and wide and when the news of his death reached Germany, an English monk who was working there to convert the heathen Saxons, wrote to tell his friends at Jarrow that Bede's name "shone like a candle in the church".

Men spoke of him as the "Venerable Bede", for "venerable" meant "worthy of respect and love". For many years, pilgrims came to pray at his grave and sick children were brought to be cured at Bede's Well. Three hundred years after his death, his bones were taken to Durham Cathedral where his tomb can still be seen in the Galilee chapel.

The Saxon Minster at York

Alcuin of York

IN the year that Bede died at Jarrow, a baby boy was born in York. He was named Alcuin and, when he was quite small, he was sent to the Cathedral School.

His teacher was Aelbert, and after the boy had been going to his lessons for some months the school was visited by Archbishop Egbert. The archbishop listened to the boys as they answered their teachers:

"The work is well done," he said to Aelbert. "Some of the thanes' sons are very slow but I see one who learns more easily than the others."

"That is Alcuin, Father," said Aelbert. "He is my best pupil. Sometimes I think that he will be a scholar as famous as our beloved Bede."

"It is hard to believe that anyone could be as clever as Bede. But you may be right. Give the boy all the help that he needs and let him see something of the world as well as the schoolroom."

Aelbert remembered this advice and when Alcuin was older he took him to Rome. It was a long journey across Frankland but the boy and his master stayed at monasteries along the way where they were always given a kind welcome.

When he came back from his travels, Alcuin stayed on at the Cathedral School. He read many books about the Church and the Bible and he also learnt the seven subjects that were taught in those days. They were arithmetic, music, geometry, grammar, astronomy and two others called rhetoric (speaking aloud) and dialect (holding a learned argument).

In all these, Alcuin was so clever that he began to teach some of the younger boys and, later, he took charge of the whole school. He was called Master of Scholars.

A few years passed and Alcuin might have stayed at York for the rest of his life. But, one day, his old teacher Aelbert, now Archbishop of York, came to see him:

"Alcuin, my son," he said, "I want you to make the journey to Rome. Are you willing to go?"

"Yes, indeed, Father," answered Alcuin. "I shall be able to see so many places that we visited when I

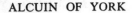

was a boy. And I can call upon some of my former pupils who live in foreign monasteries. But I forget myself. What is the purpose of the journey?"

"You know that the Pope gives the 'pallium' to every archbishop. That wide scarf of white woollen cloth is the sign of his holy office. I would have you fetch my pallium from the hands of His Holiness in Rome."

Joyfully, Alcuin gathered together the few things necessary for his journey. Then, with two monks for company, he crossed in a merchant ship to the Low Countries, travelled down the Rhine Valley and across the mountains into Italy.

The Pope welcomed the English scholar and Alcuin spent several weeks visiting churches and talking to the scholars of the Holy City. Then it was time to say good-bye and to set out on the long journey home, carrying the precious pallium and several baskets of books.

One evening, he and his companions came to Parma in North Italy. There were crowds of people and a great deal of noise in the town.

"What is happening today in Parma, brother?" asked Alcuin of the monk who let him in at the gate of the small religious house where he was to stay the night.

Celebrations during Charles' visit to Parma

"Have you not heard," replied the monk, "that Charles, King of the Franks, is here? Unlike you, my friend, King Charles does not travel quietly. Thousands of soldiers, hundreds of serving-men, cooks, scullions, merchants, jugglers, minstrels, poets, women, children, scribes, rascals and cut-throats—they all go along with the Frankish Court.

"Oh, you never saw so many people in your life! But come in now, good friends, our prior waits to welcome you at our table. We have heard, here in this little priory, of Alcuin of York."

Next morning, a messenger in a splendid blue cloak knocked at the priory gate. He had come, he said, from Charles, King of the Franks. His royal master had heard that a famous English scholar was in the town and he asked with deep respect if the Englishman would go and talk with him.

Alcuin cheerfully agreed and followed the messenger to where a two-wheeled cart awaited them. Presently, they came to the abbey where the King and his family were staying.

Alcuin was led into the hall and at once the King rose and came to meet him, throwing his arms wide in welcome. To Alcuin's astonishment, he was hugged like a bear and half-carried to the seat where the King had been sitting.

When Alcuin had got his breath back, he looked closely at this jovial king. Charles was enormous, a giant of a man, taller than any of his knights and twice as wide. Men said that he was so strong that he could break an iron horseshoe in halves like a dry stick, and lift a man in full armour above his head, with one hand.

The king was as jolly as a schoolboy. His blue eyes twinkled under bushy eyebrows and he chuckled away into a great fair beard that flowed on to his vast chest. Yet when he spoke, he had a high piping voice.

"Come, Father, sit by me," he cried to Alcuin. "Long have I wished to speak with the scholar of York. A king should know many things but I have little learning. There is much that I would have you teach me."

With a boy's eagerness, Charles asked question after question. The evening passed. Dinner was served at the high table, the knights dropped asleep

Charles welcomes Alcuin to his court

over their wine, the women slipped away to their bowers and the servants and guards stood drowsily in the shadows of the hall. But still the King sat with Alcuin, talking and asking questions.

In the weeks that followed, Charles could hardly bear to be away from Alcuin. The noisy Court left Parma and made its way slowly towards Frankland, with the King riding beside Alcuin, deep in talk with his new friend.

When they reached Frankland, Charles said to Alcuin:

"Father, I know that you must return to England. But I beg you to come back. You shall be Master of my Palace School and shall make it as famous as York. There is much to be done in Frankland, for we have few schools and much ignorance, even among the clergy."

Alcuin promised that, when he had taken the pallium safely to York, he would ask for permission to live in Frankland.

To his surprise, Alcuin found that the Archbishop and the King of Northumbria were willing to let him go. It would be good, they felt, to have the King of the Franks for a friend. Already, men were calling him Charlemagne or Charles the Great.

So Alcuin went back to Frankland to live at the King's Court. He found that Charles ruled everything and everybody like the father of a big family. He looked into the law-courts, the farms, manors,

*Charles rides with a group of scholars
while on the march*

monasteries, market-squares and even into the cooking-pots in the peasants' huts. Nothing escaped his sharp, twinkling eyes.

Alcuin came to love this huge, chuckling king who was so eager to learn and to do good. Charles would not waste a minute of the day. As soon as he woke, he sent for friends to talk to him while he dressed. At meals, he liked to hear music or to have a book read aloud. On the march, he rode with a group of scholars, talking to them and asking questions.

Yet Charles was full of fun. Sometimes he would stop by a river and order everyone to join him in a swim—courtiers, monks, ambassadors, everyone.

He loved children and was so fond of his three pretty daughters that he could not bear to lose them. When they grew up and were married, they still had to live at Court so that Charles could kiss them every morning.

In this lively kingdom, Alcuin found that there was a great deal of work to do. Even in the monasteries, many of the monks could barely read and write and the books were full of mistakes because they had been badly copied by monks who did not understand Latin very well.

First of all, Alcuin started a Palace School. The Frankish nobles were fighting-men who liked nothing better than riding to war behind the banners of their King, but they cared little for reading and writing. Now their sons had to go to school. Some of these proud youngsters, in their fur-trimmed tunics and boots of soft leather, were very lazy. Once, Charles found them admiring a hawk instead of paying attention:

"By the King of Heaven," he roared, "I care nothing for your fine looks and noble birth. Know this, unless you make up for your lazy ways, you will get nothing from Charles!"

It was among the poorer boys that Alcuin found his best scholars. When they were old enough, they went as teachers to the abbey schools that he started and, in time, some of them became bishops and abbots.

*Charles is furious with the nobles' sons
for admiring a hawk instead of studying*

Alcuin and Charles spread knowledge throughout Frankland. They remained great friends, although they were so different, the masterful king and the quiet-spoken scholar.

Charles could be very cruel. He was a Christian and he tried to convert the heathen Saxons of Germany. With fire and slaughter, he forced them to worship Jesus Christ and he made them pay heavily for the churches that he built in their fireswept land.

Alcuin spoke sharply to the King:

"You love the truth but you do evil. It would have been better if the Saxons had been told about the love of Christ, instead of being forced by hard punishments."

Charles was not angry. He loved his friend all the more for speaking out boldly. In time, he came to realize that he ought to have treated the Saxons more kindly.

Alcuin's work went on. He lived at the great palace which Charles built when he grew tired of wandering about with his Court. The Palace School was a splendid building, but Alcuin did not forget England. He went back on a long visit, partly to see his old friends and partly to patch up a quarrel between Charles and Offa, King of Mercia.

Alcuin loved the bustle of the Frankish Court and the work of being Charles' adviser but, as he grew old, he wanted peace and time to think about God.

Charles loved him too much to let him go far away, so he gave him the Abbey of Tours, a monastery so big that its lands were worked by twenty thousand serfs.

Here, as Abbot, Alcuin spent the last years of his life, still busy with a school and with the books that he was constantly writing. But there was time to walk in the gardens, to think and to listen to the birds. Charles often came to see him and, between visits, they wrote to each other about every subject under the sun.

In the year 800, Alcuin was not well enough to make the journey to Rome where Charles was crowned Emperor. He stayed on at Tours, among the flowers and trees. He died there in the spring, when the birds, especially the cuckoo that so delighted him, were returning to his garden.

Ethelfleda

THE LADY OF THE MERCIANS

"COME, daughter, sit here in the window-seat,"
said King Alfred. "Will you listen while I tell
you how you can help me and the kingdom?"

Ethelfleda looked up from her embroidery:

"Father," she said, "I will try all my life to serve
Wessex in the way that you have taught us."

The King smiled a little sadly. He loved his eldest
child and it was not easy to tell her that she must
soon leave her home and her brothers and sisters.

"You know, child, how God gave me the victory

over the Danes? How, after all seemed lost, the men of Wessex defeated the pagan host and how Guthrum the Dane was baptized at Wedmore?"

"Yes, Father," answered Ethelfleda, "I know that you forgave your enemies and they promised to go away and leave our land in peace."

"True, Wessex was saved and Guthrum has not broken his word. But the Danes were hungry for land and when they failed to take Wessex, they cast their eyes upon Mercia, the kingdom next to our own.

"Knowing that the Northmen would fall upon them, the Mercians turned to me, for their own king was a poor creature, not a man but a trembling puppet. The greatest of the Mercian earls is Aethelred and to him I gave the lands of western Mercia and the valley of the Severn."

"Then Mercia is safe, Father? What have I to do?"

"I will tell you, my daughter. Your mother was a Mercian princess, and your aunt was Queen of Mercia before she and her husband were forced to flee abroad. Yet there are many Mercians who do not trust me. They think that I would take their land, that Alfred is now a bigger foe than Guthrum.

"Wessex and Mercia must stand together or both will fall. To show my friendship and to make a bond between the two kingdoms, I would give my daughter in marriage to Earl Aethelred. What say you, will you marry Aethelred?"

England at the time of Ethelfleda

The coloured areas were controlled by the Danes

Ethelfleda bent over her embroidery to hide her tears. She was only sixteen and she knew that Aethelred was almost as old as her own father. She had heard, too, that long ago a Danish axe had split his war-helmet and gashed his face so that it was terrible to look at.

"I will do as my father bids me," she whispered.

"It is not my way to drive those who are weak, much less those who are dear to me. Do you go willingly?"

Ethelfleda raised her head proudly:

"I am your daughter, Father. I will marry Aethelred because you ask me to do so."

79

Ethelfleda meets her future husband, Earl Aethelred

So, with an escort of Wessex nobles, Ethelfleda rode into Mercia and was married to Earl Aethelred in a wooden church by the River Severn. She saw at once that the tale of his injury was true. A terrible scar ran from his forehead to his chin, splitting one eyebrow and giving him a savage expression. But his voice was gentle:

"You honour me greatly, Ethelfleda," he said. "My people and I have given our hearts to the daughter of noble Alfred."

It was true. The Earl and the Mercian folk loved the fair-haired princess from Wessex who rode to the hunt like a man, who could equal any boy with the bow and yet was as clever with her books as she was kind to the poor and the sick.

For her part, Ethelfleda was happy. She came to admire her tall, scarred husband so much that she could not bear to be parted from him. She rode everywhere with him about the kingdom, seeing to its defences, talking to the earls and the men-at-arms, the farm people and the children. To them, she was no longer a stranger. She was their own first lady in the land and they called her, "The Lady of the Mercians".

Two years after Ethelfleda's marriage, when her baby daughter was still in her cradle, a great fleet of more than 800 ships brought a fresh host of Danes to the shores of Kent and Essex. Led by Hasting, their chief, they made raids across England into the heart of Mercia, where they reached the Severn Valley and laid it waste with fire. But the Mercians would not give in.

With Ethelfleda at his side, the Earl kept his men in the field, hanging on to the fringe of the host, cutting down stragglers and giving the enemy no rest. Alfred and the men of Wessex came up from the south and also struck hard at the Danish bases near the Thames.

The invaders were baffled. Was this the soft land they had heard of? Was this the country where rich farmland and fat cattle were to be had for the taking? They pushed inland as far as the Welsh border and wintered at Chester. But although they came out of camp in the spring to burn and kill with their usual

M.W.—6

horrible zest, there was no sign that the Englishmen would allow them to settle in the land.

At last, after three years of warfare, Hasting gave up the struggle and took his host back to Frankland. Aethelred and his lady set to work to rebuild their shattered villages and King Alfred was able to live in peace for the rest of his reign.

Alfred died and his son Edward became King of Wessex. At once, the troubles broke out again. A jealous cousin fled to the north where he made friends with the Yorkshire Danes and with Eric of East Anglia whose armies came raiding as far south as Wiltshire.

They were driven back but next spring they came again and the year after that. The struggle swayed to and fro across Mercia, a buffer land crossed by armies, until the countryside became a waste of blackened fields and roofless cottages.

Ethelfleda naturally turned for help to her brother Edward. Then the Mercians, fighting shoulder to shoulder with the men of Wessex, crushed the Danish host in a great battle in Staffordshire.

But Aethelred was not there with his army. A strange illness had taken away his strength and

A messenger brings news of Aethelred's death

he lay fretting, as weak as a child, while his men
fought all day against the old enemy.

The battle was over and Ethelfleda and her
brother were at dinner in the manor-house of a
Mercian thane when a messenger brought the news
of her husband's death. Ethelfleda was silent for a
long time. Then Edward spoke:

"Do not sorrow, sister. He was a good man and
a brave fighter. There is still your family home in
Wessex where you and your child can live in peace."

"My home is here in Mercia," replied Ethelfleda.
"I am Alfred's daughter and the Lady of the Mercians
will not leave her people in their time of need."

"So be it," answered Edward. "You have only to
send and I will be at your side. Let us keep the bond
between Mercia and Wessex and, since you have no
son, let my own son Athelstan remain at your Court.
He will serve you well and your stiff-necked Mercians

will know that there is friendship between our
houses."

Ethelfleda clapped her hands. She loved her
nephew who, at seventeen, was already following
in the steps of his valiant grandfather. Had not
Alfred girded him with his own sword when the
little boy could hardly lift it? And had he not fought
with that same blade in the battle that had just
ended?

So, for eight years, Ethelfleda led the Mercians in
peace and war and at her side was Athelstan, heir
to the throne of Wessex. They rode together, the
tall woman in the blue cloak and the fair-haired
young warrior. Together, they fought the Danes in
a new way. It was the way that a clever woman
would choose.

Instead of sudden raids against the enemy and
pitched battles, Ethelfleda moved steadily forward.
She had forts built, called burghs or boroughs, as
Alfred had done, so that if her army was forced back,
there was always a stronghold in the rear.

The Danes pressed hard and they found support
from the tribesmen of Wales who came down from
the hills to attack a kingdom ruled by a woman.
But Ethelfleda routed the Welsh and chased them
into the forests. Then she ordered an advance and
her men stormed the Welsh stronghold at Brecknock
and captured the King of Gwent's wife and all her
household.

Athelstan and Ethelfleda lead the Mercians against the Danes

Leaving troops in forts that she built along the Welsh border, the Lady of the Mercians now turned on the foe in the east.

The Danes of the Five Boroughs had long kept all the land in fear. Each town was ruled by a jarl, who had his own band of followers, but Ethelfleda defeated them one by one. In 917, she laid siege to Derby and took it by storm, while her brother Edward crushed the king of East Anglia and slew him with his jarls by the river near Huntingdon.

Next year, Leicester surrendered and the Danes of York came to ask for peace. The bearded jarls knelt and swore to obey the commands of the Lady of the Mercians. Then Ethelfleda rose and said:

"I desire only peace in this ravaged land. Let there be an end to the war between your people and mine. You shall keep the lands you have settled and the customs of your forefathers. In return, you shall take as your lord and protector, not myself, lest you chafe at a woman's rule, but my brother, Edward of Wessex."

Suddenly, she grew tired. She had ridden with her armies for eight years, had planned and schemed with her nephew and her brother, had rebuilt the churches and the people's homes and now there was peace. With her nephew, she rode back towards Mercia, but she grew weaker and the men who loved her carried her in a litter to the fort of Tamworth on Watling Street.

Here she commanded them to set in her bower the high-backed seat that was carried on all her journeys.

She was sitting there when Athelstan came in, as usual, to talk over the day's events and the orders for the morrow:

"Nephew," she said, "I have little time. With your help, the Lady of the Mercians has finished her task. When I am gone, you must not take my place. No, not yet. Your father shall rule both kingdoms as one and then, in the fullness of time, you shall be king. We have beaten the Danes, you and I, and now it is your task to make them one people with the English. One day, you shall be king, not of Wessex and Mercia, but of England."

Edmund Ironside

AS the Lady of the Mercians had foretold, Athelstan carried the banner of Wessex far into the North, defeated all the Danes and made himself King of England. After him came Edgar, another of Alfred's line, and the country was at peace.

Churches and monasteries were built. The fields were ploughed, the harvests were gathered and travellers could make their way safely along the hills.

But there was peace only when the King was strong. Edgar was followed by a weak and cowardly son, so foolish that men called him Ethelred the Unready.

When they heard that England was helpless under a feeble king and jealous earls, the Danes fitted out their dragon-ships and came raiding again. Among the sea-robbers was Sweyn Forkbeard, the warrior King of Denmark.

Ethelred had no army to fight the pirate-bands, but he said:

"I will give you ten thousand pounds in gold if you will go away."

The Danes took the gold, laughing at his simple mind. Soon they came back for more and the English people groaned when they paid the Danegeld, the tax to buy off the robbers who came and came again.

At last, Ethelred thought of a plan. There were many Danes who had settled in England, most of them peaceful folk by now, though some gave help to their kinsmen when they came raiding. Ethelred made up his mind to kill them all.

Secret orders were sent to every town. On Saint Brice's Day, 13th November 1002, all the Danes, men, women and children, were to be put to the sword. This terrible deed was carried out and, among the slaughtered, was Gunhilda, sister of Sweyn Forkbeard.

News of the massacre was carried to Denmark, where Forkbeard swore a great oath of revenge for his sister's death.

For ten years, the Danish king attacked England, landing his warriors where he pleased and thrusting inland to burn towns as far apart as Norwich, Exeter, Canterbury and Northampton. The leaderless people were in despair, for their king and the Witan did nothing to protect them, they only asked for gold.

In the year 1013, Sweyn Forkbeard and his eighteen-year-old son, Canute, landed an army in Yorkshire and made it clear that they had come to conquer the land. Sick of pillage and death, the people agreed to have Sweyn for their king. Ethelred the Unready fled to Normandy.

But Sweyn was never crowned. He died suddenly in London and young Canute went back to Denmark to ask the advice of his older brother.

Sweyn Forkbeard lands with his son, Canute

Edmund was acclaimed by the Londoners

At once, Ethelred returned, full of promises to rule well and he brought with him his son Edmund, now a young man of giant strength, as brave as his father was cowardly.

Ethelred's closest friend was a Mercian noble called Edric who was so greedy that he was known as "the Grasper". These two now set about punishing the English who had made friends with the Danes. They put some to death and took their money and land. But Edmund tried to rally his countrymen to meet the invaders.

When Canute landed, Edmund naturally expected that Edric would bring his Mercian troops to help him, but the Grasper was jealous of the young prince and he marched away to join Canute.

Wessex, Mercia and all the North were lost and

Edmund had to fall back towards London, where his father's worthless life came to an end. The stout-hearted Londoners chose Edmund for their king, but he could not stay in the city:

"Like Alfred, my forefather, I will go to the West and raise an army," he told them. "Close your gates, man the walls and keep your courage high, for I will come back to you."

While Canute brought his fleet to besiege London, Edmund raised his standard in Somerset where the Men of Wessex flocked to join him. As in Alfred's day, they hurled back the Danes, for their courage returned when they saw their young King in the thick of the fight, swinging his axe and roaring:

"On, Wessex! On! On!"

That night, as they ate and rested by the camp-fires, a harper sang of the day's victory and of their King, calling him a true leader, a man of iron.

"That's right," they shouted. "An iron king at last. Edmund Ironside, that's his name!"

The Danes retreated. At midsummer, they came on again and met Edmund's army in Wiltshire. The battle went on all day and, at nightfall, the exhausted foemen drew apart. Next day, the fight was renewed as bitterly as ever and the English seemed to be slowly pressing the enemy back when Edric the Grasper, fighting with the Danes, thought of a trick to dismay the English. Hacking off the head of a fallen man, he held it up crying:

"See the head of your King! Fly, Edmund is dead!"

Unable to reach the traitor, Edmund forced his way to a mound where he tore off his helmet to show his face:

"I live!" he cried. "Your King is here!"

He hurled a spear at Edric who escaped from the field as the furious English broke the Danish ranks.

Canute fell back and Edmund Ironside was able to relieve the brave Londoners. Then he drove some of the Danes to their ships, defeated an army in Kent and followed the rest of the Danes across the Thames into Essex.

By this time, Edric the Grasper had changed sides. He came to Edmund's tent and said:

"I ask pardon for my faults and I own you as my royal lord. The army of Mercia will fight gladly at the side of Wessex."

Edmund hated a traitor, but there were others who had joined the Danes when the English had no leader. Perhaps Edric was truly sorry. The Mercian soldiers were needed, for one more victory would drive Canute into the sea. So he took Edric's hand and placed him on the right wing of his army.

At Ashingdon in Essex, the English and the Danes faced each other from two low hills with a marshy plain between. Both armies could see the river where the Danish ships were moored side by side in their hundreds. For a time, neither side moved. Then

Edric and his troops flee from the battle

Canute, seeing the Mercians take up their position, knew that he was outnumbered. He told his men to retreat across the plain to the ships.

Edmund gave the order to charge but, as the English swept down the slope, Edric's troops stood still. At a word from their lord, they turned and marched away. Canute was too good a soldier to miss his chance. He poured his troops against the deserted flank of the English army and turned defeat into victory.

Once more, Edmund made for the West. He was not beaten, for the name of Ironside rang through the shires and he raised yet another army in Gloucestershire.

Again, he faced Canute, waiting on a hillside to open the fight when daylight came.

A horn sounded; a shout was answered and guards

brought a messenger to where Edmund was sitting
with his earls. The man had come from the Danish
camp:

"I bring greetings from Canute to Edmund," he
said. "My lord would meet him, to speak frankly as
one king to another. Canute offers peace though he
stands ready for war."

The messenger was taken away and Edmund
roared with laughter:

"I never thought to hear a Dane speak of peace.
The cold air must have numbed his courage. Tomorrow, we will cut him to pieces."

But the earls shook their heads. The land cried
out for peace, they said, and this Canute was a
different man from his father. He fought with
honour and it would be wise to listen to what he had
to say.

Edmund could not fight alone, so he went to meet
Canute, unarmed, on an island in the River Severn.
Each admired the other's courage and they agreed
to share the kingdom. Canute should have Mercia
and the Danelaw, Edmund should keep the old
kingdom of Wessex. Whoever lived longest should
be king over the entire country and should rule
Danes and English as equals.

"It is better this way," said Canute, "two kings
at peace instead of two countries at war. I would
that you had been my brother, for we are too well
matched to slay each other."

Edmund and Canute meet and agree to share the kingdom

Edmund looked at the Dane. "You have been a worthy foe," he answered. "Let us now live as brothers."

So England was divided once again. Canute ruled in the north and the east, and Edmund in the south, and there was peace.

But, within a year, Edmund was dead. No one knew how he died. Some said it was a sickness, but others whispered that Edric had killed him by poison to win favour from Canute.

The Dane became king over all England, swearing to rule by the laws of Alfred and Edgar. He promised to give justice to Dane and Englishman alike and he kept faith with Edmund Ironside, for he ruled wisely and he did not forget to reward Edric the Grasper with the fate that he so richly deserved.

More about the people in part 1

PYTHEAS lived at Massilia (Marseilles), a Greek colony in the South of France. In about 310 B.C. he sailed to the Tin Islands and saw tin being taken at low tide to St. Michael's Mount, a trading centre off the coast of Cornwall. He went ashore in southern England and afterwards sailed far to the north. Trade in tin had been going on with the Carthaginians and with merchants from Gaul for many years, but Pytheas was the first visitor to Britain whose name is known to us.

JULIUS CAESAR (102–44 B.C.) was a gay and clever young man. His rich friend Crassus helped him to become popular with the common people of Rome through the circuses and splendid entertainments that he gave them. In 59 B.C. Caesar became Consul and Proconsul of Gaul. When he went there, no one imagined that he would become one of the greatest generals in history, for he had had little experience of warfare. His brilliant success added a huge province to the Empire, though his expeditions to Britain in 55 and 54 B.C. were carried out chiefly to punish the islanders and to impress them with the power of Rome.

Caesar's rival was Pompey, whom he defeated in a civil war through victories in Spain, Greece and Syria. The Romans made Caesar consul for life but he had only commenced to rule as absolute master of the Roman Empire when he was murdered in the Senate House in 44 B.C.

HADRIAN (A.D. 76–138) travelled widely as a young man and fought in the Roman Army against the Parthians. He succeeded his uncle Trajan as Emperor in 117 and continued his journeys until he knew more about the Empire than any other Roman.

He believed that the Empire was large enough and his aim was to establish peace, law and order behind such strong frontier defences as the famous Wall that he ordered to be built in Britain. Besides being a great builder of palaces, temples and libraries, Hadrian was a poet, musician and writer, but his character puzzled the people of his time. The lover of beauty and learning who was generous and just could also be sullen and monstrously cruel.

ETHELBURGA was the daughter of King Ethelbert and Queen Bertha of Kent to whose kingdom St. Augustine brought his band of missionaries in 597. Ethelburga married Edwin of Northumbria whom she converted to Christianity with the aid of her chaplain Paulinus, an Italian monk who had earlier joined St. Augustine's mission. When King Edwin was slain in 633, Ethelburga and Paulinus fled back to Kent where they founded a minster or "double house" for monks and nuns at Lyminge, near Folkestone. Ethelburga died there in about 647 and was later made a saint. St. Paulinus became Bishop of Rochester.

SAINT CUTHBERT lived from about 635 to 687. Little more is known about his life than is told in the story in this book. According to an unknown monk and to Bede, he was

M.W.—7

a Northumbrian shepherd-lad who entered the monastery at Old Melrose, served as a monk at Ripon and later went to Lindisfarne as prior under Abbot Eata.

Cuthbert preferred the stern life of a hermit on Farne Island but, in 684, King Ecgfrith of Northumbria, Archbishop Theodore and Trumwin, Bishop of the Picts, persuaded him to become Bishop of Lindisfarne. The strange wanderings of his coffin took place two centuries after his death. Eventually, his bones found a resting-place at Chester-le-Street and finally at Durham.

Saint Cuthbert was looked upon as the patron saint of Northumbria and his shrine was visited and enriched by any ruler who wished to win the hearts of the northerners. King Athelstan came there in 934, King Edmund in 945 and King Canute in 1020.

BEDE (A.D. 673–735) says in his *Ecclesiastical History of Britain* that he was born near the joint-monastery of Wearmouth and Jarrow and that, at the age of seven, he was taken by his relatives to be educated by Bishop Benedict and later by Abbot Ceolfrith. He continues, "I dwelt all my life from then onward in the same monastery and I gave all my labour to meditating on the scriptures. . . . I ever held it sweet to learn or to teach or to write."

Bede's list of writings included books about the Old Testament, the Temple in Jerusalem, the Prophets, and Lives of Saints as well as books on grammar, rhetoric and astronomy. In fact, he covered the whole field of knowledge in his time, but his fame rests upon his History of Britain from early times up until his own day.

ALCUIN OF YORK (A.D. 735–804), the most famous scholar in Europe, was much more a man of the world than Bede. He was, above all, a teacher and a trainer of teachers. A number of his letters still exist, including some to his friend Arno of Salzburg and to the Emperor Charlemagne.

For many years, Alcuin was chief adviser and Minister of Education to Charlemagne. Although Charlemagne's Empire fell to pieces after his death, the work of Alcuin did not perish, for he and the Emperor "had sowed the seeds of learning in Frankland" and the influence of their schools lasted for centuries.

ETHELFLEDA was the eldest child of Alfred the Great. At sixteen, she married Earl Aethelred of Gloucester, ealdorman of Mercia, and this alliance between Wessex and Mercia saved England when a huge force of Danes, led by Hasting, came over from Boulogne in 892 and made a prolonged effort to settle in that part of Mercia that lay outside the Danelaw.

After her husband's death in 912, Ethelfleda drove the Danes from Ireland back into North Wales, fortified Chester and Warwick and joined her brother, Edward the Elder, in a campaign to push back the Danes in the east and the north-east. Their success paved the way for Athelstan's later victories.

Ethelfleda must have been a remarkable woman. She accompanied her armies on campaign and won the affectionate respect of such doughty warriors as the men of Wessex and Mercia. Moreover, when she died, the Danish jarls who had surrendered to her were not prepared to obey Edward until he had proved himself as worthy a foe as his sister. She died at Tamworth in 919 and was buried at St. Peter's, Gloucester.

EDMUND IRONSIDE (A.D. 980–1016) was the son of Ethelred the Unready. After Alfred, the English Kings were Edward the Elder, Athelstan, Edmund I, "the Deed-doer", Edred, Edwy, Edgar the Peaceful and Edward the Martyr, who was murdered on the orders of his stepmother to gain the throne for her son, Ethelred the Unready.

The story in this book outlines the disastrous reign of Ethelred and the events that led to Canute's mastery of the kingdom. Canute reigned until 1035. His two unworthy sons ruled briefly and Edward the Confessor was brought from Normandy in 1042. He was the son of Ethelred and Emma of Normandy and his reign lasted until 1066.

Part 2

Princes and Rebels

The Empress Matilda

"HER HIGHNESS, the Princess Matilda of England!" cried the heralds. The trumpets blared and into the hall came a little red-haired girl.

With perfect dignity, she moved to where the Emperor Henry V was standing. She curtsied and looked up at her future husband. The Emperor bowed and gravely offered his hand as he escorted her to the cushioned seat where she sat at his side, facing a gathering of the greatest nobles of Germany, Flanders and Italy.

"My envoys have told the truth," murmured the Emperor. "The child is fair; she bears herself like a little queen. Teach her to be my Empress, Bruno."

Matilda, the eight-year-old daughter of Henry I,

was placed in the care of Archbishop Bruno. She learned to speak and to behave like a German princess. The rules of the Court were very strict and there was no fun or kindness in the little girl's life.

In this stiff, cold world, Matilda grew up and the Emperor was proud of his beautiful wife. She rode with him on his ceaseless journeys about the Empire and she showed no fear when battles were fought and when towns were taken by storm.

She was only twenty-five when her husband died suddenly in Flanders:

"Take my sceptre and rule in my place when I am gone," he had whispered. "The people love you . . . they will obey their good Matilda . . ."

The nobles of the Court begged her to accept the crown, but Matilda would not stay in Germany.

"I must go to my father," she said. "He has been asking for me ever since my brother was drowned in the *White Ship*."

She hurried away to Normandy, where King Henry was waiting for her.

"They are alike, those two," murmured a courtier when she arrived. "Iron-willed and both as proud as sin."

King Henry embraced his daughter and cried:

"I have lost my only son but, by Heaven, daughter, I have found him again in you!"

At Christmas, the barons and the great churchmen were summoned to an assembly. The King told them that they must swear an oath to accept Matilda as heir to the throne of England.

The Barons swear to accept Matilda as Henry's heir

The Great Council was shocked. Barons and long-robed abbots paced the hall, muttering to each other:

"Such a thing has never been known. How can a woman rule our kingdom? As for this Matilda, she is as haughty as a German."

But they did not dare to speak openly. Henry I was the Conqueror's son, with his father's temper and the same steely determination to have his way. The barons swore the oath, and among them was Matilda's cousin, Stephen of Blois.

Matilda married Geoffrey of Anjou, nicknamed 'the Handsome', and they were living in Normandy when King Henry came to see them. He was mightily pleased with his two baby grandsons and he went out hunting in the best of humours. In the forest, he was taken ill and, within a few days, he was dead.

"Will you not go at once to England to claim your father's throne?" asked Geoffrey.

105

The Londoners cheer Stephen through

"Not yet, husband," replied Matilda. "You know that I am not well since the birth of our son. The crown of England is safe, for the barons have sworn a solemn oath."

But, while she delayed, Stephen of Blois claimed the throne. He was a brave and chivalrous knight. The people and the barons liked him and they thought that he was a far better choice than his cousin, the haughty Empress Matilda.

The Londoners cheered Stephen through the streets on his way to be crowned, and although Matilda sent an angry protest, there was little that she could do. Already her husband was fighting hard against the Norman knights.

However, it was not long before the English people realized that Stephen was weak. Brave enough in battle, he did not know how to rule. He made gifts of land and titles with reckless generosity, hoping to win men's friendship. Instead, he lost their respect, and they began quarrelling and vying with each other to get what they could out of this soft king.

Matilda's English friends sent her a message:

...he streets on his way to be crowned

"When will you come to rule us?" they asked. "Your father's land is tired of a spendthrift king."

"Spare me as many men as you can find for my army," Matilda said to Geoffrey. "Look well to our sons, husband, for I shall not send for them until my kingdom is won."

In 1139, she crossed to England with a small company of knights and her half-brother, Robert, Earl of Gloucester. They landed and rode to join some friends at Arundel Castle.

Almost immediately, Stephen appeared with an army and surrounded the castle. It seemed certain that Matilda would be captured. But Stephen was a chivalrous foe:

"I do not make war upon a woman," he said. "Let my cousin be given a safe escort from the castle."

So Matilda was allowed to escape to Bristol where she and Robert had many supporters. They raised an army and took control of a large part of the West Country.

Civil war broke out between those who wanted

Matilda to be Queen and those who still followed
Stephen. Both sides robbed the countryside and some
of the barons made private war on their neighbours
and lived on pillage like robber-chiefs.

After some savage fighting, Stephen was captured
and brought before Matilda:

"Ah, usurper!" she cried fiercely. "You shall have
no mercy from Henry's daughter. Take the false
oath-breaker away."

Forgetting Stephen's generosity at Arundel, she
sent him in chains to Bristol Castle, while she rode
in triumph to London.

As she entered the capital, Matilda thought of her
husband still fighting in Normandy and of her little
sons growing up in the care of servants. The barons
had broken their oath, the Londoners had welcomed
Stephen; they were to blame for all her troubles.

"I will teach them what it means to break a
promise," she said bitterly to Robert.

When the nobles came to do homage, she treated
them with arrogant pride. She refused to listen when
Stephen's wife pleaded for her husband. Then the
leading citizens of London arrived and begged her
to rule them according to their ancient laws and
liberties.

"Dare you come here to prate to an Empress of
liberties?" cried Matilda scornfully. "Get you back
to your counting-houses and talk no more of
liberties!"

But a heavy tax caused the Londoners to rebel.
They poured into the streets like a swarm of angry

Matilda escapes to Gloucester

bees and, only just in time, Matilda fled from the capital with Earl Robert and a few followers.

They reached Winchester and captured the castle, but they were besieged there by Stephen's Queen. Food became so short that Matilda resolved to cut a way out.

Before dawn, she got away, but in the darkness, she and Robert were separated. Matilda rode all day until she was too weary to sit in the saddle; ordering her men-at-arms to tie her with ropes to a litter between two horses, she reached safety at Gloucester.

But, as he was crossing a river, Earl Robert was surrounded and captured. To have him set free, Matilda was forced to release King Stephen from prison and the civil war broke out again.

The Empress moved to Oxford but her supporters began to leave her. At length, she said to her half-brother:

"You must go to Normandy, Robert. Urge my husband to bring help without delay."

But Geoffrey could not leave.

"Tell my lady-wife that I am near to victory. All my gains will be lost if I quit the field. Nor have I many knights to spare."

Earl Robert returned but he was not strong enough to rescue Matilda who was now closely besieged in Oxford Castle.

Christmas drew near and her position was desperate. Thick snow lay on the ground and the Thames was frozen over. Supplies in the castle were very low and the famished garrison could not hold out much longer.

"If help does not come within three days, we must surrender," said the captain of the garrison.

"Surrender! I shall never surrender to my false cousin," answered Matilda.

That night, four ghostly figures peered over the battlements. All was still and there was no sign of the besieging forces. One of the knights was let down by a rope. At the bottom, he steadied the rope and Matilda was lowered to the ground. Two more knights followed. Dressed in white garments, the four

figures passed unnoticed across the snow and came to the river.

The ice was strong enough to bear them. Using the frozen river as a road, they trudged all night until they came to an abbey where horses were obtained. At daybreak, they reached Wallingford Castle where Matilda was overjoyed to find Earl Robert and her nine-year-old son, Prince Henry.

"I have come to fight for you, Mother," cried the little boy.

The war dragged on for five more years with terrible cruelties committed by the soldiers on both sides. In 1147, Earl Robert died and all the life went out of Matilda's party. Even Prince Henry could not put new heart into her supporters. They were routed and the Prince only escaped through the generosity of King Stephen. Men said he actually paid for the ship that carried the lad to safety.

At this, Matilda gave up the struggle and followed her son to Normandy. Geoffrey was there and the three of them could only wait and hope.

"If I have failed to win my father's throne," said Matilda, "I mean you to triumph, my son. Never forget that one day you shall be King of England."

She looked proudly at her son. Henry was now twenty, broad-shouldered and immensely strong, with his mother's red hair and fiery temper. In 1153, he left Normandy with her blessing and landed in England with a force of seasoned fighting-men.

This time he was successful. Castle after castle

The coronation of Henry II

was captured and when his army came face to face
with Stephen's, the weary King asked for a truce:

"If my cousin will give up her claim," he said,
"Prince Henry shall rule the kingdom after my
death."

One year later, in Westminster Abbey, the crown
of England was placed on the close-cropped head of
Matilda's son, Henry II.

But Matilda was not in the Abbey for the coronation. She would not return to the land where she had
met so many disasters and she stayed on in Normandy
at the palace that her father had built in Rouen.

Her ambitions were ended and she grew gentle and
pious. She helped the poor, looked after the orphans
and bought land for new monasteries and churches.
After so many battles and sieges, her days were
filled with kindness and prayers. The news from
England was good; her son was ruling firmly and
well. Matilda was content.

Hugh of Lincoln

TO show his sorrow for the murder of Thomas Becket in Canterbury Cathedral, Henry II gave the Church a piece of land at Witham, in Somerset.

Here, he meant to build the first charterhouse or Carthusian monastery in England. But the King was busy and the monastery did not prosper. The French monks were unhappy, for they had no money or buildings, and it seemed as if all would end in failure.

"If only I could find the right man to be prior . . ." said the King to his courtiers.

"I have heard, Sire, of the very man," replied a French knight. "He is Hugh of Avalon, a monk of the Grande Chartreuse. He is known for his saintliness, yet he is a man of affairs at that famous monastery."

"Then he shall be Prior of Witham," cried the King.

A party of clergy travelled to the south of France and came to the valley of the Grande Chartreuse. There they found Hugh, a man of about forty, tall and lean, with twinkling eyes and a courteous manner.

When he learned why the Englishmen had come, Hugh was very downcast, for he loved his life at the lonely monastery. He led them to the prior and, presently, all the monks assembled in the charterhouse. After a long discussion, they decided that

Hugh must go to England in obedience to God's will. Without a word of protest, he said goodbye to his brothers and, in 1180, he came to Witham.

His first task was to put new heart into the unhappy monks and to build the church, cells, cloisters, and a guest-house. Hugh went to see the peasants and small farmers who were very anxious about losing their land. Then he went to the King.

"My lord King," he said in his gentle manner, "Unless these poor men are given land of equal value, I cannot build God's house."

The King agreed to this and Hugh went on:

"These people will leave behind their houses and barns which now, thanks to me, a poor foreigner, are your property."

"Quite so," said Henry, with a smile. "You have presented me with some tumbledown huts and a few sheep-pens. They are great riches. What else would you have me do?"

"Why, let me give them to these people. Then they can carry away the timbers and build anew and no man shall feel robbed."

"Except me," exclaimed the King, looking around. "He really is a terrible fellow, this one. He comes here, a perfect stranger, and in the nicest way, tells me to give away my own property. Well, it seems that I must do as he bids."

Money and royal workmen were sent down to Witham, and presently the priory was finished. By this time, the King had taken a great liking to Hugh. Often, he would interrupt his hunting to call at Witham to talk about the problems of his kingdom. He came to believe that a man so honest and wise should not be hidden away in a cell on the edge of the forest.

King Henry suddenly told the canons, or clergy, of Lincoln that they must choose a new bishop, for the place was vacant. They must elect Hugh of Avalon.

The canons were not at all anxious to elect an unknown monk, but they knew the King's temper and they did as they were told. Taken by surprise, Hugh refused the honour. He had no wish to be a bishop and he was still obedient to his monastery in France.

Henry was not to be denied. Messengers were sent to the Chartreuse to obtain permission and, in 1186, in the presence of the King, Hugh was consecrated Bishop of Lincoln.

After ordering deer in his park to be killed for

Hugh, now Bishop of Lincoln, tours his diocese

the poor, the new bishop went on a tour of the area or diocese that he now ruled. Covering eight counties, it was the largest diocese in England, but Hugh travelled as humbly as a parish priest. Moreover, he made it clear that he would live and work in his diocese although, at this time, it was more usual for bishops to reside at Court or to travel abroad in great state.

In time, Hugh became famous for his courage in helping people who were looked on as outcasts. Jews were very unpopular but Hugh defended them and put a stop to the persecution of these unfortunate people; he also befriended the lepers who were numerous in East Anglia, going amongst them to feed them and to tend their sores.

One of the Bishop's chief tasks was to build a new cathedral, for he arrived at Lincoln shortly after an earthquake had badly damaged the old building. With his architect, Geoffrey of Noyers, he decided to build in a new style, with pointed arches and slender pinnacles in place of the rounded windows and square towers of the Normans.

He himself was often to be seen hewing stone, carrying hods of mortar and lifting baskets of rubble, as the splendid building rose on the hill that stands up out of the flat fields of Lincolnshire.

At the Chartreuse, Hugh's power over wild creatures had been well known and, on the day of his arrival at his manor of Stow, near Lincoln, a huge swan landed on the lake and quickly drove the other swans away. It was so fierce that no one except the

Bishop could go near it, yet it would eat from his hand, follow him into the house and often thrust its head and neck into his wide sleeves.

When Hugh was absent from Stow, the swan would retire to the lake but, just before his return, it would be seen flying up and down, beating the water with its wings and uttering joyous cries. After greeting the Bishop, it would again take possession of the inner court, stalking up and down as if to defend him from all comers.

This swan became so famous that it is often to be seen in paintings and statues of the saintly bishop.

At this time, forest-wardens had powers to punish anyone who killed the deer or drove them away from the crops. Hugh had not been long at Lincoln before he learned that Galfrid, the King's chief forester, had punished some small farmers living on land belonging to the cathedral. As tenants of the Church, the farmers were protected from the game laws and, since Galfrid would not alter his ways, Hugh excommunicated him.

The King was very angry to hear that a royal officer had been punished but, since Hugh had acted according to the law, he decided to wait for an opportunity to show his displeasure.

Hugh helps to build the new cathedral

Not long afterwards, death caused a vacant place among the canons of Lincoln Cathedral and the King sent word that he would choose the new canon:

"Tell the King," replied Hugh, "that these places are for Churchmen, not for courtiers."

These were bold words so soon after Becket's death and the priests of Lincoln trembled when their Bishop was ordered to go to Woodstock Castle. As he rode through the forest, Hugh found Henry resting from the hunt in a glade, surrounded by his courtiers. The King refused to look up and no one spoke to the visitor.

Hugh surveyed the scene. Then, with a smile, he dismounted and walked across to the gathering. Shoving a nobleman aside, he sat himself next to the King and seemed to be actually enjoying the silence. After a while, the King, who could not bear to be still, asked a servant for a needle and thread to sew a bandage on a cut finger.

The sewing proceeded in silence. Then Hugh leaned over and said quietly:

"You know, sire, you remind me of your great-grandmother of Falaise."

William the Conqueror's mother had been a humble glove-maker in Normandy and King Henry, who was not at all ashamed of his family, burst out laughing.

"Do you know what this impudent foreigner said?" he cried. "The rogue knows that my great-grand-mother was a woman of the people and he has sauce to say that my sewing reminds him of her needle-craft!"

The joke saved the situation and the King, now in a good humour, agreed that Hugh had acted rightly in his own diocese.

When Henry II died, his son Richard I soon departed to the Crusade and it was five years before he returned home. The Treasury was empty and the royal officials scurried about trying to raise money for a war against Richard's arch-enemy, Philip of France. They discovered that, by ancient custom, Hugh ought to have given the King a valuable fur-lined robe. The King hinted that only a very large sum of money could put the matter right.

But Hugh was almost penniless. All his money went to the poor and towards building the new cathedral. However, the Lincoln clergy collected 3000 silver marks to free their beloved Bishop from debt. But he was soon in trouble again.

The Abbot of Eynsham Abbey died and King Richard took the abbey's income for his own use. Hugh immediately told the King that his action was wrong. With a bad grace, Richard had to give way to the fearless bishop.

The French war was so costly that Hubert, the Archbishop of Canterbury, was ordered to persuade the bishops to pay for the upkeep of a company of knights. When Hubert announced the plan to an assembly of clergy, Hugh rose to his feet:

"A bishop is bound to furnish a due number of knights to defend the realm," he said. "He is not bound to provide men to serve across the seas. This demand is not lawful."

When King Richard learned who had defied him, he gave orders for all the Bishop of Lincoln's property to be seized. Hugh, not at all alarmed, set out to speak to the King himself.

He crossed to Normandy and found Richard in church at one of his castles. He went up to him to receive the usual greeting between monarch and bishop, but the King turned angrily away.

"Bestow on me the kiss of peace, my lord King," said Hugh gently. Richard took no notice. Hugh insisted. "I have travelled far and I deserve a greeting," he said.

"You deserve nothing," growled the King.

Taking hold of the Lion-heart's cloak, Hugh shook it.

"I ask you again for a greeting," he repeated.

Richard tried to snatch his cloak away but Hugh clung on and a tug-of-war followed. Suddenly Richard began to smile at the ridiculous situation; he loved courage and who could be angry with a man who defied Europe's most famous warrior in his own castle?

"On my soul," he cried, "if all priests were like you, no king would dare do wrong."

Unfortunately, Richard soon forgot his good intentions and demanded more money from the clergy. Once again, Hugh crossed to France but this time he was met with the news that Richard was dead, killed by an arrow when besieging a castle. He was to be buried in the family vault in Normandy but the country was infested by robbers and armed bands. It would be impossible for the Bishop to reach the place.

"I would be a coward if I failed in my duty to my lord and prince," replied Hugh. "If they rob me of my horse and clothes, I shall walk more easily."

He set off and arrived in time to conduct Richard the Lion-heart's burial service.

After attending King John's coronation and giving him a solemn warning about his conduct, Hugh went to visit his family in the valley of the Grande Chartreuse. On the return journey, he fell ill with fever and, by the time he reached Dover, he was too weak to ride a horse.

Carried by litter to London, he rested in the Old Temple at High Holborn. Here, he was visited by his friends, by the King and by Geoffrey the architect, with whom he held discussions about his beloved cathedral.

"Put my tomb where you can find a space for it," he said. "Don't let it block up the main aisle but place it close to a wall out of the way, for I do not want anyone to stumble over me."

Hugh died in London in 1200 and all England mourned for him as the funeral procession wound

Hugh and Richard struggle in the chapel

Pilgrims visit St. Hugh of Lincoln's shrine

slowly northwards. At Lincoln, two kings, John of
England and William the Lion of Scotland, helped
to carry his coffin on their shoulders into the
cathedral.

Twenty years later, 'the most fearless bishop that
England has ever known' was made a saint. His
shrine of pure gold attracted pilgrims in numbers
almost as great as those that visited the tomb of
St. Thomas of Canterbury in the south.

King John

"THE little knave has come late," said King Henry II, looking at his newborn son in the royal nurse's arms. "My lands are already promised to his brothers. This one has nothing. He shall be John—John Lackland."

Henry loved this youngest child who grew into a bright little boy with charming manners. But when the King tried to give him some possessions, there was trouble. His three older brothers were a mean and violent set and, as they grew up, their mother, Queen Eleanor, encouraged them to defy their father. Not one would give an acre to his little brother.

But Henry II was a determined man. When John was six, he gave him three castles and this caused a family rebellion. The brothers ran off to the King of France and, when Henry ordered them back, they said to his messenger:

"Tell your master that he is King no longer. Young Henry is King of the English."

Henry II captured Queen Eleanor as she was on her way to join her sons, disguised as a man. He put her into a dungeon, crushed the rebels and forced the boys to ask for pardon.

John was sixteen when his eldest brother died. Then the King said to Richard:

"You are now my heir. Anjou, Normandy and England will be yours. Give Aquitaine to John."

123

But Richard refused.

"I have fought hard and mastered the barons of Aquitaine," he said. "I will not give it to a boy who plays cards in his father's parlour."

So Henry decided that John should have Ireland which he had partly conquered some years before.

The prince was now nineteen, handsome, rather short and boyish in appearance. He was well-read, for he always carried a small library about with him, and he liked hunting, gambling and practical jokes. With his expensive clothes and jewels, he was something of a dandy, but he could be energetic when he chose. Unfortunately, he was looked upon as his father's pet, the spoilt baby of the family.

With his flashy companions, John meant to have some fun in Ireland. They hooted with laughter at the shaggy, bearded chieftains who came to pay homage, mocked the Anglo-Norman settlers and squandered the barrels of silver pennies provided for the soldiers' pay.

The expedition was a ridiculous failure and John came home to his father, full of excuses, but people at Court wagged their heads and murmured:

"A spoilt boy cannot be put to a man's work."

By this time, the third brother, Geoffrey, had died, leaving a baby son, Arthur of Brittany. The new King of France, a pale determined young man named Philip Augustus, was doing his best to foster the quarrels of the English royal house:

"Like every true knight of the Cross," he said to Richard, "you wish to join the Crusade. But how

John and his companions laugh at the Irish chieftains

125

can you go, when your father is about to give half your lands to his favourite, John?"

Stung by these words, Richard joined Philip in an attack on King Henry, who happened to be in France. Catching him unprepared, they drove him from castle to castle until, deserted by nearly all his barons, the old man asked for peace.

"My day is over," he said. "I ask only one thing. Let me but see the names of my barons who have turned against me." The list was brought and at the top was the name of John. Then the old King cried out:

"My youngest son, whom I loved above all my sons and for whom I have borne all these troubles— even he has deserted me. Let all things go, for I care no longer for the world."

Henry died and Richard hurried away to England to be crowned. His one thought was to raise money quickly and to join the knights of Europe on the Third Crusade.

Once the great warrior was out of the way, John paraded about the country as if he were already king. He put round stories that Richard would never return and when King Philip came back early from the Crusade, he was soon hand-in-glove with his brother's enemy.

News arrived that Richard had been captured on the way home and was being held to ransom in Germany. Gleefully, John and Philip made plans to share the Lion-heart's possessions and they offered to pay the Emperor a large sum if he would keep Richard in prison.

But Eleanor, the aged Queen Mother, would have none of this treachery to her best-loved son. She defended his lands, while the people of England raised the money for his ransom. At last, he was set free and King Philip sent an urgent message to John:

"Look to yourself," he wrote, "for the Great Devil himself is loosed!"

John fled abroad but Richard stayed only long enough in England to raise an army to attack Philip. Then he crossed to Normandy and happened to stay the night at the manor of an old friend. He noticed that the man was nervous:

"What is it?" asked Richard. "Have you seen my brother lately? I know he is hiding hereabouts. Well, you can tell him that I will not hold his folly against him."

John was hidden in that very house and presently he came to beg for pardon.

"Get up, brother," cried Richard with rough kindness. "You are but a child. I forgive you, but I do not doubt you will forget my words. Come to supper, lad!"

For the next five years, John seemed to have turned over a new leaf. He served Richard well and defended Normandy while his brother was fighting the rebel barons in the south. But, in 1199, Richard died from a wound and John became King.

John apologizes to Richard

To everyone's astonishment, he showed great energy, touring his dominions and forcing the barons who supported his nephew, Arthur of Brittany, to pay homage.

Prince Arthur appealed to King Philip for help and, in 1202, old Queen Eleanor was hotly besieged in one of her French castles. John raced to his mother's rescue, took the besiegers by surprise and captured all the leaders, including young Arthur of Brittany.

The prisoners were loaded with chains but no one ever knew exactly what happened to Prince Arthur. Some said he was blinded and hidden away. Most probably, he was killed by John's own hands in a fit of drunken rage when he went to gloat over his prisoner in the castle at Rouen.

This crime did great harm to John. His allies began to change sides and he seemed to lose all his energy and fire.

One castle after another fell, until Normandy itself was crumbling, but John only muttered:

"Let be, let be. One day I shall win it all again."

The truth was that he could not trust his Norman barons. They had respected Henry II and feared Richard the Lion-heart; for John, they had only contempt:

"A foolish man, he is well named Softsword," said one.

"He betrayed his father, brother and nephew," answered his companion. "I will not fight for such a one."

John hears a case in the law-courts

So Normandy was lost and John went back to England. He had no settled home but dozens of castles and manors scattered about the country and he travelled ceaselessly, never spending more than a day or two in one place. But, with all his faults, John knew how to govern.

He sat with the justices in the law-courts, hearing cases and giving judgment; he kept the sheriffs and royal officials hard at work, examined the accounts with an eagle eye, had good coins minted, granted charters to towns and built up a navy that was strong enough to beat the French. At times, he showed pity to humble people and he could be surprisingly generous to the poor.

By these methods, John had the kingdom in his grip until he picked a quarrel with the Church.

He told the monks of Canterbury to choose a friend of his as Archbishop but, on the Pope's advice, they elected Stephen Langton, an English cardinal, living abroad.

M.W.—9   129

John was furious. He drove the monks out and seized their property.

"As for Langton," he cried. "I will hang him by the neck if he as much as sets foot in my realm."

As a punishment, the Pope closed all the churches. The bells were silent and the dead had to be buried in unhallowed ground. The King himself was excommunicated. But John did not care. He took the church lands, emptied the abbey money-chests and gleefully cut down the woods at Canterbury.

With this stolen money, he hired an army and marched north to defeat old William the Lion, King of Scotland. He also defeated the Welsh and the Irish chieftains. It seemed as if this godless king and his foreign mercenaries were triumphant everywhere.

*John's men
seize the wealth
of an abbey*

John swears loyalty to the Church

In 1213, the Pope decided to turn John off his throne. King Philip of France, as the Church's champion, was about to invade England when John turned the tables on him by making friends with the Pope.

Pretending to be sorry for his sins, he welcomed Stephen Langton and knelt down and swore to be loyal to the Church. He gave England to the Pope and received it back as a vassal.

"The lord King," declared the delighted monks, "is another man, by God's grace!"

As soon as this peace-making was over, John called upon the barons to join him in a great invasion of France. They refused. John sailed with his mercenaries but, on the continent, his allies collapsed and he returned home, an angry man who had wasted his treasure. He found the barons on the point of armed rebellion.

They had made up their minds that they would stand no more from this hateful King. The root of the trouble was John's greed.

In times of war, the nobles had to serve the King

131

or pay 'shield money', and John demanded shield money more often than any king in the past—and at twice the old rate.

When a man died, his heir paid a 'relief' before he could have his father's estate. It was not a big sum—£100 for a baron—but John demanded thousands of pounds. Another of the King's rights was to give consent for a rich heiress to marry, so John forced these ladies to pay huge sums for his 'permission'. Sometimes, a lady had to pay a fine *not* to marry one of his foreign cut-throats!

The King made money in all kinds of ways. Prowling about the kingdom, he often heard of some small error and then he pounced. Barons were fined for making a false statement, for letting an outlaw escape or for breaking the forest laws. Often, they had to pay enormous sums 'for making the King angry' or 'for having the King's goodwill'.

To make sure that he was obeyed, John demanded hostages, usually younger sons or daughters. Once, hearing of a rising in Wales, he hanged twenty-eight boys, sons of Welsh princes. A month later, he said to one of his earls, with an evil grin:

"You have given your son as a hostage, therefore we require you to yield up your castle."

For no reason at all, he decided to ruin William de Briouze, a baron who had served him well. He demanded William's son as a hostage, but the boy's mother said:

"I do well remember Prince Arthur who was basely murdered."

For these words, the family was hounded from place to place until mother and son were captured and starved to death in a dungeon.

Most of all, people hated John for his mocking insults. There was no warmth or gratitude in the man. He made gifts and took them away, jeered at his nobles and insulted their wives and daughters. The chief positions of the kingdom were filled by foreign adventurers and by strong-armed ruffians who were paid to carry out the King's most brutal orders.

At last, the barons swore to obey the King no longer. In May 1215, they rode into London, where the gates were opened in welcome. But Stephen Langton cried:

"Not war, my lords. Let us urge the King to rule justly. Let us draw up a charter by which you may regain your liberty."

John was at Windsor, with only a small bodyguard, for he had paid off his mercenaries. When he read the barons' message, asking for their ancient rights, he burst out:

"They might as well ask for my crown!"

On 15th June 1215, the two parties met in a field called Runnymede near the Thames. A throne was placed upon a platform backed by a silk awning with the golden lions of England. Supported by Langton and the faithful William Marshal, King John faced the English nobles, most of them as greedy and treacherous as the King himself.

A monk read aloud the clauses of the Great Charter. There was nothing new, only the laws and customs of the land. The Church was to keep its rights, the barons were to have their liberties and to pay only what was due; no freeman was to be put in prison or punished without proper trial. All this and more was read to the silent gathering.

At length, the King fixed his seal to the parchment and the leading barons did the same. Both sides withdrew, the barons to London, the King to Windsor and then to the Isle of Wight.

Both sides were thinking of revenge. In August, a letter came from the Pope declaring that the Charter was a wicked document forced upon a King whom he had pardoned. By this time, John had collected an army.

"Now, I will make my barons howl for mercy," he cried.

In one of his moods of brilliant energy, John struck hard while the barons cowered behind the walls of London. He captured their castles, burnt their manors and loaded their treasures into his waggons.

In defeat, the barons invited Louis of France, son of John's old enemy, to accept the crown and in 1216 he landed with an army. All that summer, there was savage war in England.

A monk reads the Great Charter to John at Runnymede

"By God's teeth," swore John, "I will teach this land what it is to rebel against a king. Before the year is out, there will be so little left to eat that men will pay a shilling for a halfpenny loaf."

135

John's treasure is lost in the Wash

In his fury, John showed military skill worthy of his great brother. He made lightning marches to relieve his own castles, doubled in his tracks and outwitted his enemies at every turn. But, for all his skill, he could not win. The people of England would not help a man they despised.

In October, he was in Lincolnshire, harrying the land where the corn was still uncut. He went north and doubled back to Lynn, near the Wash. Two days later, though unwell, he set out for the north again, ordering his waggons to take a shorter route across the river estuary at low tide.

This was a well-known way over the sands but, for some reason, one of the leading waggons stuck. The others were halted and soon they became bogged down. There was not time to free them before the sea came sweeping in to overwhelm the entire baggage train.

From the Lincolnshire side, John saw the disaster.

"My treasure!" he cried in horror. "My jewels, plate, gold, even my crown and regalia—all lost!"

It was a terrible blow to a man so fond of wealth. Sick at heart and worn out by weeks in the saddle, he reached Sleaford where, said the monks afterwards, he made himself sick on peaches and cider, but he was already ill when he arrived.

Carried on a litter to Newark Castle, he was too weak to read letters from some of the barons who wished to make peace. He could only murmur his last wishes, asking that alms should be given to the poor and to religious houses for the salvation of his soul. On 18th October, John died and his followers took his body and buried him, as he had wished, in Worcester Cathedral.

His nine-year-old son, a 'pretty little knight', was proclaimed King Henry III at Gloucester but, since all the royal treasures had been lost, the boy had to be crowned with a plain gold circlet provided by his mother.

Henry III's coronation

Roger Bacon

"A RIOT, father, a riot!" cried Basil, hopping with excitement, as Master Fordham the spicer came to his door to see what all the noise was about.

The boy pointed towards the widest part of Oxford's High Street where a crowd was struggling in an uproar of shouts and screams. A group of young townsmen ran past the spicer's house, waving their cudgels.

"Can I go and watch, father?" pleaded the boy.

"And have your head split? No, boy, give me a hand with the shutters," answered his father. Turning to his relative who had also come to the door, he added, "Go in, cousin Gilbert, before the riot spreads this way."

Inside, with the door bolted, Master Fordham explained the situation to his cousin, a stranger to Oxford.

" 'Tis the students," he said. "They do as they please, with none to hinder them."

"But I saw them go by earlier," said Gilbert, "all dressed with garlands, dancing and wearing masks as for a festival."

"Ay, it starts merrily enough," replied the merchant, "but students from the south will not yield the way to the northerners. Blows are struck. Some passing townsman is tripped and set upon. Then, as you saw, the lads of the town join the fray. Last year, two men were slain in the Cornmarket."

"Can no one check these unruly students?"

"They are clerks, cousin, protected by the Church. But I hear that King Henry has ordered the sheriff to banish all who have not put themselves under a master of studies."

"How many are the students?"

"More than two thousand. Some are no more than boys but others are idle rogues who pass their time in the taverns. A plague on all students, I say!"

Like most townsmen in the Middle Ages, Master Fordham had no love for the university and he drew a black picture of the misbehaviour of the Oxford students. But not all of them were violent ruffians. There were many like Roger Bacon who came to the university to devote all their lives to learning.

In Henry III's reign, the Bacons were well-to-do landowners in Somerset. Roger's elder brother, the head of the family, saw to it that the clever youngster had enough money to manage on, unlike the poor students who shared their crusts, their books and even one gown between two or three. At this time, there were no colleges and fifteen-year-old Roger had to put his name down on the roll of a Master who was willing to teach him.

Every day, at dawn, he left his lodgings and joined the throng of students hurrying through the streets to the first lecture. He tried to reach the Master's house in time to get a stool; otherwise, he sat on the floor to listen to the lesson.

There were few books, so the Master read slowly, explaining the more difficult Latin passages, and the students wrote down what he told them and learned their notes by heart.

After two or three years, Roger had to hold a public argument in Latin with his teacher. He did well and was given his degree of Bachelor of Arts, for there were no written examinations. Then he went on studying for the next degree called Master of Arts.

By this time, the young man from Somerset was known to be one of the cleverest students at Oxford. He could choose to go and listen to the best teachers at the university, famous scholars, such as Adam Marsh and Thomas of York. Best of all, he liked to sit at the feet of Robert Grosseteste, whose surname meant 'Great-head'.

Grosseteste, son of a humble peasant, had risen to become Chancellor of the university and he was so great a scholar that the titles of his books filled twenty-five pages. He understood Latin, Greek and Hebrew and, in addition to the usual subjects, he

A lecture at Oxford University

was interested in mathematics and science. At this time, any learning beyond religion and philosophy was looked upon with suspicion but Grosseteste was so courteous and devout that he did not get into trouble.

In 1235, Robert Grosseteste left the university to become Bishop of Lincoln, and Roger was heartbroken:

"I have learned more from that good man than from all my other teachers," he said. "He alone had a true understanding of things that are hidden from other men."

With his favourite master gone, Roger made up his mind that he, too, would leave Oxford.

"Why do you wish to go away?" asked his friend Thomas.

"Because here we are taught only what is already known to learned men. I want to find out things that are not yet understood."

141

"And what are these things?"

"They are in the world, all about you, Thomas," replied Roger eagerly. "They are not just quibbles and words. They are real—stars, rainbows, comets— things a sea-captain knows more about than your Master of Arts: herbs and juices that your old country-wife understands: how a wheel turns and the way sunlight shines through a piece of glass.

"There are more truths to be learned from humble persons than from all your famous doctors. Also, I need books, for we have so few in Oxford, and I shall find them in Paris."

So Roger went to study at Paris. He read a great deal and began to make experiments. Having plenty of money, he was able to spend more than £2000 on books and instruments, while widening his knowledge by learning Greek, Hebrew and Arabic.

"I was able to seek the friendship of wise men," he said later. At a foreign university, there were many scholars to talk to—men from Italy and the Low Countries who were finding out about the anatomy of the body, Arabs from Spain who were the cleverest mathematicians and Jews who were the best physicians.

But, although Bacon became famous, he had not learned to control his tongue. He had always been sharp-tempered and when he was rebuked by his seniors for his peculiar studies, he grew very angry.

"You stand in the way of knowledge," he sneered. "You are like men walking along a narrow causeway, seeing nothing but your own feet, for you dare not

Bacon rebukes his narrow-minded seniors

lift your eyes. Knowledge is as wide as the sky but you blindly follow the old ways and you will not admit your ignorance!"

These biting words made Bacon unpopular and, after several years, he went back to Oxford to teach at his old university. When he was about forty years old, he suddenly became a friar.

The Church ruled universities, protected scholars and encouraged learning. Bacon was not a priest and he may have felt that he needed protection. At all events, the Franciscans were popular at Oxford. Many of them were scholars and Roger joined the Order and became one of the Minor or Lesser Brothers of St. Francis.

But he was never a poor friar and he certainly was not humble. As proud as ever, he went on lecturing and arguing. Students crowded eagerly to listen to a man who had new ideas, a man who taught them to think rather than to learn their lessons by heart.

Besides talking about his ideas, the 'Wonderful Doctor', as they called him, was testing out his ideas.

143

Bacon demonstrates his telescope

He invented magnifying-glasses and a pair of spectacles, he studied beams of light, made a telescope to look at the stars and even discovered how to make gunpowder, though it was said that he did not dare to reveal the secret.

People began to wonder what he was at with all these experiments. What were those strange bubblings and explosions that could be heard from 'Friar Bacon's Tower' on the old bridge over the Isis? Was he dabbling in the Black Arts? Was he becoming a sorcerer, a servant of the Devil?

The general of the Order of St. Francis did not like these rumours and when Roger rudely refused to do as he was told, he was sent to Paris. For ten years, he was almost a prisoner. The loss of his instruments and most of his books made Roger ill with vexation until he received a letter that gave him the chance he longed for.

144

Among those who had listened to his lectures was a Franciscan named Guy of Foulques and, by 1256, he had risen so high that he was elected Pope Clement IV. Remembering the brilliant friar, he sent to ask if he could study some of his writings. Bacon was overjoyed and wrote back immediately:

"Except for two years of the forty that have passed since I learned my alphabet, I have always been studying but what I have learned is not yet written down. It might be that I shall need to write it all out five or six times until I have made one tried and trustworthy book. Then I will send it to Your Holiness."

Carefully, he began to write down his beliefs and discoveries, showing how he had tried to learn by experiment. It was an enormous list, for he had been interested in mathematics, anatomy, medicine, chemistry, physics, astronomy, the calendar and music. At last, the book was finished and he called out to his favourite pupil, John of London:

"It is done," he said with pride. "I have called it my Great Work and I place it in your keeping, John. Carry it safe to Rome."

John took the 'tried and trustworthy book' to Italy but, alas, he found that Pope Clement was so ill that he was unable to study it before he died.

However, the interest of the Pope in his work did help Roger, for he regained his freedom and was able to return to his teaching and experiments. After a time, the whispers and rumours began again.

In 1277, Bacon was declared a person suspected of

M.W.—10

'strange novelties'. No one was allowed to read his books and in the following year he was suddenly arrested and put into prison.

Fourteen years passed and not until he was almost eighty was the bent white-haired friar set at liberty. He was too old now for any more arguments and he made his way wearily to Oxford. There he died in the city where he had been praised and attacked for so many years.

"They have treated me like a criminal," he said. "But all my life, I have been a seeker of truth."

No great new discovery arose from Roger Bacon's experiments but he had pointed the way in which men could find out about the marvels of the world. He was born too soon. His far-reaching mind could imagine wonders that in his day were regarded as silly or wicked: once, he wrote:

"Vessels could be made to move without oars or rowers, so that ships of great size might move at the control of one man. Moreover chariots might be made to move without animals. Flying machines might be made so that a man might sit in the midst thereof . . . like a bird in her flight."

From one of Leonardo da Vinci's drawings

After landing in Normandy Edward III knights his son

The Black Prince

A LL through the winter, the bowyers, armourers
and smiths had been busy in the workshops of
England. The King's officials had scoured the land
for money and provisions and now, on 5th July 1346,
the army was ready to sail.

With the greatest nobles of the realm, King
Edward III went aboard ship; at his side was his
sixteen-year-old son, the Prince of Wales.

As soon as the army landed in Normandy, the
King's first act was to knight his son. They stood on
a hillock near the beach so that all could see as the
King laid the shining blade upon the boy's shoulder,
buckled the belt about his waist and fastened to his
heels the golden spurs of knighthood.

When the horses and waggons were ashore, the
army moved off in three columns, ravaging the green
countryside as they went.

At Caen, a town defended by massive walls, the Prince had his first taste of real fighting when he took part in a furious assault across the bridge. The town was sacked and the English army advanced into France, as Edward III sought battle with Philip of Valois.

Marching north, the English crossed the river Seine. By this time, an enormous French army was keeping pace with the invaders, but neither king would fight until he found the position that he wanted. Edward III urged his commanders to hurry.

The march became a race to the Somme. The English reached the river first but all the bridges were destroyed. Edward sent riders to hunt along the bank for a crossing.

The weary troops moved down-river towards the sea, where the Somme became so wide that the far bank was nearly a mile off. The King summoned a council of war but his lords sat in gloomy silence until one remarked:

"In ancient times, did not the Romans have a road hereabouts?"

"By our Lady, they did!" cried another. "There must be a ford."

"Go, Edward, and fetch in every living man in the district," said the King to his son.

An hour later, the first prisoners were led in, fishermen, cowherds and trembling old peasants. The King addressed them:

"There is a ford across the river," he said. "To the man who shows me where it lies, I will give his life and the lives of twenty-five others. Otherwise, you hang at sunset."

The peasants stood in sullen misery. Then one or two whispered and pushed forward a shambling fellow named Gobin, who said:

"The ford lies two miles off at Blanchetaque. At low tide, there is a crossing of hard white chalk. How wide, did you say? Wide enough for a dozen men to pass shoulder to shoulder."

"If this be true," cried the King, "I will give you a hundred nobles."

"It is true, sire," said the peasant. "But you must cross at low tide, at sunrise tomorrow."

Trumpets called the army to readiness and, at dawn, the English watched anxiously as the tide sucked the river out to sea, leaving mud flats and pools behind. Gobin, held by two soldiers who were ready to slit his throat if he had lied, suddenly pointed to a whitish streak in the river. It was the ford.

"God and St. George!" roared the English as the first rank of archers went down the bank and waded

across with bows above their heads. The army crossed in their thousands and then the waggons lurched through the shallow water with soldiers straining at the wheels to save their precious loot.

As the King gave Gobin his reward, the banners of the French vanguard were sighted. But before their horsemen had thundered up, the returning tide had covered the ford and the English could shout derision from the far bank.

Two days later, King Edward resolved to give battle. Near the village of Crecy, his general's eye had seen the ideal place to fight a battle in the English style. Edward placed his army on the brow of a long slope; then he took the Prince with him and explained how to choose a position:

"See where the land slopes away from where we stand," he said. "There are orchards to protect our flank there and marshes to guard the other flank.

Edward explains his plan of battle to his son

Now, my son, you shall station yourself here on the right. My lord the Earl of Northampton will be over there on the left. I shall hold the main-guard there on the ridge. Set your archers forward and at either side. Then they will be free to move back out of the way when the Frenchmen come to grips."

The Prince said little but he saw the knights and men-at-arms dismount and lead their horses to the rear. He noted how the archers were busy planting sharp stakes and digging pot-holes in the ground in front of where they would stand. He felt the excitement that passed along the lines as the King rode by to see that all was well before retiring to a windmill at the rear.

It was past noon when the French scouts discovered the English position and raced back to Philip of Valois. Some of his lords advised the French King to rest his troops until the morrow, but most of the nobles would hear of nothing but attack.

At this, Philip ordered his Genoese crossbowmen to the front. Their leaders pointed out that the men had marched all day in heavy harness and were too weary to fight.

"You see what happens when you hire scoundrels," sneered the King's brother. "The cowards fall back in the moment of need."

Angered by this insult, the Genoese formed their lines and began to advance. A sudden rain-squall halted them but then the sun came out brilliantly, full in their faces. Nevertheless, the Italian bowmen gave a loud shout and marched forward in perfect

The French horsemen and foot-soldiers were hopelessly entangled

order to within about 300 yards of where the English archers stood motionless.

Crossbows were levelled but the rain had wetted their strings and most of the bolts fell short. Then the English archers began to shoot as coolly as if they were practising at the butts, firing arrow after arrow so swiftly that as soon as one was in mid-air, another was on the string. To escape this pitiless hail, the Genoese turned and fled towards the oncoming cavalry.

"Clear that rabble out of the way!" yelled the King's brother but, in a moment, horsemen and foot-soldiers were hopelessly entangled and the English arrows continued to whistle into the struggling mass, piercing armour and leather-jerkins, bringing down the great horses in screaming helplessness.

Unable to see clearly what was happening ahead, wave after wave of French knights charged up the slope, only to be brought down by their own casualties or by the goose-feathered shafts.

But courage and numbers told. Some knights reached the English ranks and broke through, so

that, from the windmill, King Edward could see a
mass of plumed crests and uplifted blades, with
mounted men smiting downwards or plunging headlong into the ruck. Presently, a man ran to the
windmill to ask for help.

"Is my son dead or badly hurt?" asked the King.

"Not so, thanks to God. But he is hard-put and
needs help, Sire."

"Nay, get you back," answered the King. "Say
that I shall not come as long as my son lives. I
command them to let the boy win his spurs."

But when the man had gone, King Edward
prudently sent the fighting Bishop of Durham forward
with a company of knights. It was just as well. The
Prince was down.

Sir Richard Fitz-Simon, seeing him slip, had
snatched the dragon-standard and thrown it over
the boy; then, straddling his body and whirling his
sword, he roared "Edward! Edward! St. George, to
Edward!" At this, the mace-swinging Bishop crashed
in so furiously that the French were thrown back and
the Prince regained his feet.

153

By dusk, King Philip, bleeding from the throat and thigh, had to be forced from the field by his knights. The battle was over and, on the hill-crest, a proud father found his son bemused with weariness:

"Sweet son," he cried, embracing him. "You are truly my son, for right nobly have you borne yourself. The honour of this day is yours."

After Calais had been starved into surrender, Prince Edward went home to a hero's welcome. Never had England known such a sumptuous round of tournaments, banquets and merry-making.

Presently, there was more excitement when a fleet was fitted out to tackle the Spaniards who were robbing English ships in the Channel. Waiting off Winchelsea for the enemy to come from Flanders, the Prince and his friends were on deck listening to the minstrels, when a shout rang from the mast-head.

"Ho! A sail! I see two–three–four–God help me, I cannot count them!"

The Prince rashly ordered his helmsman to steer for the biggest Spaniard. His ship struck the other so violently that her hull was smashed and, as the Castilians rained stones and iron bars down on to the small ship, the Prince fought furiously to lead his men up on to the enemy deck.

Seeing Edward's plight, the Earl of Lancaster brought his ship to the other side of the Spaniard and stormed aboard, crying:

"A Derby! A Derby to the rescue!"

This action allowed the Prince and his followers to

gain the Spanish deck an instant before their own
ship sank.

When he was twenty-four, Prince Edward was
sent by his father to renew the war with France. He
landed his army at Bordeaux where the lords of
Gascony met him with oaths of allegiance. Together,
they set off on a three months' tour of pillage,
ravaging the beautiful countryside as far as the
Mediterranean and returning so loaded with plunder
that the waggons could scarcely move.

A second raid was launched into the heart of
France, for the Prince expected that his father and
Lancaster would come from Calais and the west to
join him.

Each day the raiders covered a dozen miles or so,
burning a village here, looting a town there, but
there was no news of King Edward or the Duke. So
the Prince decided to retire south at leisurely pace.
He did not realize that a huge army of French

knights and retainers was already bearing down on him to wipe out the memory of Crecy.

The first inkling of danger came when a horseman dashed into his camp with news that thirty miles away the country was filled with the banners and lances of a French host four times the size of the English army. This was serious news and the Prince gave orders to move south in earnest.

John, the new King of France, was a better soldier than his father and the French steadily overhauled the English who were hampered by their plunder-laden waggons. Near Poitiers, the Prince learned that the enemy had got up with him and was closing in on two sides.

"God help us," he said to Sir John Chandos. "We must find a place where we may fight."

Like his father, he chose carefully. There was a slope guarded by a steep hill on the right; bushes, vineyards and a hedge running crosswise would provide cover for the archers. He ordered a halt and told his weary men to take what rest they could before the battle.

At eight o'clock on 19th September 1356, the French attacked. First came two columns of mounted knights who never reached the archers at the hedge. A second wave burst through and was halted among the vines. Then the main army was seen advancing on foot, for the French believed they had lost Crecy because they had not dismounted like the English.

Arrows rained into the armoured mass. Men fell in great heaps but the ranks came on relentlessly to meet the English hand to hand. But the steel-clad Frenchmen, accustomed to the saddle, had tramped half a mile uphill in sweltering heat and once their first fury was spent, the Prince thrust them back.

Then the archers and the Gascon men-at-arms, as agile as cats among the armoured giants, sallied out. Retreat became a rout and the Duke of Orleans' men quitted the field without striking a blow.

At this point, King John decided to advance with his finest knights and his twelve-year-old son, Philip. As they approached, Prince Edward had a brilliant idea. His men were tired but the horses were fresh. Mount every man that could be spared! He ordered a Gascon captain to lead a small force round the hill and take the enemy on the flank, then, with Sir John Chandos at his side, he shouted:

"Advance banners! For God and St. George!"

This was what every knight had longed for. At headlong speed, they crashed downhill into the French and, at the critical moment, the Gascon cavalry appeared on the right, charging in a cloud of dust that hid their meagre numbers. They made the victory sure.

King John fought on, with his little son behind him shouting, "Guard on the left, father! Guard on the right!"

But the boy was carried away and the King had to yield his sword.

Later, when the victors and vanquished sat down to dine, Prince Edward waited on his captured foe, called him the most valiant knight and modestly vowed that he himself was not worthy to sit at the same table.

The streets of London were hung with garlands when the Prince, clad in a plain suit and astride a little black horse, rode over the petal-strewn cobbles at the side of the royal prisoner. King John was attired in gorgeous robes and he kept his head high, but his little son wept bitterly for his father's disgrace.

Freed from affairs of state, Prince Edward married his cousin Joan, the Fair Maid of Kent, whom he had loved since she was a fatherless little girl brought up by his mother, good Queen Philippa. King Edward decided that the young couple should rule Aquitaine, the family domain in south-west France.

At Bordeaux, they set up the most brilliant court in Europe, but the Prince was soon tired of festivities. At the first opportunity, he was off to the wars.

In Spain, Pedro the Cruel had been driven from his throne by his brother and he appealed for help to the chivalrous Prince. By a great victory at Najarra, Edward won back Pedro's crown but, try as he might, he could not get a penny out of the ungrateful monarch.

Disease attacked the English camp and the Prince himself was ill when a message came from Joan, urging him to return. He struggled back but he never recovered his health and good fortune.

In Aquitaine, some of his subjects, angry at the cost of the Spanish expedition, had appealed to the King of France who claimed to be Edward's overlord. Summoned to appear in Paris, the Prince replied:

The Black Prince rides in triumph through London, with the captured French King beside him

159

"We will go willingly—but with 60,000 men in our company."

But now, he was too ill to carry out his threat and when a French scullion-boy brought an insulting declaration of war, he had to give command of his army to Sir John Chandos. Word came that Sir John was killed and Limoges, one of his towns, had surrendered.

"By the soul of my father," swore the sick Prince. "I will mete out punishment to those traitors!"

He was carried to the siege in a litter, and, when the walls were breached, he lay in silent anger, refusing to listen to the women and children who knelt down and begged for mercy.

His troops butchered three thousand people and only when he saw some French knights bravely holding out in the market-place, did his chivalry awake. Too late, he ordered an end to the killing. The massacre at Limoges remained an everlasting stain on his honour.

His illness grew worse and he went back to England, hoping to recover in his native air. Now and then, his old energy returned and, once, he even buckled on his armour again, but it was no use. He was carried back to his castle at Berkhampstead to grieve over the defeats in France and the sad condition of his father who had sunk into feeble old age.

When he knew that his end was near, the Prince asked for the doors to be opened so that his friends and servants could come to say farewell. As they filed past the dying man, he whispered:

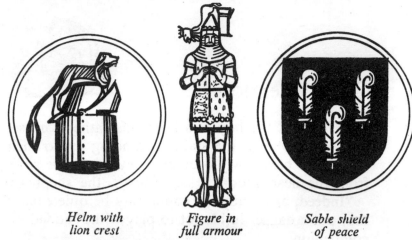

Helm with
lion crest

Figure in
full armour

Sable shield
of peace

FROM THE BLACK PRINCE'S TOMB

"Sirs, pardon me, for, by the faith, ye have served me right loyally and I cannot give you the half that is due."

Then, raising himself, he said to the lords who stood by his bed:

"I commend to you my son who is still but very young and little. I pray that, as you have served me, so you will serve him."

They buried him in Canterbury Cathedral where he still lies in his splendid tomb. On top is his figure in a full suit of armour, the feet resting on a French bulldog. Above hang his gauntlets, his helm with lion crest, his glorious surcoat with the leopards and the lilies of France and on the wall is his shield of war.

At the side of the tomb is his black or sable shield of peace with the three silver feathers. It is perhaps from this sable shield, carried in some forgotten tournament, that he gained his name, the Black Prince.

Owen Glendower

"THE night the boy was born, his father's horses were found in the stables, standing up to their fetlocks in blood. My brother, Gwyn, had the story from the head groom," said Morys, the shepherd.

"Indeed, as a baby, he could only be quietened if they put a dagger in his cot to play with," added his companion.

The two shepherds were speaking of their master's son, Owain Glyn Dwr (usually known now as Owen Glendower). Everything pointed to the boy growing into a mighty warrior, like his ancestors, the Welsh princes who had fought the English long ago.

But Owen's father sent the lad to study law at Westminster, and he only got a taste of war by running off to join the English army in a campaign against the Scots.

After this brief adventure, Owen settled down on his estates in North Wales. He lived at a moated manor-house at Sycharth with his wife Margaret and their children, and there he might have stayed for the rest of his life but for a quarrel with a neighbour.

A stretch of grazing land belonging to Owen was claimed by an English baron, Lord Grey of Ruthin, who sent a party of armed men to take the land by force. Owen went to court and won his case, so that Grey had to give up the land, though he swore to have it back as soon as the time was ripe.

His chance came in 1399, when Henry of Boling-

Lord Grey warns Henry IV that Owen Glendower is dangerous

broke overthrew his cousin Richard II and made himself King Henry IV. In such troubled times, people often took the opportunity to pay off old grudges, and Grey again seized the piece of land. Glendower travelled to Westminster to lay his complaint before the new King.

But Lord Grey was a friend of Henry IV.

"This Welsh dog is a dangerous fellow," he said privately to the King. "It is well-known that he is a supporter of Richard II."

So, when the King gave judgment, he said:

"I find no fault with my lord of Ruthin. The land is his land and Owen of Glendower has no claim."

A bishop near the throne murmured:

"Owen is well-loved in his own country, my lord King. It would be an evil day if the Welshmen rose to arms."

Henry burst out scornfully:

"What care we for those barefooted scrubs? Let Owen of Glendower return to his beggarly hills!"

Angered by the King's insults, Owen rode home and it was not long before Grey found the opportunity to do him another injury.

163

The Lord of Ruthin was told to summon the gentry of Wales to serve the King against the Scots. Craftily, he delayed sending the summons to Owen until it was too late for him to join the royal array.

"Clearly," said Grey to Henry IV, "this fellow is a traitor, since he does not come to serve you."

"He must be taken and his lands declared forfeit," replied the King.

Grey therefore decided to capture his neighbour by an old trick. He sent word to Owen that he wished to meet him in friendship and so was invited to Sycharth. Grey came with a few attendants but ordered his retainers to conceal themselves nearby. At a signal, they were to rush out and massacre all the inhabitants.

Owen had ordered his bard Iolo and some servants to keep a lookout for treachery and they soon sighted Grey's men creeping through the woods. How could they warn Owen of his danger?

Iolo went into the hall where Grey and Owen were conversing, and began to sing in an ancient form of Welsh that Grey could not understand. Among the verses, he mingled a warning that the house was about to be attacked and Owen, realizing his meaning, made an excuse to leave his guest. Then he leapt on a horse and rode away to safety.

He summoned his kinsmen and when they learned of the plot, word was passed from valley to valley until a force of Welshmen had assembled.

On St. Matthew's Day, 21st September 1400, the little town of Ruthin was holding its annual fair.

The streets, lined with stalls and booths, were crowded with people from the surrounding villages when a swarm of Owen's men burst into their midst.

They overturned the stalls, looted and set fire to the houses, but they were not strong enough to attack the stone-walled castle. From the battlements, Grey watched in helpless rage the ruin of his town.

Next, the rebel force sacked Oswestry and Welshpool but, at Shrewsbury, they were driven off by the sheriff and forced to carry their dead to the hills.

When he learned of this revolt, Henry IV brought his fourteen-year-old son, Prince Henry of Monmouth, to see how the Welsh should be punished. The royal army advanced across Wales to Bangor and on to Caernarvon Castle but, although the King put on a fine show of strength, he saw nothing of Owen Glendower, for the Welsh leader had vanished into the mountains.

Since there was little chance of catching the chief rebel, Henry confiscated his lands. Then, thinking that the country was quiet, he announced severe penalties. No Welshman was to hold high office, to marry an English wife, to own property or to live in England.

These insulting measures aroused the Welsh people. Recruits flocked into Owen's camp and, while two of his cousins captured Conway Castle by a trick and held it against the famous Harry Hotspur, Owen moved into central Wales, defeated the royal forces and carried fire and sword across the country.

He was a born leader of guerrilla troops. If the

King's commanders advanced with a strong army, he and his men melted away into the trackless mountain country. Then, like a will o' the wisp, he would reappear fifty miles away to capture an outpost or to plunder a village.

His troops were swift-footed, lightly-armed men who lived hard and knew the mountains and forest-paths. Most of them were poor husbandmen, peasants and shepherds, whose grandfathers had fought at Crecy; they formed companies of Welsh spearmen and archers in many an English army or went to the foreign wars as camp-followers, ready for any work with long knives or cooking-pots.

By 1401, Owen's revolt was so serious that the King had to send out a call to arms to almost every shire in England. Once more, he and his son led an army into Wales, laying waste the country and hanging any of Owen's friends they could catch. But they could not bring the rebels to battle.

Owen attacked the fringes of the royal army, destroyed its stores and, in one skirmish, actually captured the horses and equipment of the young

Prince. The King was forced to retire since the country was too poor to feed his army.

At once, Owen reappeared. Although he found it difficult to capture the great castles, he was now strong enough to live at his old home at Sycharth, where he held court like a prince among his captains and bards.

In the New Year, he made a sudden attack on the estates of his old enemy, the Lord of Ruthin. Then, to lure Grey from his castle, he went back, as if to plunder the town with a small force. Grey sallied out to deal with this handful of raiders, but he was ambushed by a concealed force and captured.

What would be the fate of the man who had boasted that he would hang Owen Glendower and send the quarters of his body to the four corners of Wales? Owen was too wily to take a useless revenge.

"My Lord Grey," he said, "I would not insult a noble lord by asking a paltry sum for his life. So great a man as the Lord of Ruthin cannot be ransomed for less than 10,000 marks."

It was a stupendous sum, but Grey had no choice. Somehow his family raised 6000 marks and when his eldest son had been handed over as a hostage, the Lord of Ruthin was released.

After this triumph, Owen ranged up and down the principality, harrying the south-east and all the border lands. On a hill called Bryn Glas, he defeated the enemy with terrible slaughter and captured one of the greatest English nobles, Sir Edmund Mortimer. Apart from a few castles, Owen was now master of Wales.

Henry IV resolved that he must crush this rebellion at all costs and he planned to invade the country with three armies. Bad weather, with gales and torrential rain, had brought his forces to a standstill when he received word that the Scots had invaded the north.

The valiant Henry Percy, known as Hotspur, defeated the Scots and took some noble prisoners. He expected to have their ransoms as a reward for his services but the King claimed the money for himself. In a quarrel, he struck Hotspur in the face and this was an insult that a Percy would not forget.

Hotspur thought of Owen Glendower whom he liked and admired. He also thought of Sir Edmund Mortimer, his wife's brother, now a prisoner at Owen's home. What if they joined forces? They could overthrow this ungrateful king.

The plot was hatched and Hotspur moved into Cheshire to gather supporters before advancing to capture Shrewsbury. Then he would meet Owen and Mortimer who had already married Owen's daughter.

But Henry IV acted swiftly. He raced to Shrewsbury where his son, the young Prince, gallantly held Hotspur's furious charges, until the northern troops wavered. Then, crying "St. George! Victory!" his soldiers swept the rebels from the field, leaving behind the body of Harry Hotspur himself.

This loss did not weaken Owen for the moment, because a new ally appeared when a French fleet put into Carmarthen Bay. Criccieth and Harlech were captured and, later, Cardiff Castle and Aberystwyth. In Owen's absence, Prince Henry had burnt Sycharth to the ground, so Aberystwyth now became the rebel headquarters.

The war went on, with victories for both sides. Owen's troops, brave and hardy as they were, proved to be difficult to keep together for long periods and they were of little use for sieges. On the other side, Prince Henry was becoming a very good general as he learned to use small companies of picked troops instead of cumbersome armies.

In 1405, the Welsh suffered two defeats in the south, where Owen's brother was killed and his son captured. However, the French landed a force of nearly 3000 men in Pembrokeshire and the Anglo-Welsh army advanced almost to Worcester.

But the alliance was not a happy one. The French disliked the hilly country and the shortage of food, and the Welsh were not pleased to see their own land plundered by foreigners.

Owen was still full of high hopes. He wrote constantly to the Kings of Scotland and France, planning to divide Henry IV's realm between himself, Mortimer and Hotspur's old father, the Earl of Northumberland. Yet, in truth, the tide had already turned against him.

His allies all failed him and Prince Henry was steadily wearing the rebels down. Moreover, he offered generous pardons to any who would lay down their arms.

By 1407, Glendower was on the run. He was still able to strike back but always a little less fiercely. Presently, he was reduced to wandering about the country in disguise and many stories were told of his escapades.

Once, he and his servant came to a castle commanded by Sir Lawrence Berkrolles and asked for a night's lodging. The knight was delighted with his charming guest and asked him to stay on:

"I am glad of company," he said. "As you see, the castle is well-nigh empty. My men are out searching for Owen Glendower, since he is known to be somewhere in the district."

"It would be well to capture that man," said Owen, "if anyone could do it."

After several days of generous hospitality, Owen made ready to leave and his host courteously went with him to the gate. When he and his servant had mounted, Owen held out his hand and said:

"Owen Glendower thanks Sir Lawrence for his kindness and assures him, hand to hand, that he will never take vengeance on him or on any of his people."

Then he galloped away before Sir Lawrence could recover from his astonishment.

The rebel cause grew weaker. Hotspur's father was defeated and killed in Yorkshire. Aberystwyth fell and when Harlech was captured, Owen's wife, daughters and grandchildren were among the prisoners. He and his son, Meredith, were the only members of the family left, for all his other sons had been killed or captured.

Owen Glendower thanks Sir Lawrence

But, although his strongholds were taken, his friends dead or pardoned and he was forced to live in caves and thickets, Owen refused to give in. Henry IV died and his brilliant son became Henry V.

At once, the new King proclaimed a pardon for all the Welsh rebels, and soon nearly all the most stubborn foes of England made their peace. Almost alone, Owen would not submit. Rather than accept defeat, he disappeared with his pride and his memories of the glorious days when he ruled a kingdom.

No one knew how he met his end. Some said that he went to Herefordshire disguised as a shepherd and others said that he took work as a reaper and died in a wood in Glamorgan. Only one thing was certain—that the last native prince of Wales lived on as a national hero.

James I of Scotland

IT was almost dark as the royal party approached the ferry. They bent their heads into the driving sleet and longed for the firelit hall that awaited them at the monastery of the Black Friars of Perth, where King James was to spend Christmas.

Suddenly, a figure leapt into their path, crying: "Go back!"

The foremost horses reared and the cavalcade came to a halt. In the gloom, an old woman in tattered garments could be seen barring the way with arms held wide. One of the riders approached but she cried:

"For the King alone! For the King!"

172

Queen Joan laid her hand on the King's arm but he went forward and the old woman came to his stirrup and looked up, crying wildly:

"Go back, King. If once you cross the water, you never shall return."

The King bent forward:

"Have you news for me?" he asked.

But the old woman was now muttering to herself: "Before the new year is old, a king shall die in Scotland."

"Ride on," said James curtly. Then, seeing that the Queen was looking back in alarm at the old woman, he turned with a laugh to one of his knights whose good looks had earned him the nickname, 'The King of Love'.

"Sir Alexander," he joked, "the old dame says a king shall die. You and I are the only two kings in Scotland, so look well to yourself. I think that you will die of love or too much feasting!"

The courtiers laughed and the incident was forgotten in the excitement of crossing the stormy Firth. At length, they reached the monastery and the Christmas festivities began.

For a month, there were tournaments and contests of every kind, with banquets held at night in the Great Hall. The Court danced and sang and played rowdy games, and the King and his beautiful Queen took the lead in all the merrymaking. Often, James would sing one of his own ballads from the 'King's Quair', a quire or book that he had written during his long captivity in England.

When he was a little boy, James's father, King Robert III, had sent him for safety to France but the ship was captured by Norfolk pirates who handed their prisoner over to Henry IV of England. The boy was treated well but, although his father died and an uncle ruled in his place, the English would not set him free.

Eighteen years passed before Henry V agreed to let him go and, before he left, James married Joan Beaufort, a lady of the English Court. He had fallen in love with her when he was a prisoner, watching her walk in the garden below his window.

In 1424, they were crowned at Scone and not since the days of Robert the Bruce had Scotland known such a strong and gifted king.

Although he was rather short, James I was a fine athlete and few could equal him at running, at putting the weight and throwing the hammer. But he was also a clever musician and a poet who was interested in books, painting, machines and gardens. Moreover, he had thought deeply about how to rule his stormy kingdom.

Scotland was in a sorry state. Under a weak Regent, the nobles had grown powerful and unruly and, in the Highlands, robber-barons had no respect for any man. James called a parliament and made it clear that he had come to rule.

Laws were passed to stop robbery and private wars; nobles who defied the King would lose their lives and their property, too, and those who had taken lands by force were made to give them back.

The Highland chiefs are seized

The Regent and his son were executed for the evil things they had done in the King's absence and, by a crafty trick, the Highland chiefs were seized as they entered a hall at Inverness.

For twelve years, James ruled sternly and well. But, in the kingdom, many lords hated him and yearned for the days when a baron could do as he pleased.

Among those who joined in the Christmas revels at Perth there were traitors who had vowed to kill the King. At the centre of the plot was the old Earl of Atholl who could claim the throne if James and his little son were dead.

Atholl's grandson, Sir Robert Stewart, was the King's Chamberlain and he, too, had hopes of the throne, but their man of action was Sir Robert Graham. This dare-devil youth had sworn vengeance for the punishment dealt to his relatives and nothing would appease his fiery temper.

On 20th February 1437, when the Court was at dinner, Stewart the Chamberlain left his seat as if to

175

see to the affairs of the household. Swiftly, he removed the keys and the bolts from the doors and laid planks across the moat. Then he returned to his place at the table.

The evening came to an end. The musicians retired and the guests left the hall, talking and laughing as they parted on the stairs. Sir Robert Stewart bowed and withdrew. The Queen's bower-maidens were preparing her bedroom in an alcove when the King turned to his page, Walter Straton, and said:

"Go, Walter, and fetch me some wine. I am dry from the dancing and would take a glass before I sleep!"

The lad went out and, as the King and Queen stood talking together by the fireplace, they heard noises in the courtyard below. James called the guard but the man who should have been on duty outside the Hall was not there. Could this be treachery?

"Bolt the door!" cried the King.

But the key and the heavy bar used as a bolt were missing. James looked round the room. The Chamberlain had done his work quietly and there was no sword nor anything that might serve as a weapon. The King went to the windows but the iron bars were thick and firm: there was no escape that way.

Then Catherine Douglas, one of the Queen's ladies, cried:

"The floor, Sire! The monastery vaults lie underneath!"

But how could they prise up a floor-board? The King snatched a pair of heavy tongs from the fireplace and set madly to work on the flooring while the women tried vainly to drag a heavy table towards the door.

Voices could be heard some way off and the clatter of weapons. Walter the page had met Graham and his men after they had crossed the moat and entered the monastery. Now, he was holding them at bay in the corridor with his dagger and a pewter jug.

The plank was yielding. With bleeding fingers, James wrenched it up and, with a whispered farewell to the Queen, dropped through the opening into the crypt below.

The Queen and her women were struggling to replace the board and to smooth its broken edges

when a scream told them that the page had given his life for the King. The traitors were pounding up the stairs.

"The door! Can you keep the door, if only for a moment!" cried the Queen.

Catherine Douglas rushed to the door but it was hopeless for a woman to try to hold it shut against a band of men. She thrust her bare arm through the iron loops where the bar had been. There was a push from outside but her arm held for a moment. Then the weight of several men hurled the door open and Catherine fell to the ground, fainting from the pain in her torn and broken arm.

The conspirators poured in, Sir Robert Graham at their head, the others crowding behind with torches and drawn swords. Thrusting the women aside, they searched the room, ripping down curtains and stabbing the bed.

The Queen stood quite still, her hair unbraided and a light shawl held about her shoulders. But her long robe concealed the tell-tale marks on the floor. One of the ruffians put a knife to her throat:

"Tell us, where is the King?" he cried.

Young Graham caught his arm:

"She is a woman. Leave her. We seek the King."

At length, believing that James

must have fled to another part of the monastery, the traitors clattered out and left the women alone.

For the moment, the King was safe. He could not get out, for the crypt had recently been bricked up but, if he had stayed there, all might have been well. Yet James was not the man to stay in hiding when he could rouse his friends and the loyal townsfolk.

"Help me up!" he called to the women.

It was folly but they prised up the plank and knelt down to reach the King's hands. The vault was deep and they were not strong enough to lift a heavy man through the narrow gap.

"Let down the sheets from the bed!"

They tore and knotted the sheets into a rope, but it was no use. The rope was not long enough to reach the great table and another attempt resulted in Elizabeth Douglas, Catherine's sister, being dragged down into the crypt where she lay injured.

At this moment, the conspirators were heard approaching and the plank was hurriedly dropped into place. This time, the Chamberlain came in:

"There is a vault below the Hall," he said.

Taking a torch, he and Graham began to examine the floor. Suddenly, one pointed to the splinters and a broken nail. Swords forced up the board and in a minute the hiding-place was revealed.

Graham thrust the torch into the hole. Flame and smoke were driven back by the draught, but he knelt lower, peering in. Then he leapt to his feet and cried fiercely:

"Ah! Here is the tyrant we have sought this night!"

Boards were hacked away until all could see the King standing below, unarmed, his legs straddled like a wrestler waiting for the first who should dare to leap down.

Sir John Hall was the first. Drawing his dagger, he dropped into the vault, but the King leapt on him, hurled him down and, with his foot on his throat, waited for the next.

It was Sir John's brother and he was gripped by the neck and half-strangled as the King fought furiously to reach the assassin's knife. The third man was Graham himself and he pressed the point of his naked sword to the King's chest.

"My time is come," said James quietly. "Grant me but time to confess to a priest."

"This sword shall be your confessor," cried his enemy thrusting forward with all his strength, "A Graham keeps his word!"

As the traitors put an end to the King, the monastery bell began to clang above them, pealing out its warning and rousing the townsfolk. Led by Sir David Dunbar, they hurried to the monastery, as the murderers dashed through the courtyard and escaped to the Highlands.

But if Graham and his friends thought that the people would reward them for killing a king, they were mistaken. The whole country supported the Queen in her determination to hunt them down. All were taken, even two who fled across the sea, and all were put to a most horrible end.

Warwick the King-Maker

"THERE'S a true earl for you," cried the bandy-legged groom, "free ale and as much meat as a man can carry on his dagger."

"Aye, you're a lucky fellow to wear the Bear and Ragged Staff," replied the water-seller. "A health to Warwick and his men."

In a Cheapside tavern, the groom in trim livery was boasting of his master's splendid house near the Guildhall, where six oxen were roasted daily for breakfast.

At the age of twenty-one, Richard Neville, Earl of Warwick, was the richest and most gallant noble-man in England. When he came to Court, his generosity made him the darling of the Londoners, and, in the country, his estates, castles and towns made him the envy of the barons.

Life at Court was gay and amusing but beneath its glittering surface, there was bitter jealousy. Henry VI was as gentle as his wife, Margaret of Anjou, was fiery. His nobles were divided into two parties, each trying to control a feeble king.

On one side were the King's friends, known as Lancastrians, since Lancaster was Henry's family name. Their armed retainers wore a red rose as their badge. On the other side were the Yorkists, supporters of the Duke of York, Warwick's uncle by marriage and heir to the throne. Their badge was the white rose of York.

In 1453, King Henry became mad. He sat all day without speaking, as if lost in some deep, sad dream. York was made Protector but the glee of the Yorkists quickly changed to gloom. Queen Margaret, childless for nine years, gave birth to a healthy boy, who was Henry VI's heir. On Christmas Day, the King suddenly recovered his wits and went to church as if nothing had happened.

The jubilant Queen had York and his friends sent away from Court:

"Let the Duke know that it is our purpose to make the King safe from his enemies!" she cried. With these threatening words, the Wars of the Roses began.

York called to his friends for help. Warwick and his father, the Earl of Salisbury, joined him and they set out in force towards London. King Henry,

*The jubilant Queen sends York and his friends away
from Court*

advancing to meet them, issued a proclamation:

"I, King Harry, command that no person shall take the field against me in my realm. They are traitors who do so."

Next day, the royal army took up a strong position in the town of St. Albans.

At half-past eleven, the old Abbot of St. Albans, watching from the top of the gate-house, saw the Yorkists attack the town from three sides but the barriers were strongly held. Then the Duke of Warwick led a party of his men through the gardens of some nearby houses. They broke down the doors, passed through the houses, down an alley-way and into the main street.

Behind their backs, the defenders heard the blare of trumpets and a ringing battle-cry "A Warwick! A Warwick!" The Abbot saw them turn to fight. Yorkists broke through the weakened barricades and the streets were filled with men-at-arms fighting

183

hand to hand on the slippery cobbles. The battle became a rout and, by evening, the King's forces had fled, leaving their dead in the streets.

"The King? Where is the King?" went up the cry.

Henry VI was found in the house of a tanner, having an arrow-wound in his neck dressed by the tanner's wife. Then York, Warwick and Salisbury came and knelt to him in the kitchen, begging forgiveness for what had happened. Henry said not a word, but allowed his captors to escort him back to London.

For the moment, York had triumphed. As a reward for the victory at St. Albans, he had Warwick made Captain of Calais and the Earl went to live at the seaport with his wife and two little daughters.

Life at Calais was full of interest. The town was crowded with merchants, courtiers, sailors, spies and hired soldiers; every corner hummed with rumours and plots. The French made attacks on the outskirts, the garrison drove them off and, in the Channel, pirate vessels robbed the merchant fleets.

Warwick loved Calais. His zest for adventure and his careless generosity won the hearts of the garrison so that, in the days to come, he always had a stronghold and loyal troops at his back.

Meanwhile, in London, the Queen and her favourites had returned to power. They realized that Warwick was becoming far too popular but, since they could not reach him in Calais, his father was summoned to appear at Court. Suspecting a trap, he went, instead, to the Duke of York at Ludlow. Warwick joined them there with 600 of his Calais troops.

The royal army marched into the Midlands and King Henry's heralds proclaimed a pardon for all who left the Duke of York's service. When his followers began to slip away, York knew that it was hopeless to fight.

"I will make for Ireland," he said to Warwick. "Get you back to Calais, nephew, and take with you my eldest son, Edward of March."

Warwick, his father and young Edward galloped away but the Queen's men pursued them so hotly that, in North Devon, they had to hire a small boat to take them, they said, to Bristol.

Once away from land, Warwick called to the captain:

"Can you sail round Land's End into the Channel, Master?"

"No, I can't and I ain't going to try, for you or any other fine gentleman," replied the captain.

The others looked dismayed but Warwick burst out laughing:

"Then, by Saint Jude, I can!" he cried. "Give me the tiller and I will bring you all to safety. Never fear, you shall have double-hire, master captain."

Warwick reaches Calais safely

The Earl's knowledge of the Channel brought the little boat into Calais harbour. Anxiously, he scanned the water-front to see if the port had been taken for the Queen. To his joy, he saw friends on the quay and by the time he came alongside, his wife and his daughters were there to greet him.

By now, it was open war with the Lancastrians and, in 1460, Warwick's plans were ready. With Edward, a handsome youth of eighteen whom he loved like a son, he landed in Kent, marched through London's cheering crowds and reached Northampton. There he defeated the Lancastrians in half an hour and captured King Henry but Queen Margaret and her son escaped to Wales.

Back in London, the Yorkists were still working out their next moves when word came from the north that the dauntless Queen had raised another army.

186

The Yorkists went to meet her but, at Wakefield, she scattered their troops and the Duke of York himself was killed. After the battle, Warwick's father and many other noble prisoners were executed. The Queen ordered their heads, the Duke's wearing a paper crown, to be stuck up above the walls of the city of York.

Warwick advanced to avenge his father but he was forced to retreat and Queen Margaret recaptured King Henry, who was found chuckling and babbling under an oak tree. At this point, the Queen made the mistake of her life. Instead of capturing London, she allowed her troops to move northwards, plundering as they went.

Thus, Warwick and young Edward were able to enter the capital. Both had lost their fathers and, in bitter anger, Warwick called a great meeting of the citizens at St. Paul's. He asked two questions:

"Is King Harry worthy to reign?"

"Will you have Edward of March in his place?"

The Londoners roared their answers and, at Westminster, York's handsome son was acclaimed King Edward IV. At his side stood the Earl who had made him king and on the morrow they led their army north.

At Towton, Warwick defeated the Lancastrians with the most savage slaughter of any battle ever fought in England. King Henry, Queen Margaret and the little prince escaped and the victors returned to London.

There were two kings of England. One was a half-witted fugitive somewhere along the Scottish border, the other was a gay young man enjoying himself with the elegant lords and pretty ladies of the Court. The real ruler of the country was the mighty Earl of Warwick.

Presently, the Earl arranged that the King should marry a French princess and the Council met to give consent. Then Edward, playing with a jewelled locket, remarked:

"I truly wish, as your Lordships desire me, to be wedded . . . My choice is the Lady Elizabeth Woodville!"

Warwick and the Council were flabbergasted. The lady was beautiful but the Woodvilles did not belong to the old nobility. It was impossible. Besides, what of the French match?

With an insolent smile, Edward replied softly:

"You do waste your breath, my lords. I was wedded to the Lady Elizabeth on the first day of May!"

Warwick was very angry. His plans were ruined and he was made to look a fool by this impudent youth. But he kept his temper. Edward was young and Warwick would still rule the kingdom. He did not realize that Edward was tired of being Warwick's puppet.

As polite as ever to the great Earl, Edward smiled his secret smile when poor King Henry was captured in Lancashire. He gave Warwick the honour of escorting the royal prisoner to the Tower. Then he struck.

The Earl's friends were dismissed from Court;

Edward startles the Council

the Duke of Clarence, brother of King Edward, was refused permission to marry Warwick's daughter. It was clear that the Earl himself was about to be toppled from power.

But Warwick was not ruined yet. He took his wife and daughters to Calais where the Duke of Clarence joined them and married Isobel. There was a rising of Warwick's friends in the north of England and, as soon as King Edward went to deal with it, the Earl was across the Channel and into the capital. Edward saw that he was beaten and he smilingly surrendered.

With one king in the Tower and the other a prisoner in his camp, Warwick was master of the kingdom. Edward granted everything but he also made his secret plans.

Somehow, he secured an army and suddenly proclaimed Warwick and Clarence traitors. Taken by surprise, they fled to Calais, only to find that

Edward had quietly taken the port. So they went to the Court of the King of France where Queen Margaret herself was staying.

King Louis put forward an astonishing plan:

"Since the Yorkists have played you false," he said, "why do you not put King Henry back on the throne?"

Make friends with the Lancastrians? It seemed absurd. Queen Margaret regarded Warwick as her most bitter enemy but Louis wheedled so craftily that she began to listen. After all, Warwick alone had the power and the warlike skill to bring her son to the throne. Margaret swallowed her pride and the bargain was made.

But no one thought of the Duke of Clarence. If his brother Edward IV was to be overthrown, *he* expected to be king in his place. Clarence secretly made up his mind to change sides when the time was ripe.

Suspecting nothing, Warwick and the Queen laid their plans and when King Edward awoke one morning, he found his army so riddled with treachery that he could only leap on a horse and ride furiously to the coast to escape to Flanders.

Then the King-maker entered London and brought King Henry from the Tower. They rode together through the streets, the magnificent Earl and the poor crack-witted monarch. Once more, Warwick was absolute master but, in his pride, he still forgot Clarence.

In 1471, came news that Edward had landed in

Warwick brings Henry from the Tower

Yorkshire. Warwick coolly collected his retainers in the Midlands and waited for Clarence to arrive with his forces. But Clarence threw away the red rose and went over to his brother's side.

At dawn, on Easter Sunday, the Battle of Barnet began in a thick mist and, by ten o'clock, Warwick was getting the upper hand when a force of Lancastrians came to support him. They wore the Earl of Oxford's badge, a star with rays, but in the mist Warwick's men mistook the star for the rising sun worn by Edward's soldiers. They attacked their own allies. The cry of "Treason! Treason!" was heard and panic followed.

Oxford fled, Warwick's brother was slain by his own side and the Earl, seeing his army in ruins, started to fight his way to where the horses were picketed in a wood. He lost touch with his friends but had almost reached the horse-lines when a Yorkist slipped through the trees and struck him a heavy blow from behind.

191

King Edward finds Warwick's body after the battle

Meanwhile, on the field at Barnet, King Edward stood victorious. The mist was lifting and he could see his men pursuing the defeated foe, stripping the slain and bringing in the noble prisoners.

"For the sake of an old friendship," he called to his lords, "the Earl of Warwick shall be spared and brought to me."

There was shouting from some way off, a man came running pointing back towards a wood. The King and his party moved across to see the cause of the excitement. On the ground, a body lay stripped of its armour. Edward went nearer. There was no mistaking that proud face.

"There lies the last of the barons," said Edward, "Warwick the King-maker is dead."

Margaret Paston

MARGARET and John stood nervously in the window looking out at the Norfolk countryside. They felt uneasy, for they knew that John's mother, old Agnes Paston, seated with her needlework by the fire, was watching them with hard, calculating eyes.

Both were relieved when the visit was over and Margaret and her servant rode back to her father's house at Mauteby.

That evening, Agnes wrote to her husband, Justice Paston, in London:

"Right worshipful husband, I pray that you are well and safe arrived in London. As for the first meeting between our son and the daughter of John Mauteby, she hath pleased him by her gentle manner. The business goeth well and I think we shall have no great trouble in the making of a marriage."

If Margaret pleased John, her father's rich manors were even more pleasing to Justice Paston and his wife. The Justice had risen high in the world from a humble beginning; he had married Agnes for her money and now the pair of them were happy to have found a wealthy bride for their son.

The match was made and Margaret went to live at the Paston home. A few years later, Justice Paston died and John became the head of the family. Shrewd old Agnes was still very much alive, but Margaret was now mistress of the household with all its

Margaret tells John to fight his enemies in the courts

servants, dairymaids, children and unmarried relations.

When he was alive, many people had been jealous of the great Justice and, now that he was dead, they began to claim some of his estates. Margaret told John that he must fight his enemies in the law-courts:

"I will look after things in Norfolk," she said. "Make all haste to London, husband, for it is said that Lord Molynes has his eye upon our manor at Gresham."

John rode to London and Margaret, leaving her children with old Agnes, went with a few servants to take possession of the manor-house at Gresham.

Next day, they were putting the house in order when a boy came in crying:

"Mistress, an army of Lord Molynes's men is coming!"

Margaret ran to an upper room and looked out. Sure enough, a column of men was winding past the church not a mile off and, from the south, another force could be seen approaching, the winter sun glinting on their mailed coats and helmets.

"Bar the doors! Close the shutters!" cried Margaret.

But, while the Paston men did their best to defend the house, a party of Molynes's retainers, using a tree-trunk as a battering-ram, broke down the front door and crowded inside. Margaret faced them furiously:

"I know you, John Partridge," she stormed. "Get you from my house with your down-at-heel ruffians!"

"Take her outside," was all that Partridge replied.

So fiercely did Margaret resist, that the retainers had to drag her from the house by the hair. Then they drove out her servants and began to smash the household goods, while others pulled the thatch from the roof and, finally, sawed through the main door-posts so that part of the building collapsed.

Bruised, her garments torn and muddy, Margaret

made her way home and wrote an indignant account of the attack to her husband. John complained to Parliament and to the Lord Chancellor and, although Lord Molynes was a powerful noble, he was made to give the manor back.

By 1451, Margaret had repaired the house at Gresham but, when John wanted to sue Lord Molynes for damages, the Sheriff of Norfolk told him bluntly that he dared not be his friend. At this, John went to Norwich to see what might be done but, to Margaret's horror, he was set upon by a gang and only saved from a dagger-thrust by the thick doublet that he was wearing.

It was clear that he needed a great nobleman as a friend. The country was now so lawless under Henry VI's weak rule that only a strong protector could save a man from ruin.

One day, Margaret said:

"I do recall my cousin, Sir John Fastolf. He is home from the French wars where he has made a great fortune. I suppose, if he were spoken to, he would be gladder to serve his kinsfolk than strangers."

John went to see Fastolf who took an instant liking to his cousin's husband. He realized that Paston was a clever man who knew the law and all the affairs of Norfolk. As time went by, he used John's advice in every business matter and could not bear to be parted from him.

So the Pastons were often at the old knight's magnificent castle at Caister, near Yarmouth. Even when John was away in London, Margaret would

Caister Castle

stay on there with her four sons and her daughters, Anne and Margery.

In 1459, when the Wars of the Roses had begun, Sir John Fastolf was taken ill.

"God send me soon my good cousin Paston," he murmured. "I hold him a faithful man and the best friend and helper in all my life."

John hurried up from London but, two days later, Fastolf died. When his will was read, John Paston found himself one of the richest men in England, for his friend had left him Caister Castle and all his vast estates.

It seemed as if nothing but good fortune came to the Pastons. They were entertained by the nobility, and Margaret met the Queen at Norwich. John took his seat in Parliament and it was rumoured that he was to be knighted. He managed to arrange that this honour should go to his eldest son who therefore became Sir John.

But powerful enemies were biding their time. They said that the will was false and that Paston had no right to so many manors and pastures. The Duke of Norfolk actually seized Caister Castle but Edward IV, who had recently triumphed over King Henry, made him hand it back. Margaret saw the danger to her family:

"Can you not find a way to get our eldest son into the King's household?" she asked her husband. "He is now of age and can make friends with the young lords about the King."

This was done and Sir John, a handsome young scapegrace, went happily off to enjoy the tournaments and gaiety of King Edward's Court.

But Paston's moves were closely watched by his enemies who also had friends in high places. Soon it was necessary for John to spend nearly all his time in the law-courts. He was so busy that once he forgot to obey a summons to attend the King and was put into the Fleet Prison by the offended monarch.

To Margaret's relief, he was soon set free but the struggle went on. In London, Norwich and in local courts, lawyers argued the Paston claims for weeks and months on end. John was rarely at home for he had to speak up for his rights and his enemies used every trick to defeat him.

Margaret Paston buying herrings

In this situation, Margaret was left to take charge of affairs in Norfolk. She dealt with lawyers, bailiffs, farmers and cottagers, settled their arguments, collected the rents and faced the retainers of powerful neighbours who sometimes attacked her property.

All this time, she was managing her family and a large household that moved from one manor-house to another in order to keep up the Paston claims and also to eat the produce of the farms.

The supplying of a big household was a task in itself. Margaret had to see that bread was baked, meat salted, hams cured, fruits preserved, wine and ale laid in stock. She kept an eye on the markets and planned ahead, for, in winter, there was no fresh meat and dried fish was needed during Lent. In her letters, she would tell her husband:

"I have bought a horse-load of herrings for 4s. 6d. but I can get no eels yet."

Her bailiff told her one day:

"Mistress, I have got me a friend in Lowestoft to

buy seven or eight barrel of herring at a cost of 6s. 8d. a barrel. I have also laid in beef to last from autumn until the spring."

There were some things that could not be bought locally, even in Norwich. So, when Margaret wrote to her husband and sons in London, she usually added a note:

"I pray you that you will buy some frieze (woollen cloth) to make your child's gowns. You shall have it best cheap and best choice of Hugh's wife."

She liked fine clothes for herself and asked John to buy "three yards of purple cloth, price to the yard 3s.; a bonnet of deep purple, price 2s. 4d.; a girdle of blue ribbon, price 6d.; three dozen laces with red and yellow, price 6d.; three pairs of pattens (wooden clogs to protect shoes from the mud), let them be long enough and broad upon the heel."

In everything, Margaret's first duty was to her husband; children mattered far less. She was not so unkind as old Agnes who beat her daughter unmercifully because she would not marry a rich old man, but Anne and Margery were sent 'to learn manners' in other households and she had no patience when Anne was unhappy.

As for Margery, she committed the crime of falling in love with a man of lower rank, Richard, the Pastons' bailiff. Margaret refused to have her in the house and when, despite threats and punishment, Margery married her faithful Richard, the family would not forgive her.

A powerful new enemy appeared when the Duke

London merchants

of Suffolk suddenly claimed two of the Paston
manors. Margaret at once went from Caister to
Drayton where, to prove her rights, she collected
rents from the farmers. One refused to pay and when
two of his horses were taken, he got the Duke's
bailiff to come with 160 men to take property and
animals from the Paston tenants.

At this, Margaret sent her servants to drive off
seventy-seven of the cattle that the enemy had taken.
When threatened, she refused to budge and all
through the summer of 1465, the battle went on,
until she was almost worn out:

"What with sickness and trouble, I am brought
right low and weak," she told her husband, "but I
will do what I can in your matters."

With John again in prison, she had to carry on.
While her son defended Drayton, she went early one
morning to the Shire House and laid the whole case
before the Judges and the chief men of the county,
telling them she was surrounded by armed men and

had only two supporters left, her chaplain and Thomas Bond. Her enemies had captured Bond and tied him up like a thief.

The judges ordered that Bond should be released and the Duke's men were to depart peaceably.

It was a short-lived triumph, for matters were soon so serious that Margaret had to make the journey along robber-infested roads to London in order to consult her husband. While she was away, the Duke attacked the Paston property and completely wrecked their house and the village of Hellesdon.

Margaret returned to Norfolk but, in the spring of 1466, she received terrible news. Worn out by his troubles, her husband had died in London.

Margaret states her case at the Shire House

The eldest son, Sir John, became head of the family and poor Margaret's worries increased. The spendthrift bachelor enjoyed himself and squandered the money that his mother and her second son, also named John, collected for the family lawsuits. In little more than a year, all the Fastolf possessions were lost, apart from a few manors and Caister Castle.

When it was known that the Duke of Norfolk was determined to have Caister, even Sir John was alarmed. He began to gather a garrison but, in 1469, he was away in London when Edward IV was captured by Warwick the King-maker. The Duke of Norfolk immediately took advantage of the troubled situation to attack Caister with 3000 men.

The castle was defended by young John who did his utmost with a handful of retainers and meagre provisions. Margaret raised every penny to send him aid but no help came from Sir John. In the autumn, the brave little garrison surrendered.

With Caister lost, Sir John came to his senses and made an effort to recover his property. But, by now, the Pastons were desperately short of money. Margaret did not know which way to turn, for she was penniless and much too proud to sell an acre of land.

"I fear me I shall be obliged to borrow or else to close my house, or both," she said to Sir John. His only remedy was to sell manors and even the family silver.

Young John and his mother were made of sterner

stuff. They scrimped, saved and fought their enemies all along the line. Gradually, things took a turn for the better. The Duke of Norfolk died and Sir John was persuaded to send a petition to the King.

In May 1476, after seven years of struggle, the King's Council restored the castle and lands to the Paston family.

"Blessed to God, I have Caister!" cried Sir John to his mother.

Three years later, Sir John died and Margaret lived out her old age knowing that all was safe in the capable hands of young John. He was so much more like his father than his gay brother. She did not live quite long enough to see him made Sheriff of Norfolk, for she died in 1484, a year before the Wars of the Roses ended, but she was happy in the knowledge that John would safeguard all that she had fought for.

In her will, she left money for a priest to sing and pray for her soul and for 'the said John Paston, late my husband'. It is good to know that she did not forget Margery who had married the bailiff for love, for she left the sum of £20 for Margery's eldest child.

Margaret and young John

More about the people in part 2

MATILDA (1102–67), also known as Queen Maud, was the daughter of Henry I, called 'Beauclerc' or 'Good scholar', and of Matilda, daughter of Queen Margaret of Scotland. King Stephen was the son of Henry I's sister, Adela.

It was the loss of his son, William, that caused Henry to make Matilda heiress to the throne. Prince William sailed from Normandy in 1120 in the *White Ship*; he gave the sailors too much wine to drink, so they kept a bad look-out and wrecked the ship on a reef. William got safely into a small boat but was drowned when he tried to put back to the wreck to rescue his half-sister.

SAINT HUGH (*c*. 1135–1200) was the son of a nobleman of Avalon in the south of France. His mother died when he was eight and his father had him brought up in a nearby monastery. As a young man, he joined the Carthusians, a very strict Order in which the monks lived almost like hermits. After he became Bishop of Lincoln, Hugh still went back to Witham every year to spend some weeks in his tiny cell.

After his death, so many pilgrims visited his tomb that the eastern end of the cathedral had to be enlarged. His body lay in a shrine and his head in a separate casket. The gold plates and jewels were taken at the time of the Reformation but the stone floor and steps are still deeply worn by the feet and knees of countless pilgrims. Hugh's famous swan may be seen as part of a statue of the saint at New College, Oxford.   *c*. (*circa—Latin*) *means 'about'*

Was KING JOHN (1167–1216) really 'the worst king who ever reigned in England'? Most of the stories of his wickedness were written by monks long after his death and we know that some of these were untrue. John was clever and, at times, a terrifyingly good general; he was no harsher to his subjects than William the Conqueror or Henry II and no more wicked than many medieval kings.

His bad name seems to be due to the fact that, unlike other kings, he had no lovable qualities—Stephen was generous, Richard I brave, Henry III pious, but no one could admire John or pity him when he turned out to be a failure. His son, Henry III, though not wicked, was a feeble monarch and it was left to Edward I to restore respect for the Crown.

When ROGER BACON (c. 1214–92) became a Friar Minor at Oxford, the Franciscans were different from the barefooted followers of St. Francis who had come to England fifty years before. Many were scholars who did not preach or follow the rules of poverty and humility.

For centuries, Bacon was looked upon as a wizard and, later, as a martyr punished because he would not keep silent about his scientific discoveries. Nowadays, he is seen as a brilliant thinker born at a time when few people could understand his ideas. Robert Grosseteste was one of the noblest men of medieval times. Like St. Hugh, he was buried in his cathedral at Lincoln.

THE BLACK PRINCE (1330–76) was not known by this famous name in his lifetime. He was called Edward of Woodstock. Nor is it likely that he took his motto 'Ich dien' and his badge of three ostrich plumes from the blind King of Bohemia who fell at Crecy.

The marvellous 'achievements' (the name for his armour, surcoat, shields, helm and gauntlets) that can be seen above his tomb in Canterbury Cathedral were placed there in 1954. They are exact copies of the originals which are now kept in a glass case.

Crecy and Poitiers were two of the chief battles of the Hundred Years War that lasted, on and off, from 1340 to 1453. By the end, France had won back all the English conquests except Calais.

OWEN GLENDOWER (c. 1350–1416), rightly a national hero of Wales, was far more than a rebel leader. At the height of his power, he called a Welsh Parliament, made alliances with France and Scotland, corresponded with the Pope and made plans to build two Welsh universities.

Unfortunately for him, he was opposed by a young soldier of genius, the future Henry V and, in the fighting, Wales became a poverty-stricken land. About seventy years after Glendower's death, the grandson of a Welsh gentleman named Owen Tudor became King Henry VII.

The murder of JAMES I (1394–1437) was a tragedy for Scotland, for his son, James II, was only six years old. The nobles were soon behaving with their usual treachery and greed. When James II grew up, he showed his father's spirit in subduing the earls but, during the Wars of the Roses, he decided to recover Roxburgh Castle from the English and was killed when a siege-gun that he was working blew up in his face. His heir was a nine-year-old boy and the old troubles broke out again.

WARWICK THE KING-MAKER (1428–71) held more land than any subject had ever held, for he and his father both married wealthy heiresses. Warwick's magnificent household, his naval victories and his open-handed friendliness to ordinary people made him very popular but he could not be satisfied with less than the power of a king.

After his death at Barnet, Queen Margaret was defeated and her son slain at Tewkesbury. Henry VI died soon afterwards, almost certainly by the hand of a murderer. Queen Margaret, after four years in prison, was ransomed by Louis XI and she died in France. The Duke of Clárence was put to death for treason, being drowned, it was said, in a butt of wine. Having got rid of his enemies, Edward IV reigned until 1483.

The story of MARGARET PASTON (died 1484) comes from the Paston Letters, written by and to members of the family between 1422 and 1509. This great collection was sold in the 18th century and passed through many hands before the letters were published in several volumes.

Most of the letters were penned by a secretary but sometimes, Agnes, Margaret or John would write themselves in haste, apologizing for the lack of a scribe. The writing-paper was made in France or Italy, for there was no English paper-making industry yet. Each sheet was 10–12 inches wide and nearly 18 inches long; it was folded several times into a small packet, sealed and addressed but no envelopes were used.

Part 3

Discoverers and Adventurers

John and Sebastian Cabot

IN the year 1493 a piece of exciting news spread through the seaports and capitals of Europe. A Genoese adventurer named Christopher Columbus had reached the Indies by sailing westwards across the Atlantic Ocean.

No one doubted that the new islands were part of Asia. They were sure to be rich in spices and gold and, since Columbus was in the pay of the King of Spain, their wealth would belong to Spain. The Portuguese, too, were growing rich. Their sailors had made voyages into the Atlantic and along the coast of Africa where, it was said, the rivers ran with gold.

No discoveries had been made by English seamen. So far, they had done little more than sail their fishing-boats to Iceland.

Living at Bristol, however, with his wife and three sons, was a black-bearded foreigner who knew more about the oceans than most men. He was Giovanni Caboto, otherwise John Cabot, a citizen of Venice who, like Columbus, had been born in Genoa.

Like Columbus, too, Cabot was a man with an idea. For years he had wandered from city to city, trying to interest people in a new way to reach the spice-lands of the East. The world, he said, was round. He showed people a globe made of metal; he produced charts and maps to prove that it was easier and quicker to reach the East by sailing *west*.

"When I was a young man trading between Damascus and Mecca," he would tell the Bristol merchants, "I often saw the spice-caravans arrive from the East. The camels were half-dead from weariness, the men were burnt black from crossing the hot deserts. Months, even years, it took them to reach the markets where I bought spices for my masters of Venice. Now, see for yourselves, on this globe. Since the distance by land is so great, the distance by sea must be shorter."

King Henry VII needed money badly. He envied his fellow-monarchs of Spain and Portugal who would soon have gold by the shipload and he wished that he could send out sea-captains to discover new lands.

The King and his Court visited Bristol where John Cabot was invited to explain his ideas for a voyage of exploration. Without delay, Henry VII agreed to provide a ship and he gave Cabot a royal letter, sealed with the Great Seal. It granted "to our well-beloved John Cabot, citizen of Venice, to Lewis, Sebastian and Sanctius, sons of the said John ... leave and power to sail to all ports, countries and seas of the East, of the West and of the North, under our banners and ensigns . . .".

In 1497 Cabot sailed from Bristol in a ship called the *Mathew*. It was so small that the crew numbered only eighteen men and we do not know if John's sons went with their father. Perhaps they did, for Lewis and Sanctius were never heard of again and they may have died at sea or have been washed overboard. In later years, Sebastian used to say that he went on the voyage. He even spoke as if he, not his father, had

"Land Ho!"

been the captain. But Sebastian was probably no more than fourteen or fifteen years old at the time and he was not always careful about telling the truth.

The *Mathew* left Ireland behind and sailed out into the Atlantic.

"Our course is due west now," said John to the helmsman. "Keep the North Star on your right hand."

Long, anxious weeks went by before the look-out at the masthead shouted "Land-ho!". There on the horizon lay the "new-found land", a bleak headland that Cabot named Prima Vista—first view. In his opinion, he had reached the northerly tip of Asia and he had only to sail on to come to Cathay where he would find the sun-lit cities and measureless riches described by Marco Polo.

It was not China that Cabot had reached, but North America, probably Cape Breton Island. He sailed along the coasts of Newfoundland and Labrador and he went ashore to claim the territory for King Henry VII. In all probability, he set foot on the American mainland before Columbus.

The country was silent and empty. There was no sign of people or houses. The sailors found some snares for trapping animals and a few bone needles that were used, they thought, for making nets, but if there were any inhabitants in the area, they stayed hidden. Cabot was puzzled but not downhearted. He had proved that he was right and, with a larger ship, he could go on to find the Spice Islands. Meanwhile, he would return home to report the discovery of a new land.

If the country lacked riches, the sea was teeming with fish. The sailors had only to let down a basket to have it filled with cod—"England will have no more need of the old trade with Iceland," they cried.

The Mathew *reaches the icy seas of Labrador*

When the *Mathew* reached Bristol, the King was sufficiently pleased with Cabot to give him £10. This seems a very mean reward but in those days it was quite a large sum of money and Henry soon followed it up with a pension of £20 a year. Meanwhile, he gave orders to prepare a bigger expedition.

In May 1498 John Cabot left Bristol on his second voyage. This time he commanded a fleet of five or six ships, one provided by the King and the others by Bristol and London merchants, with local captains on board. Again, we cannot be certain that his son Sebastian was with him.

"I shall follow the coast of the new-found land until I come opposite Cipango (Japan)," John told the ambassador of Milan. "From there, I shall sail straight to the country of the Great Khan and trade with his subjects for spices and silks."

Once more Cabot reached North America and sailed hopefully along the coast, expecting to find a strait that would lead him into warmer seas. Foiled by ice and probably by the fears of his sailors, he had to turn back. For several weeks he coasted down the eastern shore of America, far enough to alarm the Spaniards. He found no gold or spices but he made the name of Cabot renowned among mariners.

The strange thing is that we do not know when John returned home or what happened when he reported that he had found neither treasure nor the way to Cathay. Perhaps the merchants were so disappointed that they cold-shouldered John. Until recently, people believed that he perished in the northern seas but we know now that he was still alive in 1499, for he drew his £20 pension in that

Sebastian impresses the Bristol merchants

year. It seems certain that he died soon afterwards.

By this time his son Sebastian was well known in Bristol. Pleasant, energetic and charming, he impressed people by his knowledge of geography and navigation. He was here, there and everywhere. He visited Spain and France, he knew important people and all about the latest discoveries. He often hinted that he himself had taken part in these adventures and there was hardly anyone who doubted a young man so knowing and clever as Sebastian Cabot.

It was not surprising that the King should award him a pension of £10—not for any voyages, but "for diligent services in and about our town and port of Bristol".

In 1509 Sebastian sailed to Labrador with two ships fitted out at the King's order. He pushed north until he came to a strait leading to the west. Presently, it broadened out and turned southwards. Surely the strait was the North-West Passage and this broad sea was the Pacific Ocean? Cathay must lie ahead.

217

But the sea was thick with floating ice and, as the perils increased, the sailors mutinied and Sebastian was forced to turn back. Like his father, he sailed along the coast examining every inlet in case it should prove to be a channel leading to the cherished spice-lands. Having thus explored a large part of the North American coast, Sebastian came safely home to Bristol.

At least, that was his story. It seems to be true but no one has ever found a single English document that

The seamen compel Sebastian to turn back

mentions this voyage. The foreigners who wrote about it had heard of it from Sebastian himself!

By this time, Henry VII was dead and, since young Henry VIII showed no interest in voyages of discovery, Sebastian left England and entered the service of the King of Spain. At once he was an important person. He lived at Court where the King made him Pilot-Major of Spain, with a handsome salary and splendid apartments.

Every Spanish captain had to report to the Pilot-Major when he came home from an ocean voyage and no expedition was undertaken without Sebastian Cabot's advice. He examined captains in navigation, gave them their licences to sail, kept records of voyages and supervised the making of maps and charts.

The Pilot-Major of Spain became so celebrated that Henry VIII and Wolsey asked him to return to England to lead an expedition to the North-West. At this, the London merchants protested, saying that "the said Cabot was an impostor, well-known as such, without any real knowledge of the North-West countries, though a glib reciter of other men's tales".

Back in Spain, Sebastian remained in high favour. The King had complete faith in him and nothing could be more natural than to give him command of a great expedition to the Moluccas—the Spice Islands, far away in the Pacific Ocean.

The learned navigator proved to be a complete failure as a commander. After wasting three years in disastrous attempts to find gold in South America, he came back to Spain to stand trial for disobeying orders and for losing his ships and men. Found guilty, he had just been sentenced to banishment in Morocco, when the King of Spain returned from abroad and gave him a complete pardon.

Restored to the post of Pilot-Major, Sebastian remained in the royal service for many years, though he seemed always to have a secret desire to return to England. At length, when he was approaching the age of seventy, the invitation arrived.

The ministers of the boy-king, Edward VI, had decided that they must do something to stir the unadventurous spirits of English mariners. They paid £100 to a ship's captain, Master Peckham, "for the transporting of one Cabot, a pilot, to come out of Hispain to serve and inhabit in England".

As soon as Sebastian arrived, he was given a salary of £166 13s. 4d. "for good services done and to be done" and, from time to time, there were special gifts of £200, doubtless to keep him happy. It was well known that the King of Spain was trying to tempt his celebrated Pilot-Major back to Seville.

But Sebastian was happy in England. The unkind remarks of the London merchants had been forgotten and, among people who knew so little about the oceans, who could doubt the wisdom of Cabot? He was a most jovial old fellow and he entered into his new duties with the utmost goodwill.

England's trade was poor and new markets were needed. Very well, he would speedily put things right. Unfortunately, the Spaniards and the Portuguese had divided the New World between themselves and the way to the East was barred—except by the North-West Passage, and that was both difficult and dangerous. Why not try the North-East Passage and sail to India and Cathay that way?

Sebastian dances at the Christopher

Thus, as Governor of the Merchant Adventurers, Sebastian was "chief setter-forth" of the voyage. He was too old to go himself but he drew up a long list of instructions for Willoughby and Chancellor, the commanders, who set off from Greenwich in 1553.

They found that there was no sea-route to India, only icy seas and a vast frozen land-mass. Willoughby died, frozen to death with his crew, but Chancellor made his way overland to Moscow and he came home with a treaty of trade signed by the Czar, Ivan the Terrible.

English spirits rose. Here at last was a new market for hardware and woollen cloth. The Muscovy Company was formed and its white-bearded Governor went down to Gravesend in high spirits to speed the departure of a new expedition.

The captain of the *Searchthrift* wrote in his journal,

"The right worshipful Sebastian Cabot came aboard our pinnace, with many gentlemen and gentlewomen who, after they had viewed our ship, went ashore and the good old gentleman gave most liberal alms to the poor to pray for our good fortune. At the sign of the *Christopher*, he and his friends feasted and made me and my ship's company great cheer. And, for very joy, he entered into the dance with the young people, which, being ended, he and his friends departed, commending us to Almighty God."

So, at the end of his long and rather mysterious life, "the good old gentleman" played his part in awakening Englishmen to the opportunities for trade and adventure across the seas.

Lady Jane Grey

"AND if my Lady will stand still for but one minute, all shall be finished," said Mistress Ellen, as she tried to fasten the little girl's head-dress so that it stood out like a halo round the fair head of the Marquess of Dorset's daughter.

Jane laughed and stopped twisting her head to read her book. The nurse smoothed the bell-shaped overskirt and Lady Jane was ready to make her morning visit to her parents.

She walked sedately across Bradgate's great hall and entered the winter parlour where her parents were seated by the carved fireplace. Jane curtsied and said:

"Right reverend and worshipful parents, I bid you good morning and I beseech you of your blessing."

Henry Grey, Marquess of Dorset, answered briefly, but his wife, Lady Frances, eyed the child coldly and began to chide. Jane's curtsey was ill-done. She mumbled her words. What of her lessons? Was her Greek as far advanced as her cousin's? Had not Master Harding rebuked her for playing too long on the lute?

Lady Frances ended by giving her seven-year-

223

old daughter a sharp blow between the shoulders:
"Get you to your lessons," she snapped.

As soon as she left the parlour, Jane's meek
expression changed. She hurried eagerly along to the
schoolroom where Doctor Harding was waiting. She
loved her lessons and could read Latin with ease
already. Now she was beginning to learn Greek,
French, Spanish and Hebrew.

Between her eighth and ninth birthdays, Jane was
sent away from home to live with Queen Katherine
Parr, Henry VIII's last wife. Happy with her books
and music, Jane knew little of the happenings in the
royal household. Henry VIII died and the new king
was her cousin, Edward VI, a boy of her own age
with whom she often played. Like Jane, he was
clever but he was much too young to control the
nobles who surrounded the throne.

One of these was Lord Seymour, the High Admiral,
a bold, handsome man whose charm so attracted
Katherine Parr that she married him within a few
months of the old King's death.

The Admiral smiled jovially at the little girl in his
wife's household. He went to have a quiet talk with
her father.

"She shall be placed in marriage much to your
liking," said the Admiral.

"With whom shall you match her?" asked Dorset
craftily.

"Why, she might be wife to any Prince. Should His
Majesty, when he comes of age, be minded to marry
within the realm . . . But, my Lord Marquess, to
make so great a match, I must needs have the Lady
Jane in my keeping."

For £2000, Dorset gave Jane into the Admiral's
care so that he might arrange to marry her to King
Edward. But Katherine Parr died suddenly at
Gloucester and, soon afterwards, the Admiral's folly
brought about his ruin. After his execution, poor
little Jane was sent home to her parents. The disappointment made her mother more sharp-tempered
than ever.

One day, Master Ascham, Princess Elizabeth's
tutor, happened to visit Bradgate. The servants said
that all the family were out hunting and only the
Lady Jane was at home.

Ascham walked into the house and found the
thirteen-year-old girl reading Greek, "with as much
delight as if it were a merry story".

"Why, Madam, are you not in the park with the
others?" he asked.

"All their sport is only a shadow of the pleasure
I find in Plato," answered Jane with a smile.

"But, tell me, how is it you take such delight in
books that few men can read with ease?"

"I will tell you," said Jane. "God gave me such
severe parents and so gentle a schoolmaster. When I
am with my parents, all that I do is wrong and I am
so cruelly punished with pinches, nips and blows that
I think myself in hell. But when I go to Master
Aylmer, he teacheth me so gently that I am happy
all the time that I am with him. So you see why
books are my pleasure."

Ascham had a long conversation with Jane and,
later, he encouraged her to write regularly in Latin
and Greek to scholars in England and Switzerland.
They wrote back as if to an equal and they found

M.W.—15

Master Ascham finds Lady Jane reading Greek

that, like themselves, Jane believed passionately in the new religion of the Protestants.

While Jane was writing to her learned friends, a struggle for power was going on among the lords of the Council. The cleverest of these treacherous men was John Dudley, Duke of Northumberland, who planned to overthrow Protector Somerset.

Having won the young King's admiration—he was
a great archer and the best jouster in England—
Northumberland made himself all-powerful. Edward
and the Council stood in dread of this dark ruthless
man who was the real ruler of England. He dominated
everyone and he laid his plans to raise his family still
higher—as high as the throne itself.

If Edward should die, the heir to the throne was
Princess Mary and, after her, Princess Elizabeth.
Lady Jane's mother, now Duchess of Suffolk, was
next in succession. She was made to give up her rights
to her daughter and Northumberland arranged that
Jane should marry his son, Guilford Dudley. If
anything should happen to Edward VI, it might be
possible to see that the crown came to the Dudleys.

So far, Edward seemed to be healthy. He worked
hard at his books and he enjoyed outdoor sports. In
1552, however, he caught measles and, although he
recovered, he seemed always to be tired. By summer,
he was seriously ill.

The Duke increased his hold on the sick boy's
mind. Day after day, he spent long hours talking to
him about State affairs, voyages of discovery and,
above all, religion, for Edward was an ardent
Protestant.

In April 1553, Northumberland announced the
betrothal of Lady Jane Grey and his son. Jane
herself had been told nothing. She hardly knew
Guilford Dudley and she liked him less. Elegant and
handsome like all his family, he was a conceited
booby, a mother's spoilt darling.

"I will not marry Lord Dudley," she said.

The Suffolks stormed at her and struck her until

Northumberland bullies King Edward into altering his will

her spirit was subdued. On 25th May, Jane was married to Guilford Dudley in London.

But the King was dying and Northumberland had to work fast. He spoke continuously to Edward about the succession, working on the boy's fears, wheedling, threatening. If Princess Mary came to the throne, the Protestant religion would be crushed . . .

"But, by my father's will, Lady Mary stands next to me," said the King.

"Where God's glory is in peril, a good prince will set aside a son, a brother or a sister. Think, Sire, of your immortal soul, if you do not do God's Will."

"What then of my sister Elizabeth? She is of the Reformed Church."

"Your Highness does well to ask. If you put aside one, you must put aside the other. Their births were not legal. It is not God's purpose for them to reign."

At last, Edward gave way. Too ill to argue any more, he agreed to leave the crown to his cousin, Lady Jane Grey.

Three judges were summoned to the royal bed-chamber to witness the King's will.

"It is not legal," quavered the Lord Chief Justice. He was taken outside to receive the full flood of Northumberland's anger. Next day, the judges returned with the Privy Council to Greenwich Palace where the dying King ordered them to sign. Weeping, they did as they were told and so did a hundred of the chief officials of the realm. Eight days later, Edward VI died.

Meanwhile, Northumberland invited Princess Mary to London. But, as she was setting out, an unknown man stepped forward to whisper an urgent warning. Mary turned her horse and rode away to Framlingham Castle in Suffolk.

Cursing himself for not having seized Mary earlier, Northumberland summoned the Council to attend Lady Jane Grey at Syon House.

On 9th July 1553 Jane entered the great room and was bewildered at being led to a dais under a canopy. She had no idea of the reason for this gathering, for Northumberland had kept the King's death a secret.

With sonorous words, the Duke announced the death of King Edward VI. Jane felt sorrow for the boy whom she had once known so well . . . but what was the Duke saying? The Lady Mary . . . the Lady Elizabeth . . . disinherited—what could he mean?

"His late Majesty hath named your Grace as heir

to the crown of England. Therefore, you should cheerfully take upon you the name, title and estates of Queen of England, France and Ireland!"

Queen of England? In terror, Jane saw that the lords were kneeling. She tried to speak, to run away. Almost fainting, she cried through her sobs:

"No! No! The crown is not my right. The Lady Mary is the rightful heir!"

The Duke and Guilford Dudley tried to calm her. Her parents lost all dignity and ranted at the white-faced girl until she fell upon her knees and begged God to tell her what to do. There was no answer and she took the silence to mean that she must obey. She rose and the lords came forward, one by one, to kiss her hand. She was Queen of England.

Next day, to the boom of cannons and the harsh blare of trumpets, Jane entered the Tower of London in state. She was so small that she was made to wear clogs with three-inch soles, but she held herself like a monarch, smiling prettily, as she walked from the Water Gate on the arm of her gorgeously decked husband. She was too excited to hear the vintner's boy cry:

"The Lady Mary hath a better title!"

In the royal apartments of the Tower, they brought Jane the crown and the jewels, but it was some time before she would allow the Lord Treasurer to try the crown on her head.

"Another shall be made for your husband," he said. Jane looked up. Now she realized why Northumberland had made her Queen—so that a Dudley should be King!

"No," she said firmly, "that cannot be. I would be

The Lords of the Council kiss the hand of Lady Jane

content to make my husband a duke. But I will never consent to make him King."

"I *will* be King!" cried the spoilt youth, bursting into tears. In the furious storm that broke over her head, Jane remained calm. When Guilford's mother declared that she would take her son home, the fifteen-year-old Queen said quietly:

"He shall not leave. His place is here and, whether he likes it or no, he shall remain."

Two days passed without trouble from the Londoners, but Northumberland's sons were routed when they took a force into East Anglia to capture Princess Mary. At this, the Duke decided to send Jane's father, the Duke of Suffolk, but once again Jane was obstinate.

"My father shall stay here in my company," she said. Because he dared trust no one else, Northumberland rode angrily out of London at the head of his army. By the time he reached Newmarket, there was news that men were up in arms for Mary. His troops began to desert and, at Cambridge, the Duke panicked.

Seeing that the game was up, he tore down the notices proclaiming Lady Jane and shouted, "Long live Queen Mary!". Nothing could wipe out his treason and Northumberland was arrested and brought to the Tower through a crowd of jeering Londoners.

Nine days after the Council had knelt to kiss Jane's hand, Suffolk hurried to the room where Jane was at supper:

"Daughter," he said, "I am here to tell you that you are no longer Queen. You must put off your royal robes and be content with a private life."

Northumberland on his way to the Tower

"I shall put them off more willingly than I put them on," replied Jane. "I did so out of obedience to you and my mother, but I sinned and I gladly relinquish the crown."

Then she added piteously:

"May I not go home?"

But Suffolk had already gone. To save his own neck, he sneaked out of the Tower to add his voice to those who shouted for Queen Mary.

Placed under arrest, Jane was moved to a small house on Tower Green where the Gentleman-Gaoler looked after important prisoners. Her husband was in another part of the Tower and she saw nothing of him or her parents. However, her attendants were kind, she had her prayer-book and she wrote a long letter to Queen Mary, confessing that she was wrong to have accepted the crown.

She learned that, although she and her husband would have to stand trial for treason, the Queen would not allow her to die.

There was no pardon for Northumberland. He went to the block in grovelling misery, admitting that he had even betrayed his religion and was never at heart a Protestant. Jane watched from her window as he went to his death:

"I pray God," she said scornfully, "I nor no friend of mine die so miserably."

Six months passed. Jane wrote letters and prayers, while Guilford occupied himself with carving his family arms on his prison wall. They had stood their trial and both were under sentence of death, but they fully expected to be pardoned.

From time to time, news filtered into their prison. Queen Mary was determined to marry Philip of Spain and the people were angry. There were riots in the City; Catholic priests had been stoned and there was talk of rebellion.

In Kent, Sir Thomas Wyatt led an armed rising that was meant to be a protest against the Spanish marriage, but Jane's father foolishly joined in. The affair was bungled and Wyatt was captured at Temple Bar. Two days later, Jane was told to prepare herself for death.

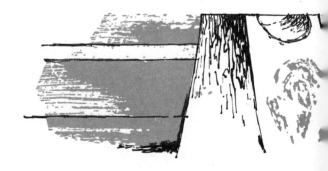

*"Master executioner, I forgive you
for what you have to do."*

Mary was not a harsh woman and she had no wish to end her cousin's life. But, whispered her advisers, as long as Jane Grey lived, there would be plots and rebellions. The Queen sent a priest to see if the girl would become a Catholic; that alone might save her.

Jane was young and she did not want to die: "I am innocent and I do not deserve this sentence," she said. "Lord and Saviour, suffer me not to be tempted above my power."

Her Protestant religion meant more to her than life and, although she liked the priest and kissed him farewell at the end, she did not yield.

On 12th February 1554, at ten o'clock in the morning, she caught a glimpse of her fair-haired husband as he passed beneath her window on his way to Tower Hill. Shortly afterwards, still watching, she saw the cart return with his headless body. She closed her eyes for a moment, picked up her prayer-book and went downstairs into the open air.

The scaffold was on the Green and she walked towards it, a tiny figure in black, holding the Lieutenant's arm. She was quite calm, "her countenance nothing abashed, neither her eyes moisted with tears".

She spoke briefly to the spectators and forgave the executioner. Without assistance, she tied the handkerchief about her eyes. Then she stretched out her arms, crying:

"Where? What shall I do?"

Someone guided her towards the block and she knelt down. The people heard a clear, girlish voice cry out:

"Lord, into thy hands I commend my spirit."

John Hawkins of Plymouth

WHEN Queen Elizabeth came to the throne, a young sea-captain was trading out of Plymouth. He was John Hawkins, younger son of William Hawkins, a leading merchant of the town.

John and his brother William were partners in the family business but, so far, the warehouses and the shipyard held no attraction for John. He preferred to go to sea and had already made several voyages to Spain and the Canaries where his fair dealing and his ability to speak Spanish made him popular with the local gentry.

At this time, England and Spain were allies and Queen Elizabeth was anxious to keep on good terms with Philip of Spain.

Thus, for a young man with a good knowledge of the Spanish trade, there might be opportunities to increase his business. John Hawkins left Plymouth and went to London, taking with him £10,000, his share of the family fortune. Soon he married Katherine, daughter of Benjamin Gonson, Treasurer of the Navy, and was introduced to some gentlemen of the Court and of the City. They were interested in taking shares in a trading venture and they asked about his plans:

"Sirs, I intend to sail to the Gold Coast," said Hawkins.

"Doubtless to trade for gold, ivory and spices like your father?" remarked Sir Thomas Lodge.

"No, sir," replied Hawkins. "The Portuguese make great difficulty in that trade. I have in mind to buy negroes to sell them to the King of Spain's subjects in America."

"But doth not His Majesty forbid all trading by foreigners in those waters?"

"It is true, sir, that a licence is required. But I have friends in Spain who can ease such matters. The plain fact is that the planters need negroes most urgently and will pay handsomely for them."

In the 16th century no one saw anything wrong in buying and selling slaves. The trade was well established and King Philip levied a tax on each negro sold to his settlers. Even so, slaves were scarce and expensive in the Spanish colonies.

In 1562 Hawkins sailed to West Africa with four ships. By capture and by purchase from Portuguese traders, Hawkins collected 400 negroes and set sail for the West Indies. At Hispaniola, the Spanish

Hawkins and the Spanish officials

governor and officials were surprised to hear themselves addressed courteously in Spanish.

"Honoured and excellent sirs," began Hawkins, "I am come to offer you merchandise at fair prices. You may assure yourselves that I intend no harm to you or to the interest of the King's Majesty of Spain whose servant I am."

The officials were taken aback. They ought not to trade with a foreigner, but this Englishman was richly dressed and well spoken—perhaps he had powerful friends in Spain. A little trading in a quiet place along the coast could do no harm—and they would tell Captain Bernaldez to conceal some soldiers in hope of taking the stranger unawares.

But Hawkins was too wily to walk into a trap. He met Bernaldez in the open, with his own men close behind, fingering their weapons. The Spaniards smiled and bowed. The trading was completed with

239

goodwill on both sides and the Englishmen sailed for home, satisfied with their profit.

In London, the success of this first voyage led to preparations for a bigger expedition. This time, the Queen provided one of her own ships, the *Jesus of Lübeck*. It was an old vessel, leaky and difficult to handle, but Hawkins felt honoured to sail in her as his flag-ship, and even more honoured to be summoned to the Queen's residence at Enfield.

If Elizabeth had expected to meet a bluff Devon sea-dog, she was disappointed. The captain was as elegant as any gentleman of her Court in his fashionably padded doublet of black velvet, with cuffs and collar of fine cambric. But it was his charm and eager loyalty that impressed her most. As for Hawkins, for the rest of his life he was to see Elizabeth as she was then—still young and handsome, with the dazzling air of majesty that entranced her poets, statesmen and mariners.

On his second voyage, Hawkins again collected slaves in West Africa and crossed the Atlantic to the Spanish Main. By a mixture of charm and veiled threats, he again sold his goods and negroes at a good profit. Then, after giving generous assistance to a distressed French settlement at Florida, he returned to England and thankfully brought his leaky old flag-ship into Padstow.

From his cabin he wrote to the Queen, "Thanks be to God, our voyage is reasonably well accomplished".

The Plymouth captain was now in high favour with everyone, except the Spanish Ambassador who wrote privately to his master, King Philip.

Elizabeth receives John Hawkins at Enfield

"I saw him at the palace and invited him to dine with me. The vast profit of his voyage has excited other merchants and Hawkins is going out again next May . . . I might tell the Queen he has traded in ports forbidden by Your Majesty and ask her to punish him . . ."

Elizabeth refused to punish her famous captain but, to avoid a quarrel, she would not let him sail in the following year.

For once, Hawkins may not have minded. There were business affairs with his brother in Plymouth and his own son Richard was now five years old. The boy was big enough to trot after his father through warehouses, into a ship's hold and upon the poop-deck where he could play at being a sea-captain and could learn from his father how things should be corded, stowed and made ship-shape on a Hawkins vessel.

Meanwhile, there was a good deal of mystery about the preparations for the third voyage. Stories went about that Hawkins had agreed to serve King Philip in the Mediterranean, that two Portuguese runaways were going to lead him to a gold-mine in Africa and that a Spanish admiral tried to stop his ships leaving harbour.

However, in October 1567, Hawkins left Plymouth with six ships—the *Jesus*, the *Minion* and four small vessels supplied by the Hawkins family, including the *Judith*, soon to be commanded by their nephew, young Francis Drake.

It was more difficult than ever to collect slaves in West Africa. Nor were things any easier in the West Indies and along the Main. Stern warnings from Spain had made the planters unwilling to buy and, in one place, Hawkins had to capture the town in order to do business. However, almost everything was sold and, with a great sum in gold, pearls and silver stowed aboard the *Jesus*, it was time to go home.

Almost at once, the little fleet ran into a hurricane. The *Jesus* was leaking so badly that she could hardly be kept afloat and, at all costs, Hawkins had to find a haven where he could make repairs.

In the Gulf of Mexico, he came to San Juan de Ulua. Flying the faded royal standard instead of the Cross of St. George, he was able to slip past the fort that guarded the harbour-mouth because the Spaniards mistook his ships for a Spanish plate-fleet, expected at any time.

Hawkins made himself clear to the astonished Governor:

"I desire only to repair my ships. I will pay for

Hawkins and the Governor of San Juan de Ulua
"I desire only to repair my ships!"

victuals and I will not take a pennyworth of your silver or gold."

The Spaniards made no difficulty and work began at once.

Next morning, a lookout sighted the Spanish fleet approaching. What was to be done? Hawkins had taken the fort and his guns were ready, so it would be possible to keep the fleet out. But that would be an act of war.

"There is no help for it," he said to Drake. "Our two countries are at peace. I must let them in and trust to the Spaniards' honour."

Both sides promised not to molest the other but, as soon as his fleet was inside, Don Martin, the newly arrived Viceroy of Mexico, prepared for action. Two days later, in a sudden attack, the men working ashore were massacred, and Spanish guns opened fire on the English ships at their moorings.

Hawkins ran on deck to see that the *Minion*, alongside, was being boarded. "God and St. George!" he roared, "Upon the traitorous villains!" Leaping down, he drove off the attackers and turned to repel a similar assault on the *Jesus*.

"Cut the head cables!" he ordered. "Haul off into the harbour."

Clear of surrounding craft and, having told Drake to take the *Judith* outside, he attacked the Spaniards so fiercely that two of their galleons were sunk and the rest silenced. But the shore batteries continued to pour shot after shot into the *Jesus* until she was in a pitiable state. Hawkins therefore used her to shield the *Minion* while the gold and silver were transferred

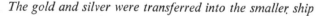

The gold and silver were transferred into the smaller ship

into the smaller ship. This work was not quite finished when two fireships came blazing towards them.

Frantically, the men cut the *Minion* free and, as the ships parted, Hawkins was the last to leap to safety. By tremendous efforts, they got out of the harbour and anchored for the night near to the *Judith*.

Next morning, for some reason never explained, Drake had vanished, leaving his commander in the lurch. Hawkins, who never liked to blame an officer, merely reported later that "in the night, the *Judith* forsook us to our great misery".

They were indeed in misery. The *Minion*, badly damaged, had two hundred men on board and very little food and water. It would have been suicide to try to sail home, so a hundred seamen volunteered to be put ashore along the coast in hope of surviving until help could arrive from England.

It was a nightmare voyage for the others. Only fifteen men were alive when they sighted Devon and they were too weak to bring their ship into Plymouth. A relief crew was sent out and, from the rail, a gaunt figure thanked them. Dressed in his finest clothes and wearing a gold chain, John Hawkins came bravely into his home port.

He found that Drake had already arrived and all England was buzzing with the story of the treachery at San Juan. From this time on, no matter what Elizabeth and Philip pretended, there was unofficial war with Spain.

At home with Katherine and young Richard, Hawkins soon recovered his strength. By summer, he was at sea again, this time commanding a fleet that

helped the Dutch and French Protestants in the
Channel. But he constantly put his own plan to the
Queen's advisers.

"With God's grace and a good squadron at the
Azores," he told the Earl of Leicester, "I can take
the King of Spain's treasure-fleet and avenge the
wrongs done to this realm."

The Queen gave him permission to fit out ten
warships at Plymouth but she always found reasons
to prevent his sailing. The truth was that she needed
her wily captain at home and Hawkins became
Treasurer of the Navy, guardian of all the royal
ships. Faithfully, tirelessly, he toiled to create the kind
of Navy that he knew was needed, bringing the old-
fashioned ships up to date, rebuilding half-decayed
galleons, introducing more powerful guns and better
pay for the seamen.

Instead of going to sea as he longed to do, he
found himself dealing with shipwrights and timber
merchants, with the fitting-out of fleets for other
commanders, and he saw his nephew Drake take his
own place as England's most celebrated sea-captain.

For his great work, he earned hatred and suspicion.
By putting a stop to the dishonest practice of over-
charging the Queen for timber, ropes, canvas and
every kind of naval stores, he made enemies in high
places. They accused him of "cunning and craftiness
to maintain his ambition and pride and for the filling
of his own purse".

In fact, Hawkins grew poorer, not richer, in the
Queen's service, but he stuck to his task:

"The true test of my work will be seen when
Her Majesty's ships meet the Spaniards," he said.

Hawkins in the Shipyards

In 1584 Hawkins managed to get to sea but he was only allowed "to ply up and down the Channel and guard the coast" instead of going to intercept the treasure-fleet as he hoped. However, he was pleased that his new ships handled so well and when, four years later, the Armada came sailing up the Channel, they did not fail.

Hawkins commanded one of the four squadrons that dogged the Armada like terriers and finally broke its formation. Thanks to their seaworthiness, their guns and the luck of the weather, they saved England from invasion.

With the danger past and the kingdom frantic with joy, Hawkins, who had been knighted on the Lord Admiral's flag-ship, was still hard at work. Off the coast of Kent and in the seafaring towns, he was trying to cope with thousands of sick and starving sailors for whom there was little food and no pay. Somehow, he got the survivors back to their homes but he never forgot the plight of those seamen.

In later years, he and Drake founded the Chatham Chest, a fund to help distressed mariners, and he also built the Sir John Hawkins Hospital for old seamen and shipwrights.

By this time Hawkins was going on for sixty. He was tired and he wished to resign from the Navy to go back to Plymouth where his brother and his wife had died and his son Richard was now a sea-captain in his own right. But the war with Spain continued and the Queen would not release him, so he continued to serve her for the rest of his life.

He built some fine new ships but he grieved at the waste of money on unsuccessful land operations. For

half the cost, he could have taken a fleet to sea to
cut off the King of Spain from his Empire and his
gold.

The Queen grew ever more obstinate and tight-
fisted, so that even Drake was half in disgrace and
Hawkins was constantly in trouble over the expenses
of the Navy.

Perhaps this was why the two ageing sea-captains
put forward a plan to rob the Spaniards in the old
style. Permission was given and in 1595 they sailed
from Plymouth as joint-commanders of a powerful
fleet.

It was a disastrous expedition. The two men, never
close friends since San Juan, were entirely different—
Hawkins, thorough and methodical, Drake, fiery and

The fight at Porto Rico

impatient of another's ideas. They did not quarrel openly but there was no harmony and the Spaniards, better armed and stronger than ever, had already learnt of their coming.

At Porto Rico, the English met so fierce a reception that even Drake's genius could not prevail, and by this time Sir John Hawkins was dead. On the day before the attack, he had died on board the *Garland* and his last thoughts were for the Queen. "Assure Her Majesty," he murmured, "of my love and loyalty." Since he was not able to bring her the treasure that he had intended, he left her £2000 to make amends.

In his own ship and serving his Queen to the end, Hawkins died as he had lived, a loyal Englishman.

251

Sir Philip Sidney

"THIS child may save us yet from all our perils," said Sir Henry Sidney, looking fondly at his new-born son.

His wife, Lady Mary, smiled a little sadly.

"I pray God that he may do so," she replied. "Then he will be the first of my luckless family to aid my husband."

Lady Mary was the daughter of John Dudley, Duke of Northumberland. Barely a year had passed since her father's execution for treason. Her brother, Guilford Dudley, had gone to the block on the same day as Lady Jane Grey, and four other brothers were still in the Tower.

Yet Queen Mary was not a vengeful woman and she sent Sir Henry Sidney to Spain to escort King Philip to England. Two weeks later, Sir Henry rode into the courtyard of Penshurst Place, his grey manor-house in Kent. He dismounted and ran to his wife's room:

"Great news!" he cried. "The King himself is coming to our child's naming!"

So, in December 1554, at a magnificent christening ceremony, King Philip of Spain was godfather to an English baby. Naturally, the child was named Philip in his honour.

While little Philip Sidney and his sister were learning to walk and to explore the rooms and gardens of Penshurst, their father was away in

Philip and Fulke Greville at school

Ireland, trying to subdue the rebels. Just before Philip's fourth birthday, Queen Elizabeth came to the throne and at once showed that she had not forgotten that the Dudleys were her childhood friends.

Lady Mary was called to Court. Her brilliantly handsome brother, Robert Dudley, became Earl of Leicester, the Queen's favourite, and Sir Henry Sidney was made Lord Deputy of Ireland and Lord President of Wales.

Philip went to Shrewsbury School, not far from Ludlow. A boy called Fulke Greville started there on the same day and they became friends for the rest of their lives. Both were good at lessons and at the school sports of tennis, archery and running. Philip was more serious than his friend but he was so friendly and generous that all the boys seem to have looked upon him as their leader.

253

After four years at Shrewsbury the two friends went up to Oxford, and in the long holidays there were visits to Ireland and to the magnificent London home of Philip's uncle, the Earl of Leicester. Sometimes he stayed at the home of William Cecil, the Queen's minister. Cecil was very fond of his friend's son and wrote to Sir Henry:

"Your Philip is here; he is a boy worthy to be loved and so do I love him as he were mine own son."

In 1572 Philip obtained the Queen's permission to travel abroad. Walsingham, the English Ambassador in Paris, gave him a cordial welcome and introduced him to Catherine de Medici, the Queen Mother. This terrifying woman smiled graciously upon the nephew of the great Earl of Leicester, for she was hoping to marry one of her sons to Queen Elizabeth.

Meanwhile, tremendous preparations were afoot for the marriage of Catherine's daughter to Henry of Navarre and Paris was thronged with people who had come to attend the royal wedding.

During the night of 24th August, St. Bartholomew's Eve, Philip was awakened by screams and the clash of weapons. Hundreds of French Protestants were being dragged from their beds to be butchered in the streets. As a foreigner, Philip was safe in the English Embassy but, as an ardent Protestant, he was horrified by the massacre.

"If the Protestant countries do not bind themselves into an alliance," he cried to Walsingham, "they and their religion will be overthrown."

"Softly, Philip, it is not wise to speak such thoughts aloud," replied the Ambassador. "For the love I

St. Bartholomew's Eve

bear your parents, I would have you leave Paris at once. An escort will ride with you to Frankfurt."

After Philip had made his farewells to the Walsinghams and their pretty daughter, he departed to Germany and continued his travels into Italy.

People were enchanted by the slim young Englishman. Princes, merchants and scholars welcomed him into their homes. He studied languages and science and talked to learned men about politics and religion. He became an expert fencer and, under the tuition of the Emperor's riding-master, a brilliant horseman.

At last, the Grand Tour came to an end and Philip went home to Penshurst to see his parents and his admiring young brothers. He was nearly twenty-one and eager to begin his career as a statesman. Mary, his favourite sister, was already a maid-of-honour at Court and it was not long before Leicester, his uncle, introduced Philip into the circle of elegant young men who attended the Queen.

Her Majesty was about to set out on one of her progresses through part of the kingdom. Her sharp, green eyes looked approvingly at Leicester's nephew and she gave him a jewelled hand to kiss. "I do require you to accompany our progress," she murmured.

By October, the Court returned to London and Philip went to live at Leicester House. Sea-captains and soldiers of fortune came in and out, with talk of voyages and alliances, but, for a young man thirsting for adventure, there was strangely little to do.

Philip hated idleness and he obtained permission to assist his father to rule Ireland. Often, he carried despatches to the Queen and one day, to his delight, she chose him to go abroad as her representative.

It was an important mission for a young diplomat. He travelled to Prague to greet the new Emperor and he had also to find out how things stood in Europe. Philip needed all his charm when he called, first, upon the Spanish Viceroy of the Netherlands and then upon William the Silent, leader of the Dutch.

After his return, Philip was sure that the Queen would find some splendid task for him to carry out. It might be a voyage, an armed expedition, the founding of a colony . . .

"And it please Your Grace," he suggested eagerly, "I would raise a company to aid our friends in the Netherlands against their oppressors . . ."

The Queen smiled and asked him to arrange a hunting-party for the morrow.

"Within a month, Master Frobisher doth sail to the New World. I beg leave of Your Majesty to accompany him."

Elizabeth changed the subject. No matter what Philip suggested, she always found a reason to keep him at Court. It seemed as if she could not bear to let him out of her sight. Rather than lose him, she wasted his brilliant talents.

One day, Philip protested so hotly about this boring existence that the Queen rebuked him angrily.

Feeling himself out of favour, he went down to Wilton, the lovely home of his sister Mary, now Countess of Pembroke.

Mary and her brother had remained close friends since their childhood. Both loved books, poetry and the countryside. Both were clever and high-spirited, but this summer Mary was unwell and Philip was bored.

M.W.—17

To amuse his sister and to pass the time, Philip began to write a long story-poem.

"This is my joyful book," he told Mary. "It is to be full of quaint things, all written as prettily as your most flowery poet. It will magic away our melancholy."

"This is my joyful book."

Set down on odd bits of paper and passed laughingly, a page at a time, to Mary, the poem was never finished. Years later, as he lay dying, Philip remembered his "joyful book". It had been written carelessly for fun and he asked his friends to burn it. They could not bear to do so but had it published with the title *Arcadia*.

The Queen restored Philip to favour. He had just been knighted when he heard that Drake and Frobisher were preparing an expedition to the West Indies. Eagerly, he offered to take part.

It was secretly arranged that Drake should command the fleet and that Sir Philip Sidney should lead the land forces.

When all was ready, Philip and Fulke Greville rode down to Plymouth. To their dismay, Drake refused to sail unless they had the Queen's permission and he insisted on writing to London to inform Her Majesty of the gentlemen's intention.

"There is but one thing to do," said Philip to his friend. "I will post my men outside the town to seize the Court messenger. If the letter is not to our liking, we will send it back!"

The Queen was furious when she heard of this defiance. She sent for a peer of the realm and ordered him to bring Sir Philip Sidney back. If he did not come, he would be banished for ever.

"Tell him," she added softly to the royal messenger, "that I have other work for him to do."

Six weeks after Drake sailed, Philip was made Governor of Flushing, the Dutch sea-port. He was also to be second in command of an English army that was about to leave for Holland under the Earl of Leicester. William the Silent had been murdered and it seemed as if the Spaniards were about to overrun the country.

Sidney found the defences of Flushing in a poor state and most of the soldiers were sick and ill-armed. He put new heart into the garrison and sent to Leicester, urging him not to delay in England.

The attack on Axel

Unfortunately, when Leicester arrived, he seemed more interested in banquets and costly ceremonies than in fighting the Spaniards. Little was done in the winter of 1585, and when spring came the Dutch situation was desperate. The Spaniards, under their brilliant general, the Duke of Parma, were pressing across the country towards the coast. If the seaports fell, all was lost.

Sidney and Count Maurice, William the Silent's valiant son, felt that they must act. To distract the Spaniards, Maurice asked Sidney to lead an attack on the town of Axel.

With a thousand men, Philip left Flushing by night and rowed up the Scheldt for twenty miles. He joined forces with Maurice and the allies marched through the darkness towards Axel.

Near the town they halted. With forty picked men, Philip went ahead until the moat was reached. In the darkness, he and his men slipped quietly into the water, pushing ladders as they swam. They scaled the gates, overpowered the sentries and opened the gates to their comrades before the defending garrison realized what had happened.

This exploit revived the spirits of the Dutch people and Leicester began to show signs of his old energy. He moved his headquarters to Arnhem and agreed to attack the nearby towns of Doesburg and Zutphen.

The smaller town, Doesburg, was captured by assault, with Sir Philip leading a storming party that included his brother Robert and the young Earl of Essex.

Realizing that the allies would attack Zutphen next, Parma despatched a convoy with food and ammunition to enable the garrison to hold out. Hearing of this plan from a prisoner, Leicester sent five hundred men to ambush the convoy, but he did not know that it was accompanied by a powerful escort.

Very early in the morning, Sidney and a number of cavalry officers left camp to inspect the ambush-party. Despite a thick mist, they found the men well positioned on a hillock near to a church.

As they prepared for action, Sidney noticed that two of his brother-officers were not wearing thigh-pieces because of recent wounds. Not wishing to go into battle better armed than his friends, he threw aside his own leg-armour.

The rumble of waggons and the clatter of men and horses could be heard. Suddenly the mist lifted.

There, below the knoll, was the convoy moving towards Zutphen with its heavy escort of pikemen, musketeers and cavalry.

Outnumbered six to one, the Englishmen charged. A series of savage hand-to-hand encounters took place. The English withdrew, formed up and charged again and then a third time.

In the second charge, Sidney's horse was killed. Flinging himself upon another animal, he dashed in again and cut right through the enemy. As he wheeled, a musketeer fired at him from short range. The ball struck his unguarded thigh, smashing the bone. His terrified horse plunged wildly, but when a trooper came up and offered to lead him to the rear, Sidney waved the man away.

"Look to yourself, let them not see I am wounded," he said.

He got the horse under control and rode in agony back to his uncle's camp. Seeing that he was badly hurt, men ran to aid him: he asked for water and a bottle was brought. As he raised it to his lips, a soldier, fearfully wounded in the same engagement, was carried by. Sidney saw the dying man's eye light up with longing and he handed the bottle to him.

"Thy necessity is yet greater than mine," he said.

Leicester was appalled by his nephew's appearance:

"Oh, Philip!" he cried, "I am truly grieved to see thy hurt."

"My lord," answered Sidney, "this have I done to do you honour and Her Majesty some service."

They took him by barge to Arnhem where he lay for twenty-five days in the house of a Dutch widow. His young wife, Walsingham's daughter, was brought

Sir Philip at Zutphen

from Flushing to nurse him, his brothers came whenever they could leave the war; Leicester was constantly at his bedside and the Queen wrote a comforting letter and ordered the messenger to return immediately with news of his health.

For a time, it seemed as if he might recover. He was so calm and cheerful that his friends did not suspect the terrible condition of his wound. The surgeons had been unable to reach the musket-ball and, though he joked with them, composed verses and set them to music, he knew that his life and all his hopes were ended.

On 17th October 1586, scarcely thirty-two years old, Sir Philip Sidney died at Arnhem.

Protestant Europe mourned him. Philip of Spain when he received the news in a despatch wrote at the bottom of the page, "He was my god-son".

In England, people felt that they had lost the brightest and noblest of their young men. They gave him the stateliest funeral that ever filled the streets of London and his father-in-law Walsingham ruined himself to pay for it.

Thirty years later, his friend Fulke Greville asked that no words should be written on his own tomb, except:

"Fulke Greville,

Counsellor to King James I. Servant to Queen Elizabeth" and then, the highest honour that he had ever known,

"Friend to Sir Philip Sidney".

Captain John Smith

MASTER George Mettham looked severely at the tousled, sunburnt boy who stood in front of him:

"Thou are a grief to me," he said mournfully. "Thy father, God rest his soul, entrusted me to keep thee at thy books and afterwards to put thee to farm his land. But I find that all thy days are taken up with horse-riding, wrestling and sword-play. Hast thou no wish to be a farmer?"

"Sir, my mind is set upon the sea," replied the lad.

"I feared as much," continued his guardian, "but I would make more of thee than a common sailor. Therefore I have spoken to Master Sendall, ship-merchant of Lynn, and he will take thee as apprentice. Tomorrow, we shall ride to Lynn."

John Smith left his Lincolnshire village with a light heart. He was sixteen, a strong unruly lad, determined to see the world and to make a name for himself.

But King's Lynn was a sorry disappointment.

Instead of going to sea, John found that his master set him to work in a warehouse. This was no life for an adventurer so, one day, he threw down his pen, packed his clothes into a bundle and set out on foot to London.

In time, he reached France where he worked for a while as a nobleman's servant and then he enlisted in a company that was leaving to fight in the Low Countries.

"In the two years that I served the Dutch," said John afterwards, "I learned to ride a horse in battle, to use lance, musket and axe. But I had no taste for killing fellow-Christians, so I took my pay and made for home."

In 1599 he was back at Willoughby in Lincolnshire. His gruff guardian had managed the farm well and there was money to fit himself out like a gentleman, so John purchased some first-class weapons, several suits, shoes, books and a couple of iron-bound chests to pack them in. He was ready for anything that offered travel and adventure.

At this time, the Turks were pressing into eastern Europe and when John learned that the Emperor was raising an army to defend his territory, he decided to set out for Vienna to enlist as a soldier of fortune.

On the way, he fell in with three rascals who stole his chests containing all his money and clothes. However, he reached Marseilles and managed to obtain a passage to Italy. After a series of adventures, including a spell as gunnery officer on board a French pirate ship, he came to Vienna and joined the Imperial Army as a soldier of artillery.

John Smith and the Turkish champions

In the war against the Turks, the young Englishman
soon gained a reputation for bravery and cunning.
Promoted to the rank of captain, he entered the
service of Prince Sigismund whom he greatly admired.
During the siege of a town called Regall, Captain
Smith became the most renowned soldier in the
army when he killed three Turkish champions, one
after another, in single combat. For this feat, he was
awarded a pension of three hundred ducats and the
right to wear on his shield-of-arms the three Turks'
heads.

The Christians pressed the enemy back but one of

267

their armies, advancing too rashly, became trapped in a valley by a horde of Tartars.

Some of the cavalry escaped but the rest of the army was slaughtered by the half-savage tribesmen. Next day, some Tartar soldiers were stripping the bodies of the dead, when they came across Captain Smith, lying fearfully wounded among the slain. Noticing that he was still breathing, they carried him to their camp and tended his wounds in order to sell him in the slave-market.

John soon recovered, only to find that he had been bought by a Turkish noble who sent him in chains to Constantinople as a gift to the Lady Tragabizanda, a maiden to whom this nobleman was betrothed.

The young lady took an interest in the handsome slave and she was talking to him one day when her mother chanced to come into the courtyard. Horrified to find her daughter conversing with an infidel, the old lady declared that she would get rid of him at once. At this, the fair Tragabizanda sent John to her brother who was the Pasha or Governor of a distant province.

Fettered to a servant, John arrived in Cambia in southern Russia. The Pasha, having heard from his mother, had decided to punish the Christian for daring to speak to a high-born Turkish maiden. John was beaten unconscious, an iron ring was riveted round his neck and, presently, he was put to the hardest tasks on the estates.

One day, he was alone threshing corn in an out-lying barn when the Pasha came by and began to revile him and to beat him with a heavy riding-whip. John defended himself and, in a terrible struggle,

Smith's escape

killed his persecutor. Quickly, he threw off his rags and put on some of the dead man's garments. He filled a sack with corn and, mounting the Pasha's horse, galloped away into the open plains.

For days, he rode in a north-westerly direction, not daring to approach the occasional encampment that he sighted on those vast grasslands. At length, he came to a broad track that was used by trading caravans and this led him to a town on the Russian frontier. The Governor received him kindly, provided him with food and lodging and sent him on to the next town.

Across Russia and Poland, John travelled from city to city until he reached Leipzig in Germany. To

269

his surprise, he found that his old lord, Prince Sigismund, was living there in exile. The Prince gave him his discharge from the army, with 1500 ducats in gold and a document granting him a coat-of-arms.

"It is right that you should return to your own country after suffering so many hurts in my service," he said. "Do not forget, brave captain, to wear the three Turks' heads for ever."

In 1605 Captain John Smith came home to England. He had been away for five years and his career as a soldier of fortune was ended.

*   *   *

With James I on the throne, war with Spain was ended and all the talk in London was of colonies and settlements in North America.

In a tavern, John was talking to Captain Gosnold who had recently returned from America.

"This land named Virginia is a goodly land," said Gosnold. "It hath great forests and broad meadows. The Indians are few in number and appear to be a kind, loving people."

"Then surely this will support many Englishmen who have no work to do?" cried Smith. "With God's help, you and I shall plant a settlement in Virginia!"

Men, ships and stores were needed. John Smith and Gosnold found a number of gentlemen willing to put money into the venture; the London Virginia Company was founded and in December 1606, three ships were ready to sail with 150 pioneers on board. Commanding the ships was Captain Newport.

The leaders of the expedition were Captain Gosnold, Master Wingfield, Captain Archer and Ratcliffe.

From the start, Smith was unpopular. The ne'er-do-wells and down-at-heel gentlemen disliked his plain speaking, for he made no secret of the fact that he despised their laziness.

"This fellow means to make himself captain over us all," complained his enemies. Despite Gosnold's

Smith in irons during the voyage to Virginia

protests, they had Smith put into irons for most of the voyage. Indeed, some wanted to hang him then and there.

On arrival in Virginia, the Company's orders were unsealed and it was found that Captain Smith was named as one of the seven Councillors appointed to rule the colony. Naturally, he had to be set free and, to his enemies' relief, he merely laughed in their faces and said:

"I do not doubt, gentlemen, that ye will show as much zeal with spade and axe as ye did in locking me up!"

The ships anchored in Chesapeake Bay and a landing-party went ashore to choose a place for the first settlement, called James Town, in honour of the King. While they were examining the countryside, a file of Indians crept unnoticed towards them and let fly a shower of arrows. Two sailors were wounded and, although a volley from the muskets sent the Indians shrieking into the woods, it was clear that the first task must be to protect the settlers. Smith, the experienced soldier, soon had trees felled and hauled into position to make a triangular fort in which he mounted several cannons on platforms of logs and earth.

Meanwhile, the stores were unloaded from the ships and, in June, Captain Newport sailed back to England leaving the colony to fend for itself under Master Wingfield, the first President.

Summer in Virginia was very hot. The river almost dried up and, at low tide, it stank, as did the marshes nearby. Most of the stores were found to be mouldy and, since it was unsafe to go far in search of game, the settlers had to live mainly on fish, crabs and berries. Many of the men fell sick and there was much grumbling, especially by those who had never been used to hard work out of doors. Archer and the grumblers deposed President Wingfield and put Ratcliffe in his place. During these events, Smith and Gosnold were seriously ill. Gosnold died but Smith recovered and helped to nurse the sick.

Building the fort

Ratcliffe proved to be a weak, idle man, and Smith could see that the colony was doomed unless he himself could obtain food. Boldly, he went to the Indians, holding out coloured beads, axes and pins to their fascinated gaze. In exchange, they gave him venison, corn and pumpkins that helped the sick to recover.

"Our troubles are not ended," warned Smith. "How shall we live unless we provide for ourselves? I shall place you in companies, one company to hew trees, another to clear the land and to make it ready for seed. We must have better houses and a church. Let every man take on the hardest task as his own share!"

As winter approached, Smith built up a store of food. He traded with the Indians, learned their language and came to respect their courage and skills. But he did not trust them. He knew that they hated the white men and would wipe them out if it were not for their fear of the muskets.

North America was still unexplored and, whenever he could leave the settlement, Smith would take a party by barge up-river to trade and to increase his knowledge of the country.

On one of his expeditions, he persuaded an Indian, by gift of a copper kettle, to act as a guide. He chose two companions and, having ordered the rest of his company to keep watch and not to leave the barge, he set off into the woods.

Several miles inland, Smith and his Indian guide were walking some distance ahead of his two companions when he heard a ghastly cry behind him. Quickly whipping a cord round the guide's arm to bind him to his own wrist, Smith drew his pistol and turned back, thrusting the man before him as a shield. He found that his friends were already dead and that he himself was surrounded by two hundred Indians. The guide called out that this was the chief of the white men whom they ought to take alive.

Seeing the Indians pause, Smith slipped the cord off his wrist and made a dash for freedom, only to plunge up to his armpits in a swamp. The warriors pulled him out half-dead with cold and dragged him to their village.

He was brought before the Chief, a splendidly built man with an air of majestic dignity, who gazed at the prisoner for a long time. Smith gazed calmly back and then, with the utmost gravity, drew from his jerkin a pocket-compass and solemnly presented it to the Chief. The Indian was fascinated. He and his warriors tried to touch the quivering needle but could not because of the glass. What was this thing? What did it say? John explained the use of a compass. He told them about the stars and the tides, how the earth moved and how the white men had found their way across the great ocean.

The Indians were awe-struck by this wise man who spoke their own language and explained such great mysteries. Food was brought for him and presently he was led to a wigwam and invited to rest there.

After many days, during which John was treated almost like a god, the Indians told him that they were going to take him to their Great Chief.

They set out, travelling across country, and came to the village of Great Chief Powhatan who actually lived only about twelve miles from James Town. His 'palace' was a long barn-like building made of branches covered by bark and John's guards thrust him inside, forcing a way through the dense throng of warriors, squaws and children to an open space at the far end where Powhatan, surrounded by his wives and counsellors, was seated upon a pile of embroidered cushions.

Gravely, the Chief questioned the prisoner. Why had he come to this land? What was the secret of the white man's magic? How did the rods speak with thunder? Smith's answers seemed to please him, for Powhatan ordered dishes of meat and bowls of sweet corn to be brought in, and he invited the prisoner to join him in eating. Growing bold, Smith began to speak of King James, boasting of his cities, his ships and his armies. Powhatan's expression changed to alarm. He turned to his counsellors and, in a moment, two large stones were brought in and placed on the ground. Four men came forward bearing heavy clubs. The white man was to be killed by having his brains dashed out.

All this time, a graceful, dark-eyed girl of about fourteen had been eagerly listening and watching from her place among the royal wives. She was Princess Pocahontas, Powhatan's favourite daughter, and when she saw that the prisoner was condemned to death, her eyes filled with tears of pity. Smith, intending to show that he could die as bravely as any Indian, looked round calmly and then knelt down and placed his head upon the stones. As the clubs were uplifted, Pocahontas darted forward and threw herself beside the Englishman so that the warriors dared not strike.

"Spare him!" cried Pocahontas

"Spare him!" she cried to her father. "Spare the stranger! It is not good to kill so wise a man."

There was silence. As Powhatan recovered from his astonishment, the thought came to him that the girl was right. It would be foolish to kill this man when he might exchange him for gifts that would make him lord over many more tribes.

"Let the white man stand up," he said at last. "I shall have further talk with him tomorrow."

A few days later, on condition that he gave them two cannons from the fort, Captain Smith was escorted to James Town by twelve warriors. He had been away for five weeks and the colony was in a worse plight than ever. All the stores had been eaten and only thirty-eight men were left alive. When they saw their one real leader striding towards the fort between his guards, the settlers rushed out and embraced him.

"We believed you to be dead!" they cried. "How did you survive among the savages?"

"Almighty God and a little Indian maid preserved my life," replied John. "But, first, let me deal with these guards."

He turned to the Indians and took them to see the cannons mounted on their platforms:

"Take them to your Great Chief," he said.

But of course the warriors could not budge the great guns that each weighed more than a ton.

"Ah, I forgot. They have big stones in their mouths," said Smith, smiling. "We must empty them."

He ordered both guns to be fired and the Indians fell terrified to the ground. When they had recovered, they declared that they would much rather take some blue beads to Powhatan and soon they left happily, with beads, hatchets and a special gift for Pocahontas.

As soon as they had gone, Captain Smith began to put the colony in order. He arrested Archer and some of the troublemakers and he summoned the others to a meeting.

"Do not despair," he said. "I have seen much of this land and if we but play our parts like men, we shall prosper yet."

Next day, a party of Indians arrived, carrying great baskets filled with venison and bread. With them was Pocahontas who had come to see the English town and to talk to her brave captain. After he had shown her all the houses and the church he thanked her most courteously and presented her with the prettiest ornaments in his store.

Throughout the winter, the little princess brought many gifts of food to the settlers. She saved their lives and they came to look upon her as an angel sent by Heaven to preserve them.

When spring came, Captain Newport sailed into Chesapeake Bay with a ship-load of stores and a hundred new settlers. Unfortunately, they were another batch of down-at-heel gentlemen, servants, soap-boilers and glass-blowers:

"Twenty good workmen would have been better than them all," growled Smith.

Ratcliffe and Archer were delighted to have fresh allies, for the newcomers were soon grumbling about the bearded captain who never ceased badgering them to sow crops and to stand guard.

"By order of the London Company, we are here to discover gold," they retorted. "Furthermore, it is

Indians caught stealing weapons

well known that you have dealt harshly with the
Indians but we are to treat them with gentleness."

In their folly, the new settlers tried to curry favour
with the Indians who began to come in and out of
the fort as they pleased, stealing hatchets, knives and
even muskets.

One day, Smith caught some of them as they were
carrying off armfuls of weapons. Promptly, he
clapped them in the town jail and when Powhatan
sent his warriors to the rescue, they were scattered by
the thunderous cannons. To appease the terrible
captain, the Indians soon brought back a large
number of stolen weapons as well as gifts of food.

Gradually, the colony began to prosper. John
Smith's work was recognized at last, when the
settlers elected him President in 1608. He had the
church rebuilt, the fort strengthened and new store-
houses prepared for the harvest. Fresh fields were
planted and every Sunday the whole colony was put
through their armed drill so that they would be able
to defend themselves in time of need.

More settlers arrived in the autumn and, once
again, Smith had to teach them that they had come

to Virginia to make homes and not to pick easy riches. A few Dutchmen tried to betray the colony by giving arms to the Indians and the settlement had to withstand some fierce attacks as well as the more serious threat of starvation.

Smith was undaunted. He overcame every difficulty, defeating the Indians, sometimes by force and often by cunning. Pocahontas saved his life a second time when she warned him of a surprise night attack and, at length, his stubborn spirit so impressed Chief Powhatan that he made terms and, for as long as Captain Smith remained in Virginia, the English and the Indians lived together in peace.

By 1609 the colony was thriving so well that John began to think of building a new settlement up the river. He was returning to James Town by boat one evening, when he fell asleep resting his head on a bag of gunpowder. One of the men, in lighting his pipe, dropped a spark and the powder exploded. In flames, John leapt overboard and when his men rescued him and lifted him tenderly into the boat, his injuries were so terrible that they believed he was certain to die.

For weeks he lay at James Town more dead than alive, but gradually his strength prevailed and he began to recover. However, he was very weak and his injuries were so severe that he was persuaded to return to England to be treated by skilled doctors.

In October 1609 John Smith left Virginia for ever.

"Alas!" cried his friends, as the ship stood out to sea, "We have lost the man who built this colony and saved all our lives."

*   *   *

The founder of Virginia recovered his health and, less than three years later, he was commanding an expedition to New England. This was so successful that a Company was formed to establish a colony there but, on his way out as Admiral of New England, Smith was captured by French pirates and his crew came back with the story that he was dead. However, he escaped in a small boat, was wrecked on the coast of Brittany and reached home penniless. Unable to find support for yet another expedition, Smith took up a new way of earning a living. He turned author and settled down to write the story of his travels. In addition, he prepared maps and leaflets about America and these were used by many travellers, including the Pilgrim Fathers.

From time to time, some of his friends from Virginia would call to see him and, one day, to his great delight, two soldiers who had served with him against the Turks turned up at his home to talk over their old adventures and escapes. On another occasion, he actually met Pocahontas who had married an Englishman in Virginia and was visiting London. The little princess was so overcome by the sight of her brave captain that she could not speak at first but could only weep for joy.

Smith did not live to a great age, for he died in 1631 at the age of fifty-one and he was buried in the parish church of Holborn in London.

William Harvey

THE body of a well-built man lay on a table in the anatomy theatre. Tiers of wooden seats, rising one above another in circles, were crowded with students who looked almost straight down at the dissecting-table where neat rows of knives and probes were laid next to the body.

Two college officials entered the theatre, walking side by side with solemn tread. The Clerk followed, carrying a white rod. All the students rose as the great Doctor Fabricius came in and seated himself in a high-backed chair opposite the body. The Masters of the Anatomy, his assistants, positioned themselves at either end of the table with the instruments ready.

With a low bow, the Clerk presented the white rod to the Doctor; the officials withdrew and the Anatomy Lecture began.

Deftly, the assistants opened the body of the criminal who had been executed for robbery a few days previously. They exposed the lungs, heart and liver as their Master directed by pointing with the rod.

During his lecture, Doctor Fabricius did not fail to mention his notable discovery that in the veins of the body there were valves like tiny trap-doors whereas the arteries had no valves at all. As the Doctor proceeded to explain this little-known fact, a student, seated with the Scots and the Englishmen,

The Anatomy Lecture

leaned forward as if anxious to catch every word. Noticing this movement, the old Doctor smiled benevolently for the student was one of the most brilliant pupils he had ever taught.

After one hour, the Demonstration ended and the Clerk cried aloud:

"This lecture, gentlemen, will be continued at five of the clock precisely!"

The white-aproned, white-sleeved Doctor and his assistants left the candle-lit theatre and the students, breaking up into noisy groups, followed them into the bright Italian sunshine.

Deep in thought, the student who had leaned forward so eagerly walked away by himself. He was William Harvey, twenty-two years old, a native of Folkestone in Kent. He was the eldest of seven boys, the "week of sons" born to Thomas Harvey, a prosperous merchant engaged in the Turkey trade.

In the year of the Armada, the merchant had sent William, aged ten, to the King's School at Canterbury and, six years later, to Cambridge. Having gained a good knowledge of Latin and Greek at the university, William went to study medicine and the sciences at Padua, near Venice.

Harvey was still thinking about the lecture when his friends, Fortescue and Darcy, sighted him by the river, gazing thoughtfully at the water.

"Hey, Will! Will, I say, art thou deaf?" hailed Fortescue. " 'Tis dinner-time. If the Doctor had me on the table, he would open an empty belly!"

Harvey laughed and turned to his friends:

"Yet, still I do not see how the blood can ebb to and fro like the sea, as our masters tell us. Does it not flow perhaps, in a stream like this river?"

"It is foolish—aye and dangerous—to question the teaching of centuries, Will," replied Darcy. "Let be and come to thy dinner."

Not long afterwards, Harvey gained his degree as Doctor of Medicine and returned to England. In 1602, he settled in London as a member of the College of Physicians.

At this time, the best-paid and most highly respected medical men were physicians. They were well educated but nearly all their knowledge was based on the teachings of the Ancient Greeks. It was almost a crime to suggest that Aristotle or Galen might ever have made a mistake.

In Harvey's day, the common diseases were leprosy, ague, smallpox, influenza and the "sweating sickness". The remedies for illness were curious. Even the College of Physicians approved such strange medicines as crabs' eyes, buttered live spiders, partridge feathers, baked mice, ants' eggs and powdered human skull!

Harvey bought a house in St. Martin's parish, near Ludgate, and here he brought his bride, Elizabeth, daughter of Launcelot Browne, who had been physician to Queen Elizabeth.

The young Doctor built up a good practice and among his patients were the Lord Chancellor, Sir Francis Bacon, the Lord Treasurer and many of the gentry in the capital.

When he went about London, the Doctor rode in style, with a "foot-cloth" draping his horse almost to the ground, while his servant trotted along behind. Known to everyone as "little Doctor Harvey", his short spry figure, his curly hair, olive complexion and dark eyes, as bright and quick as a bird's, gave him a foreign air. He walked and talked quickly, waved his hands about in conversation and, rather to the alarm of some people, had the habit of playing with a small dagger that he wore at his belt. Although he gave the impression of being a fierce little man, he was really gentle, full of jokes and acts of kindness.

Dr. Harvey in London

As a physician, Harvey dressed soberly in doublet and breeches of a purple-brown colour, with a large turned-down white collar in place of the old-fashioned starched ruff of Elizabeth's reign. Outdoors he put on a long cloak and a broad-brimmed hat, but when lecturing or seeing patients he wore the small black cap of his doctor's degree. On two or three mornings a week, the little doctor would step briskly through the narrow lanes of the City until he came to St. Bartholomew's Hospital. There the Hospitaller would have patients brought to him in a room with a big open fireplace.

Seated at a table, he would gaze intently at each patient on the settle opposite him. Then he felt his pulse, asked him a few questions and prescribed the treatment and medicine for his illness. As always, he made careful notes in a large book that was kept locked when not in use—though his handwriting was so terrible that no one could have read it if he had left it open!

After this, he would go into the wards to see patients who were too ill to be moved. Unlike most physicians, he did not think it beneath his dignity to

Harvey at work in his "museum"

examine patients closely. Far from despising the
surgeon's art, he took every opportunity to increase
his knowledge of the body and he often performed
operations with his friend, Master Woodhall, the
leading surgeon of the day.

Each evening, after he and his wife had dined
together, in the company of Elizabeth's pet parrot, a
fine bird that was a renowned talker, Harvey would
retire to a room behind his study. Here, in his
"museum", as he called it, he spent all his spare time,
dissecting every creature that he could lay hands
on—rats, mice, eels, frogs, rabbits, birds and snakes.
Their pickled remains filled the jars that stood on
shelves round the room. In cages and fish-bowls were
dozens of live creatures that he studied.

Sometimes, at night, with only his servant for
protection, he would go to a hospital or a prison in

order to discover the cause of a person's death. Having opened the stomach or the skull, he would conceal his investigations by skilful sewing and leave for home before daylight.

Harvey pursued this work in secret because, in his search for knowledge, he would have aroused the anger of those who believed it was wicked to question the age-old beliefs. For centuries, men had believed that the blood was produced in the liver and that two kinds of blood, one in the veins and the other in the arteries, moved slowly up and down the body.

In men and animals, Harvey studied the heart; he worked out the amount of blood in the body and he observed the working of the lungs. The old theories seemed to be wrong, but he knew that he must *prove* his own opinions.

He remembered how his old Master at Padua had pointed to those little valves in the veins, but Fabricius had never been able to explain why they were there. After much thought and experiment, Harvey saw the explanation. The valves meant that blood could flow in one direction only and that direction was *towards* the heart. There were not two kinds of blood after all. There was one mass of blood that was pumped by the heart round and round the body "in a kind of circle". The blood, he said, was "cleaned" in the lungs and the arteries carried this bright red blood to the farthest parts of the body. Then it travelled in the veins back to the heart and began its journey all over again.

This was a tremendous discovery. It was to provide a new and real understanding of the living body but, for the time being, Harvey said very little about it.

By Act of Parliament, the College of Physicians was allowed to dissect the bodies of four criminals a year and, in 1615, Harvey was appointed Lecturer in Surgery for a fee of £40 a year. He was to lecture on Wednesdays and Fridays at ten o'clock until eleven, speaking at first in Latin and then in English.

He planned his work carefully. During the first year, he dealt with ulcers, wounds and broken bones and, in winter, when a dead body would keep longer, he dissected "the inward parts" of a man. In the second year, before a gathering of doctors and privileged visitors, he dissected the trunk; in the third year, the head; in the fourth year, a leg and an arm; in the fifth year, he dealt with the skeleton and the setting of broken bones and in the sixth year, with general surgery. After that, he began the course again.

When Harvey gave his first lecture in April 1616, we know that he had already discovered the circulation of the blood because his notes still exist. This is what he said:

"It is plain from the structure of the heart that the blood is passed continuously through the lungs to the aorta. . . . It is shown that the passage of the blood is from the arteries into the veins, whence it follows that *the movement of the blood is constantly in a circle* and is brought about by the beat of the heart."

In public, Harvey had contradicted the teaching of 1500 years and, curiously enough, there was no immediate outcry. Perhaps he spoke briefly and quietly. The rest of his lectures were brilliant and it only got out gradually that the little doctor had some

"It is finished!"

quaint idea about the blood. The rumour reached a
master-printer in Germany who published medical
books.

One evening, Harvey laid down his pen and turned
to his wife while her favourite parrot (that he was to
dissect one day) strutted up and down the arm of her
chair:

"It is finished," he said. "After twelve years I have
written in full my account of the circulation of the
blood."

"And will thou send it now to Master Fitzer at
Frankfurt?" asked Mistress Harvey.

"Tomorrow," replied her husband. "He hath begged for it this long time in order to have it printed in time for the great Book Fair. He saith in his letter that it will make a stir in Europe."

The book caused a sensation. Opponents poured ridicule and abuse upon the author. Books were published in Venice, Holland and France to prove him wrong, and in London the attacks were so fierce that, for a time, Harvey believed that he was ruined.

"I have fallen mightily in my practice," he said ruefully. "All the physicians are against me and many persons declare that I am no better than crack-brained!"

However, he soon recovered his spirits and remarked to his wife:

"I shall not answer my enemies. Time will prove me right and, when it does, I need say nothing more."

But his brother-physicians had not forsaken him. In 1629 he was elected Treasurer of the College, and shortly afterwards King Charles I commanded him to travel abroad with the Duke of Lennox.

The doctor was delighted to visit the Continent for the first time since his student days. He was away for a year in France and Spain where he noted that the effects of war and plague were so bad that

"by the way, we could scarce see a dog, crow, kite, raven or any other bird *or anything to dissect* . . ."

After he came home, Harvey was honoured by being made Physician-in-Ordinary to the King at the huge salary of £300 a year and this was later increased to include an apartment at Whitehall and £200 for his food and wine. Charles I became very fond of his little doctor and liked to have his company when travelling and hunting. Naturally, Harvey obtained permission to dissect the bodies of deer in the royal parks and, in Scotland, he was far less interested in His Majesty's political troubles than in animals, birds and the way a chicken develops in the egg.

When Charles left London to prepare for war, Harvey was over sixty but, as the King's doctor, he went with his master. Yet, even when Charles was collecting troops, Harvey rode off to Derby to visit an old friend in order to discuss child-birth and illnesses of women.

In due course, he found himself with the royal army at Edgehill where he was given charge of the King's sons, the Prince of Wales, aged twelve, and the Duke of York who was ten. Prudently, he persuaded the excited boys to accompany him to the shelter of a wide ditch and, while the princes peered through the hedge to see how the battle was going, Harvey took a book out of his pocket and began to read, quite unaware of the gunfire and thundering cavalry no great way off. Suddenly, a cannon-ball whistled through the hedge, ploughing into the ground and spraying the doctor with earth.

At this alarm, Harvey closed his book and led the boys to the rear where he was soon busy with the wounded. An observer wrote afterwards that a certain cavalier was lying on the field among the slain "as a dead person but, brought off by his son, he was recovered by the immortal Dr. Will Harvey who was there under a hedge when the battle was at its height".

After Edgehill, the King made his headquarters at

At Edgehill

Oxford and here Harvey spent the rest of the war, content to be able to continue his work. He was grieved, however, to learn that in London a mob had broken into his house:

"I here give vent to a sigh," he wrote sadly. "Certain persons not only stripped my house of all its furniture but, what is matter of far greater sorrow to me, my enemies took from my museum all those papers and things on which I have spent years of toil."

After the surrender of Oxford, he returned to London. His wife had died, he had no children and his home was destroyed. But his brothers, five of them still alive and all prosperous merchants, welcomed him to their homes and he passed the rest of his life visiting them in turn.

He was particularly fond of his brother Eliab who, for many years, had looked after the doctor's money since he himself had no head for business. At Eliab's house in the City or at his country residence at Roehampton, the now white-haired doctor was happy with his nieces and their children.

As he grew older, he became rather odd in his habits. When gout pained him, he would go up to the flat roof of the house in frosty weather and sit with his feet in a pail of water until they were numb; at meal-times, he would sit himself down and start eating whether or not the company was seated and he insisted upon having a great salt-cellar filled with sugar which he sprinkled on his food—meat, vegetables, everything! Often, he was to be seen walking about the fields, observing insects and small creatures in the grass, all the time combing his white hair with great energy, and then he would go and sit in a cave in the grounds, declaring that he could think better in the dark.

In his eightieth year the little doctor died at Roehampton surrounded by his brothers and their children. His body was taken to the family vault at Hempstead in Essex where, more than two hundred years later, the College of Physicians placed his coffin in a white marble tomb in the church.

Harvey has been called the greatest genius of English medicine, and his discovery has been likened to that of Christopher Columbus. Both men proved that the old ways of thought were wrong, both opened the door to knowledge. Columbus discovered a continent, Harvey laid the foundation of modern medicine.

Prince Rupert

"HE is still a little giddy, though not so much as he has been. Pray tell him when he does ill, for he is good-natured enough—but he does not always think . . ."

Elizabeth, "the Winter Queen", sighed as she paused in the middle of her letter to a friend in England . . . if only Rupert were as steady as his brother Charles-Louis . . . but he had always been a wild boy . . . no wonder his sisters called him Rupert-the-Devil . . . She hoped that he would behave himself in England at the Court of his uncle, Charles I . . .

The widowed Queen need not have worried about seventeen-year-old Rupert. Charles I and the English Court were delighted with the massive young Prince who was so much more lively than his solemn brother. He rode and shot superbly, he was unbeatable at tennis and as interested in drawing and chemistry as in sport.

Rupert enjoyed himself so much that he did not wish to leave and his mother had to command him to return to Holland.

On his last day, as he rode out to hunt with the King, he turned to his uncle and exclaimed:

"Sire, I wish that I might break my neck in the field, so that I would leave my bones in England!"

Back at home, he soon forgot his disappointment

Rupert returns home

when his mother allowed him and his young brother Prince Maurice to join a Dutch regiment. They took part in a daring attack on a Spanish garrison, and in the following year Rupert went to Germany to try to win back his father's estates. He was serving as a colonel-of-horse with the Swedes against the Austrians when he was captured and taken to a castle overlooking the Danube. During a long captivity, his kindly jailer allowed him to paint, to study and to ride out on parole with Boy, a white poodle given him by the Ambassador at Vienna.

Three years passed before his uncle succeeded in persuading the Emperor to set him free.

On Christmas Eve 1641, with Boy scampering ahead, Rupert rode into the courtyard of his mother's house in Holland. He asked for news. Where was Maurice? How were his sisters? Was Charles-Louis in England again?

When he learned that England was on the brink of civil war, he cried to his mother:

296

"I will leave at once to offer my sword to my uncle."

It was August, however, before Queen Henrietta Maria handed him his commission as Captain-General of the Royal Horse. With Maurice and the white poodle, he reported to the King at Leicester and immediately went to inspect the cavalry.

He was twenty-two and some of the senior commanders looked down their noses at this youngster promoted over their heads. But the Prince had eyes only for his men. He rode down their ranks, a splendid figure in crimson silk with lace at his wrists, raising his plumed hat as they shouted:

"King Charles! King Charles! Hang up the Roundheads!"

Yet, for all their enthusiasm, they did not impress Rupert. He had seen enough of professional soldiers to recognize that these eight hundred young bloods, squires' sons and pink-faced farmers had everything to learn. They were laughably ill-equipped and had little notion of discipline.

As the royal army moved westwards, Rupert worked like a fiend to train the cavalry. Soon, the very name of Rupert began to alarm the Parliamentmen:

"This diabolical cavalier flies with great fury through the counties," they complained, "raising men for the King in the most rigorous way. It is impossible to bridle his fierceness!"

By the time the army approached Shrewsbury, Rupert had increased his command to 3000 well-mounted horsemen who, for the next two years, were to prove themselves the finest cavalry in Europe.

In September, the Earl of Essex, Parliament's general-in-chief, marched from London with a large army. The King withdrew from Worcester and Rupert, commanding the rear, took four hundred horse to discover the enemy's intentions. Resting in a field at Powicke Bridge, he realized from the glint of steel through the hedgerows that a force of cavalry was advancing ahead of the Parliamentary army.

In breeches and shirt, he ran to his horse, shouting to Maurice and the rest to follow. They leapt the hedge and fell upon the unsuspecting Parliament troops as they emerged from a narrow lane. Someone shouted "Wheel about!". The lane became choked with panic-stricken horsemen who broke formation and fled across the fields.

In a few minutes, a thousand men were routed and four hundred killed by a handful of cavaliers without body-armour or pistols.

At Ludlow, the King was overjoyed by his nephew's success:

"Let your Majesty but give the command and we shall take London within a month," cried Rupert.

The King was doubtful but, yielding to his nephew's pleading, he ordered the advance. Meanwhile, Essex hurried up to bar the way and the two armies came face to face at Edgehill in the centre of England.

In the King's camp a fierce argument took place. Lord Lindsey, the elderly commander-in-chief, proposed cautious tactics while Rupert urged a shock attack in the style of the Swedes. The King supported his nephew, whereupon Lindsey threw down his baton angrily:

Powicke Bridge

"If I am to be overruled by a boy, I will die a
colonel at the head of my own regiment!" he cried.
Rupert had already gone out to his cavalry.

"Ride close, sword in hand, until you break in
amongst the enemy. Not until then shall you use
your fire-arms," he ordered.

The young cavaliers could hardly contain their
excitement. At the word of command, they hurtled
down the slope and broke clean through the opposing
ranks. Hallooing for joy, leaping hedges and ditches,
they hunted the fleeing enemy across country with
never a thought for the battle on the slope behind
them.

Against orders, the reserve cavalry had followed
Rupert, so there was no cover for the King's infantry.
In hard fighting, the Royal Standard was lost,

The King's Council

Lindsey was killed and those around the King begged him to fly.

At this critical moment, Rupert returned, having frantically rounded up some of his scattered troopers. The Standard was re-taken and, as darkness came on, the exhausted armies drew apart, both claiming the victory.

Next day, Rupert strode into the King's council of war to urge boldness.

"We are between the enemy and the capital," he said. "Let me ride with three hundred horse and I will be in London and have Parliament dissolved before my Lord Essex has his breath back!"

The King hesitated. Hoping to avoid any more bloodshed, he listened to half a dozen plans. Lord Digby, a tricky, dangerous man, disliked Rupert;

300

Wilmot and Goring, a pair of brave but drunken officers, opposed him at every turn.

"This fire-eating Prince will pillage London as if it were some German town," they warned. "He speaks to no one but only cries "Pish" to gentlemen who were soldiers when he was at his mother's knee."

Ignoring Rupert's plan, Charles made a leisurely march to Oxford and set up his headquarters there before advancing in gingerly fashion towards London.

Rupert raced eagerly ahead, attacking outposts and probing the enemy's defences. His cavaliers sacked the little town of Brentford but, by now, the Parliament-men had recovered their nerve.

At Turnham Green, they stood firm in gardens and orchards where cavalry were useless. They had plenty of ammunition and they would not budge. The King retreated to Oxford.

Hesitation had cost him the war but, for the moment, no one believed it. The Royalists seemed to be successful everywhere and Rupert covered himself in glory as he raked the home counties with the cavalry and organized a ring of strong-points round Oxford.

While the Court settled itself comfortably in the colleges, he was hardly ever out of the saddle. He captured Cirencester, Lichfield and a dozen smaller towns, won a brilliant engagement at Chalgrove Field and joined forces with Prince Maurice outside Bristol. Together, they stormed the defences and captured the great seaport.

Colonel Fiennes, the Parliamentary commander, was granted the honours of war and was permitted to

march out of the city with his men. Some of the
Royalists began to taunt and plunder them as they
passed. Horrified by such behaviour, Rupert and
Maurice dashed in among their own men, beating
them left and right with the flat of their swords.
Having restored discipline, Rupert apologized to
Colonel Fiennes and rode with him until he was clear
of the crestfallen Royalists.

Soon after the capture of Bristol, Queen Henrietta
Maria arrived from abroad with a hundred waggon-
loads of stores and weapons. The King's fortunes
were at their peak and victory seemed certain.

But, in truth, Charles was far from strong. He
could not give the supreme command of his armies
to Rupert because of the jealousy of his senior
officers. His Court was filled with quarrelsome
schemers, money was running out and ammunition
was always short. Although Rupert won one engagement after another with the cavalry, the King lacked
the infantry to win a war against such men as
Fairfax and Cromwell.

By 1644 the Royalist cause was beginning to fail.
With Digby, full of bad advice at his elbow, Charles
left Oxford and marched about the west country
with little purpose. In the north, Lord Newcastle
and the last remnants of the King's forces were
closely besieged in York.

Rupert was sent to save the situation. Like a
whirlwind, he tore through Cheshire, relieving garri-
sons and capturing towns until he came to Bolton.
On foot, he forced his way into the town to win one
of the most savage victories of the war. While his
soldiers ransacked the houses for food, he took from

Rupert and Maurice beat their own men for plundering the Parliamentarians

his pocket the King's letter. His orders were clear:

"I command and conjure you that, laying all else aside, you immediately march with all your force to the relief of York."

His army was too small for the task but, by a brilliant manoeuvre, he evaded three Parliamentary armies and entered the city.

"He does not always think . . ." wrote Rupert's mother years before. It was still true. The Prince assumed supreme command of all the troops in York without a thought for the feelings of Lord Newcastle, a strange, touchy nobleman who was practically a king in his own northern county.

"You have no choice in the matter, my Lord"

"Tomorrow, we meet the enemy at Marston Moor. Have your men ready to march at dawn," said Rupert curtly.

Newcastle eyed this arrogant youngster in a sweat-stained tunic:

"My troops are worn out from the siege and Your Highness's men would look the better if they were clean and rested. I do not choose to fight tomorrow."

"The King's position demands it," snapped Rupert. "You have no choice in the matter, my Lord."

Next day, Newcastle's men had not arrived when Rupert was positioning his own troops. An officer remarked:

"The enemy outnumber us two to one, sir. Besides my Lord Fairfax and the Scots, they have Cromwell commanding the Horse."

Rupert brightened. He had never met this squire whose skill with cavalry was said to equal his own:

"Is old Ironsides here?" he cried. "Will he fight?"

A Puritan trooper who had just been brought in for questioning, nodded grimly. Rupert turned to the man:

"So he will? Here, my friend, go back and tell the Lieutenant-General that he shall have as much fighting as he likes."

The trooper was released and presently Cromwell's answer came back:

"By God's grace, so shall Prince Rupert!"

Newcastle's whitecoats arrived so late that they had to be stationed at the rear but it was almost dusk and too late for a battle. Rupert gave the order to stand easy and went to his supper. At that moment, Cromwell charged.

The Royalists never recovered. To his horror, Rupert saw his own cavalry fleeing in confusion.

" 'Swounds, do you flee?" he roared. "Follow me!"

He rallied his second line. Goring fought magnificently on the left but the odds were too great. Many of the infantry threw down their arms but the whitecoats refused to fly and died fighting where they stood.

It was night when Rupert came across Lord Newcastle and some officers at York.

"What will you do?" asked one.

"I will go to Holland. I will not endure the laughter of the Court," growled Newcastle.

Prince Rupert spoke briefly:

"I will rally my men."

He went out into the darkness and mounted his horse. He had met defeat for the first time. The King's cause was ruined but he was still a soldier. He would rally his men and he went alone, for Boy, the white poodle, had perished somewhere in the fighting.

M.W.—20

By dawn, he had collected together the greater part of the cavalry and, beating off their pursuers, they rode to the Welsh border. As Parliament's army steadily wore down the Royalists, Rupert fought on. He captured Leicester but when the enemy came up with superior forces, he advised the King to retreat. Charles and Digby overruled him.

At Naseby, Rupert beat Ireton's cavalry but Cromwell had sufficient reserves to turn his terrible Ironsides against the King's infantry in the centre. Charles lost his army, his guns, baggage and even his private papers. The end of the war was in sight.

Ordered to hold Bristol with the remnant of the cavalry, Rupert looked at the city's crumbling walls and remarked to Maurice:

"His Majesty has given us a task here, brother."

Sir Thomas Fairfax surrounded Bristol. His troops easily breached its defences and, to prevent the slaughter of the unhappy citizens, Rupert offered to surrender. Fairfax allowed him to march out "with colours, pikes and drums" and, as he courteously accompanied the Prince out of the city-gate, they passed Cromwell, sitting grim and silent on his horse.

The loss of Bristol was a bitter blow. In the agony of defeat, some of the Royalists declared that Rupert had betrayed the cause. Some even whispered that he had surrendered the city for money.

King Charles refused to see him. Instead, he removed him from his command and told him to leave the kingdom.

"I will not submit to such base treatment," cried Rupert. "This is Digby's doing. With the friends we still have, let us go to the King."

Rupert passes Cromwell after the surrender of Bristol

By speed and cunning, he crossed four counties and came to Newark Castle. Without ceremony, he burst into the King's presence, demanding to be heard. Charles continued to eat his supper without so much as looking up.

Four days later, after Rupert had been tried by court-martial, the King signed a document stating that his

"right dear nephew was not guilty of cowardice or disloyalty!"

But the Prince was not restored to his command and, having taken a cold leave of his uncle, he rode away from Newark with Maurice and two hundred gentleman of the cavalry. Charles stood at a window and wept to see them go.

Rupert was deeply hurt but, once he had recovered his temper, he knew that he could not desert the King in the hour of defeat. He swallowed his pride and asked to be pardoned for his ill-mannered conduct. They were together at Oxford when Charles decided to escape in disguise in order to give himself up to the Scots. Rupert begged to be allowed to accompany his uncle.

"Nay, your great height would give us away," replied the King.

With the war ended, Parliament treated Rupert and Maurice generously. They were permitted to leave the country and, in July 1646, the Prince reached St. Germain, near Paris, where Queen Henrietta was keeping up a threadbare Court.

          *   *   *

Rupert received a hero's welcome in France. The boy-king, Louis XIV, made him a Marshal and presented him with command of an army in Flanders. However, he was so severely wounded in the head that he was obliged to return to Paris to recover his health.

One day, word arrived that some of Parliament's sailors had mutinied and had sailed their ships to Holland. With Maurice and Charles, the young Prince of Wales, Rupert went aboard in the hope that they might win over the entire Navy. Once at sea, it was clear that the unpaid seamen were much keener on piracy than on rescuing the King from the Isle of Wight.

In disgust, Rupert returned to Holland. At least, he had nine ships and he resolved to continue the war in his own way.

Sea-outlaws

His mother sold the last of her jewels to equip the little fleet and, in January 1649, Rupert and the ever-faithful Maurice sailed to southern Ireland.

For a time, they cruised about, capturing Parliamentary ships and dividing the booty between their crews and the exiles in France. At Kinsale, they were horrified to hear of the King's execution and startled to find that Admiral Blake, Parliament's great naval commander, was lying in wait for them with a powerful squadron. For three months, they were trapped in harbour until a gale scattered Blake's ships and allowed them to slip across the Bay of Biscay to Portugal.

Blake chased after them and the sea-outlaws had to make for the lawless waters of the Mediterranean where they supported themselves by piracy until Blake's relentless pursuit made them decide to try their luck in the West Indies.

Off the Azores, two ships went down in a storm, one with three hundred men aboard, and Rupert had a narrow escape when transferring to the *Honest Seaman*. The survivors made for the west coast of Africa where they not only obtained meat and fresh water but succeeded in capturing four English vessels. The largest of these, the *Defiance*, became Maurice's flag-ship and, in good heart, the buccaneers again set course for the West Indies.

They were disappointed to find that all the English islands were now in Parliament's hands. However, they cruised about, adding steadily to the plunder below decks until a hurricane scattered the fleet.

When the wind dropped, the ships were terribly battered. The *Honest Seaman* was a total wreck and the *Defiance* had vanished. Dull, faithful Maurice, who had stood by Rupert since childhood and had never once questioned his leadership, was never seen again.

Sorrowfully, Rupert sailed for France in the *Swallow*, the only sound ship that was left. His ill fortune continued to the end, for the *Swallow* went aground and the Prince reached St. Germain with hardly a penny to show for three years' buccaneering in the name of the King.

Once again, he was met with rapturous compliments and Louis XIV sent his own coach to carry the hero through the streets of Paris. Once again, the old jealousies came to the surface as soon as the cheering had died down.

Young Charles II and his courtiers were desperately poor and they had been longing for Rupert to return with shiploads of gold. Where was the money? What had Rupert done with the treasure? Charles II, a debonair spendthrift, half believed rumours that the Prince must be concealing a fortune.

People began to say that Rupert had changed. His old gaiety had turned into a brooding melancholy:

In exile, Rupert returns to his old hobbies

"Prince Rupert goes little abroad," reported one of Parliament's spies, "and is very sad that he can hear nothing of his brother Maurice."

In fact, Rupert was ill. Fever had weakened his great body and the wound in his head caused unbearable pain until it was relieved by opening his skull to remove a piece of metal.

Hurt by the King's attitude and disgusted by the company of men like Digby, Rupert left Paris. He was heard of in Heidelberg, Cologne, Holland, Hungary and Vienna. Rumour had it that he was commanding an army for the Emperor in Eastern Europe.

The truth was that he had returned to his old hobbies of chemistry and drawing. Among his inventions was a method of engraving pictures on metal that is called *mezzotint*, and he was living quietly, in semi-poverty, trying to perfect this process when he learned that Cromwell was dead.

Charles II gained his father's throne in 1660 and he at once invited Rupert to England. On his arrival, he rewarded him with a pension of £6000 and the posts of Vice-Admiral of the Fleet and Governor of Windsor Castle.

As if by magic, Rupert's gloom vanished. At long last, his loyalty was recognized; he had a home and work to do. With all his old zest, he threw himself heart and soul into the business of the Navy and into encouraging merchant ventures, especially the Hudson's Bay Company and the exploration of Canada.

During the Dutch War Rupert commanded a squadron and took part in several sea-battles. His great raid on the Dutch coast when over a hundred enemy vessels were destroyed led to the famous attack on Chatham. The Navy was blamed for this disaster but Rupert, in a towering rage, told the King why the war went badly:

"The fault lies not in His Majesty's officers and men," he bellowed, "but in the horrible neglect of provisions, pay and the work of the shipyards. Damn me if I can thrive at sea until some have been hanged on land!"

As in the old days, his blunt words and fiery temper earned the enmity of some people. But the men adored him, especially when he threatened to take a cane to the Navy Commissioners and when he actually sent a shot through the rigging of a captain who flew the wrong flag! Poor little Mr. Pepys, Clerk to the Navy, trembled in his shoes and wrote spitefully, after a committee meeting:

"Prince Rupert do nothing but swear and laugh a little, with an oath or two and that's all he do."

Even the King stood a little in awe of his fire-eating cousin for he remarked ruefully:

"With the Prince coming here today, I must expect a chiding."

But the fierce old Admiral had a quieter side to his nature. He took delight in showing people the improvements he had made at Windsor, his collection of old weapons, his horses and the splendid hounds in his own pack.

He never married and the Court bored him, so he took himself off to Windsor to his workshops. Besides cannons, firelocks and nautical instruments, he invented a revolver, a new method of boring gun-barrels, a powerful kind of gunpowder and he even experimented with a torpedo and amused himself by forging coins to annoy the Master of the Mint! Some of his finest mezzotints are still at Windsor Castle.

Prince Rupert died in 1682 and was buried in Westminster Abbey. He was the bravest, cleverest and most faithful of all the Stuarts.

William Dampier

ONE morning in the early years of Charles II's reign, a thin dark boy received a thrashing for not having learned his Latin grammar. He was William Dampier, son of a Somerset farmer, and, instead of memorizing Latin verbs, he had been poring over the pages of a book called *Voyages touching the Discovery of America*.

The schoolmaster's stick was heavy. It interrupted a day-dream of distant lands where brilliant birds flashed in the forests and dark men drove canoes along unknown rivers. But it did nothing to weaken the boy's determination to be a traveller.

William's parents died when he was about sixteen, and within a year he had left farming to his older brother George and was sailing to Labrador in the charge of a Weymouth skipper. By the time he was twenty-one, he was a hardened seaman who had voyaged to the East Indies and had seen some hot fighting against the Dutch when serving with Prince Rupert's squadron.

William was at home on sick leave when a local landowner offered him the chance to manage a plantation in Jamaica. He accepted the offer because, as he said:

"I have ever had a thirst for knowledge and experience."

Up country in Jamaica, life was so dull that he

314

Log-cutting in Campeachy Bay

threw up planting and went down to the water-
front to look for a ship.

He spent a year on a coaster, trading in and out of
the lovely islands of the West Indies before joining a
band of the toughest ruffians on earth. They were
the logwood-cutters of Campeachy Bay and, for
two years, Dampier cut and hauled the valuable
timber, working in tropical heat, knee-deep in water
with his hard-drinking companions.

By this time he was keeping a journal. At night, when his workmates were carousing, he would write up his notes about the strange plants, birds and animals that he had seen:

"The monkeys that are in these parts are the ugliest I ever saw. The fowls are humming-birds, a pretty little feathered creature no bigger than a wasp."

He described things that people at home had never heard of—garr-fish, sea-devils, "tiger cats"—and he noted the difference between alligators and crocodiles, the taste of turtles and cooked snake, the way to plant coconuts and the Indians' methods of making canoes.

When a hurricane swept away all his hard-earned cash and possessions, Dampier was forced to do what many another unlucky man had done. He joined the buccaneers.

His crew-mates included criminals, mutineers, gentlemen-of-fortune and escaped slaves. There was an old soldier who had served under Cromwell, a couple of drunken doctors and a few educated men who had fallen on hard times.

As always, Dampier made the best of the company he was in. He was strong and he did his work with the best. There was something aloof about him, and his dark face and thrust-out underlip warned the roughest cut-throat that he might be a dangerous man to cross.

His first buccaneering was brief and bloody. There was an attack in open boats on a Spanish town where a dozen men were killed but the only loot was a quantity of salt-beef and some red and yellow parrots. These pleased Dampier "because they would prate very prettily".

The buccaneers captured a few ships and shared the plunder. Having some money in his sea-chest, Dampier left them, bought a passage to England and reached his brother's farm after an absence of four and a half years.

Dampier writes his journal

In Devonshire he fell in love with Judith, a lady's maid from the Duke of Grafton's household. They were married and, in the spring, Dampier said good-bye to his bride and sailed to Jamaica. He took with him a consignment of saws, axes, hats, stockings, shoes and rum.

On landing, he sold his goods on the quayside and sent the money home to buy a small estate in Dorset. He was about to go back to join Judith there when he fell in with a Mr. Hobby who proposed a short trading voyage.

Never able to resist the chance of "knowledge and experience", Dampier set off with Hobby but, in the first bay they came to, they found a dozen ships lying at anchor. Their own vessel was quickly boarded by a jovial set of ruffians who broached a cask of rum and revealed that they were about to sack the town of Porto Bello.

Hobby's crew immediately deserted to the bucca-neers and it was not long before Dampier realized that he must join them or starve.

Porto Bello was captured without much trouble. The buccaneers crept through the woods and surprised the garrison with a sudden dash. When the booty was counted, it came to £40 a man.

A council was held to decide the next step and it was resolved to try their luck across the Isthmus of Panama.

Leaving a party to guard the ships, 330 men set off into the tropical forest, a coloured flag at the head of each company. Dampier was there with two friends, Basil Ringrow and Lionel Wafer, a young chemist who was now the surgeon's mate. Like the rest, they were clad in seamen's jackets, blue waistcoats, wide breeches and black stockings. On their heads they wore red caps and, besides weapons, each man carried several "doughboys"— hard dumplings baked in sea-water. Wafer had his medical chest and Dampier his precious journal that he kept in a piece of bamboo stoppered at either end with wax.

Aided by the Indians, who hated the Spaniards, the buccaneers crossed the Isthmus but, at Panama, they were repulsed with the loss of forty killed and wounded. However, they seized a Spanish ship and made off down the coast in search of easier prey.

At this point quarrels broke out. Captain Coxon, accused of cowardice in the fighting, withdrew in a huff and recrossed the Isthmus with seventy men.

Sawkins, a most valiant man who had made his ruffians observe the Sabbath and give up gambling, became the new leader. When he was killed in a headlong attack on a Spanish fort, Captain Sharp, a smooth-tongued rogue, took command.

Crossing the Isthmus of Panama

There were more raids, another mutiny and a desperate affray at Arica, the silver port of Peru. The buccaneers stormed into the town but they were driven back with heavy losses.

The survivors drew off to an island.

"Rather than serve longer under Captain Sharp, I will desert this crew," cried one. "Who is with me?"

More than forty raised their hands, including Dampier and Wafer. They resolved to cross the Isthmus by a roundabout route.

It was a terrible journey. They had no food, except a little flour, chocolate and sugar. The route lay through dense forest criss-crossed by rivers, so they could hardly make six miles a day.

"We gave out that if any Man faltered on the journey, he must expect to be shot to Death, for we knew that the Spaniards would be after us and one man falling into their hands might be the ruin of us all," wrote Dampier. Soon, their sufferings were greater than their fear of the Spaniards.

Two or three laggards were lost, one man, weighted down by his bag of dollars, was drowned crossing a river and Wafer, having had his kneecap blown off, could only hobble in agony. Fortunately the Indians befriended them and sheltered Wafer in one of their villages with some others who could go no further.

The rest struggled on to the coast and were taken aboard a French privateer.

Before long, the Englishmen were reunited with Coxon and their old companions in a nearby anchorage. They cruised along the Spanish Main, taking prizes, quarrelling and drinking in their usual style until some of the more sober characters decided to make north to Virginia where they could sell their share of the booty without too many questions.

After a spell ashore, Dampier joined the crew of the *Revenge* with Wafer and Ringrow who had turned up none the worse for their adventures. Fresh water was taken aboard but no meat except "shark that was boiled and stewed with vinegar and pepper". Undismayed, the buccaneers rounded the Horn and came to the coast of Peru.

Here they joined a pirate fleet of ten sail and rampaged up and down the coast capturing ships and pillaging towns to their hearts' content.

Between raids Dampier found plenty to interest him:

"The Sea-lion is a large creature about 12 to 14 foot long . . . it hath a broad face with many long Hairs growing about its lips like a Cat. It has a great goggle eye . . . The 9th of May we arrived at this Isle where there is a small Cove or sandy Bay where ships may careen . . . there are Fowls in great multitudes called Boobies but mostly Penguins, a Sea Fowl about as big as a duck and such Feet, but a sharp Bill, feeding on Fish. They do not fly but flutter . . . their Flesh is but ordinary Food but their Eggs are good Meat. There are 4 sorts of Sea-Turtle which I shall now describe . . ."

After a year of raiding, Dampier decided to leave his ship to throw in his lot with Captain Swan of the *Cygnet*.

Swan, a fat blustering man, took Dampier aside and whispered:

"I am resolved to quit buccaneering lest it bring us to the gallows. Wilt thou pilot my ship across the

M.W.—21

Pacific that we may resume honest trade in the East
Indies?"

Downcast by Ringrow's death and Wafer's transfer
to another ship, Dampier agreed to go, though the
Cygnet's crew looked even more villainous than his
own.

It was a hard voyage with provisions down to a
handful of maize daily per man. One sailor, caught
stealing food, was given three lashes from every man
on board and when, after fifty-two days, the *Cygnet*
reached the Philippines, there were three days'
rations left and the crew had secretly planned to kill
the captain and officers and eat them. Hearing this,
Swan remarked to his lean pilot:

"Ah, Mr. Dampier, you would have made them
but a poor meal!"

At Mindinao, the Englishmen were so well entertained by a friendly Sultan that Swan spent all his
time ashore, growing fatter and more brutal every
day. At length, the buccaneers decided to abandon
him.

Being unwilling to sail without a doctor, they
tricked Mr. Coppinger, the assistant surgeon, into
coming aboard. By chance, Dampier happened to be
with him. Both were seized and the *Cygnet* put to sea,
leaving Swan and thirty-six others stranded on the
island.

From the piracy point of view, the voyage was a
failure and by the time they reached the Nicobar
Islands in the Indian Ocean, the men had become so
violent that Dampier decided to escape at all costs.

He obtained a canoe and, with two Englishmen, a
Portuguese and four Malays who fitted outriggers to

The escape of Achin

the tiny craft, he set out to cross 150 miles of sea to
Achin, an English trading post.

A storm came up so gigantic that even Dampier
was terrified:

"I have been in many dangers," he wrote, "but the
worst of them was but a Play-game compared with
this."

Praying for God's help, he steered night and day,
while the others baled for their lives. On the fifth
day, they staggered ashore on the island of Sumatra

and collapsed from exhaustion and fever. Two of the adventurers died but the rest managed to reach Achin where they were treated kindly by the merchants.

Anyone but Dampier would have accepted their offer of a passage home. Troubled by fever, as thin and ragged as a scarecrow, he still could not bear to leave this part of the world that he knew little about. His boyhood dreams led him on and he took ship with a Captain Weldon to go trading to Indo-China. He made journeys far inland to study strange tribes, became mate to a crew of Moors, sailed to India and the coast of China and back again to the East Indies where he took the post of gunnery officer to an English trading fort.

Finally, he obtained a passage home "and we luffed in for the Downs where we anchored on September the 16th, 1691".

The ex-buccaneer had been away for twelve and a half years and his sole possessions were his journal and a much-tattooed native named Prince Jeoly whom he had befriended in the East Indies when, as a prisoner-of-war, the man was put up for sale. Needing money to reach Devonshire, Dampier had to part with his servant who went on show in London as "The Famous Painted Prince, the Wonder of the Age".

For the next few years, Dampier seems to have lived quietly at home with Judith, earning what he could and putting into order those smudged tattered notes that he had kept in a bamboo tube as he swam rivers, had dried over fires on deserted beaches and had carried inside his shirt through all the tempests, fights and adventures of twelve years round the world.

The story of his travels was published in 1697 with the title *A New Voyage* and, within days, Dampier was famous.

All London wanted to read his book. New editions were printed and the modest author found himself taken up by fashionable people, by scientists, geographers and merchants. His portrait was painted, his advice was requested for voyages and overseas ventures. Everyone wished to meet him; Mr. Pepys of the Navy Board invited him to dinner one evening and John Evelyn noted in his diary:

"I dined with Mr. Pepys, where was Captain Dampier who had been a famous buccaneer, had brought hither the Painted Prince and printed the story of his very strange adventures. He was now going abroad again by the King's encouragement . . . He seemed a more modest man than one would imagine."

"The modest man" was appointed captain of the *Roebuck* with George Fisher as his lieutenant. Their mission was to explore the unknown land of Australia "a country likely to contain gold".

From the start Dampier was unlucky. He had never commanded a ship before, his crew were a surly, timid lot and Fisher, a regular Naval officer, made no secret of his contempt for a captain who had been a low-down pirate.

When they got to sea, Fisher quarrelled violently with the bo'sun and thrashed a midshipman unmercifully. At the first taste of bad weather, he showed pitiful ignorance and cast such doubt upon his captain's skill that he made the crew even more panicky than they would have been.

"The ignorance and obstinacy of some under me occasioned me a great deal of trouble," wrote Dampier in his mild way when he was actually facing a mutiny led by his own lieutenant. There was a scene on deck when Fisher called the captain:

"Old Rogue! Old Dog! Old Cheat!"

Sent to his cabin, he continued to bawl threats until Dampier had him put into irons. He would have to get rid of Fisher.

When they reached Brazil, the lieutenant was taken ashore and lodged in a Portuguese jail until a ship arrived to carry him to England. Unperturbed, Dampier sailed on and on 6th August 1699, dropped anchor in Shark's Bay, Western Australia.

The crew were suffering from scurvy and the ship was showing signs of being unsound, but the land looked attractive and there seemed to be every prospect of success. Parties went ashore but, try as they would, they could find no fresh water and the aborigines, whom Dampier approached with great courage, were murderously unhelpful.

Had he now turned south, Dampier must have made a thorough discovery of Australia seventy years before Captain Cook. As it was, he sailed northwards out of Dampier Bay to search for water along the barren coast.

By this time, the men were almost dying of thirst. Reluctantly, Dampier steered away from the land to Timor where he could obtain water. For several weeks, he "jogged on", exploring the coast of New Guinea, naming capes and islands and recording his

Dampier with the Aborigines

notes on the natives and vegetation of unknown islands.

The *Roebuck*'s timbers were found to be so rotten that it was impossible to return to Australia. The sole hope was that she would last out the voyage home. Dampier nursed her skilfully round the Cape but, in February 1701, she foundered off Ascension Island.

The captain got his men ashore on rafts and they lived on turtles and shellfish until a passing vessel took them off and carried them to England.

At once, Dampier had to face a court-martial. Lieutenant Fisher had returned long since to make his tale good and the Court found Dampier guilty of "Hard and Cruel Usage against Lieutenant Fisher". He was fined all his pay and was declared "not a fit person to be employed as Commander of any of His Majesty's ships".

It was a harsh decision against a captain who had made important discoveries and had managed to control a difficult crew once Fisher was off the ship. Perhaps their Lordships felt that they had been unfair for, within a year, Dampier was given a new command.

War with Spain had broken out and, in 1703, the *London Gazette* announced that Captain Dampier, being about to depart in the *St. George*, "had the honour to kiss the hand of Her Majesty, Queen Anne".

He was given a roving commission and, with Captain Stradling of the *Cinque Ports*, he made for the old buccaneering coast of Peru. Several Spanish vessels were taken but the treasure town of Santa

Maria proved to be too tough a nut to crack. As usual, failure led to quarrels. Stradling went off alone, and after a bitter wrangle with his mate, Alexander Selkirk, left him on the uninhabited island of Juan Fernandez. This brutal act was to supply Defoe with his immortal story of *Robinson Crusoe*.

Meanwhile, Dampier put into a quiet bay to careen his ship. To his dismay, he found that she was as rotten as the old *Roebuck*, for her timbers were "eaten like a honeycomb" and, in places, the carpenter could push his thumb clean through the planks! Repairs were going on when the mate and twenty-one malcontents stole the longboat and sailed away with most of the provisions.

Dampier had plenty of pluck. With a leaky ship and a weakened crew, he ordered a desperate attack upon a Spanish treasure galleon known as the "Manila ship". This failed and thirty-five more of the crew deserted in a captured barque.

With only twenty-eight men left, the tough old captain actually captured the town of Puna, seized a Spanish ship into which he transferred his crew, crossed the Pacific and got back to England in 1707.

Not surprisingly, poor Dampier was now regarded as "an unlucky captain". At fifty-six, he was hard-up and out of a job when Captain Woodes Rogers of Bristol invited him to join a privateering expedition as "Pilot for the South Seas".

The *Duke* and the *Duchess* left the Downs with crews that were mostly "tailors, tinkers, pedlars, fiddlers and haymakers". But Rogers was a breezy, masterful commander. He put down a mutiny and licked these landlubbers so thoroughly into shape that they endured a terrible passage round the Horn, captured a Spanish town with immense booty and 30,000 pieces-of-eight and, wonder of wonders, actually took the "Manila ship", the prize that for so long had drawn every buccaneer to those waters.

But the most famous exploit of the voyage was the rescue at Juan Fernandez. Nearing that lonely island, the men espied:

"a solitary person, running on the beach with a white ensign. He was clothed in a goatskin jacket, breeches and cap, sewed together with thongs of the same."

They hailed him and he gave them directions to land in a strange, stumbling voice and ran along the shore like the wind. It was Alexander Selkirk, who had been marooned by Stradling four years previously. Naturally, Dampier went ashore to examine the castaway's hut and the manner in which he had survived for so long.

In October 1711, the expedition returned home with £170,000 on board. For the first time in his life, Dampier had made a profitable voyage, but a lifetime of hardships had wrecked his health and he did not live to receive his share. The buccaneer who carried a note-book as well as a cutlass and pistol had realized all his boyhood dreams.

Celia Fiennes

IN the 17th century, young gentlemen made the Grand Tour and girls stayed at home. Travel for adventure and knowledge was not for women and there was no such person as a lady-explorer until Mistress Celia Fiennes* set out to visit every county in England.

Celia was brought up in a family, not of Puritan kill-joys, but of sober Dissenters or, as we should say, Nonconformists. Her grandfather was Lord Saye and Sele, nicknamed "Old Subtlety" for his wily opposition to Charles I, and her father was the Colonel Fiennes who surrendered Bristol to Prince Rupert. The entire family supported Parliament and no fewer than eight of Celia's uncles fought against the King.

The Fiennes were moderately rich and very well connected. There were baronets, knights and even an earl in the family and, during her travels, Celia called upon uncles and cousins who were prosperous squires and well-to-do business men in London and the towns. Nor were the Fiennes ruined when Charles II came back. They kept their estates and Colonel Fiennes died unmolested in 1669 when Celia was seven years old and her sister Mary was six.

* Fiennes is pronounced "Fines"

Mistress Fiennes and Celia set out, riding side-saddle

The two little girls grew up at Newton Toney in Wiltshire. Girls of good family hardly ever went to school and Celia and her sister received their first lessons from their mother and afterwards from a tutor.

Celia did not care much for lessons. At the beginning of her Journal, she writes:

"Wiltshire is a fine champion country, pleasant for all sports—Rideing, Hunting, Coursing, Setting and Shooteing",

making it clear that she preferred outdoor sports to spelling! Certainly, the Journal is full of mistakes in grammar, history and geography, but "I speak and write with freedom and easyness" she remarked gaily, as she scribbled away.

When Celia was twenty-two, her sister married Mr. Harrison, a rich merchant, and went to live in London, leaving Celia and her mother in Wiltshire.

Naturally, they missed Mary. The house and the park seemed dull without her and Mrs. Fiennes noticed that Celia appeared to have lost interest even in exercising her horses. She had always liked to be out and about, to watch the wheelwright at work, to help in the brewhouse and harness-room. Now she

332

was listless and bored, forever complaining of headaches and colds. Alarmed lest her daughter should become genuinely ill, Mrs. Fiennes proposed a change of air.

"We will take a journey to view the countryside," she said. "Thomas shall ride with us to be our protector and I have in mind to call upon our relative, Sir William Constantine, and upon Cousin Collier in Dorset."

Mother and daughter set out, riding side-saddle. Thomas and a lady's maid followed, with the spare horses and enough baggage to provide for a change of clothes.

They rode first to Salisbury to see the cathedral and on to the great house at Wilton where Sir Philip Sidney wrote *Arcadia*. Celia, already beginning to brighten, was much amused by some devices in the gardens that sprayed water over unsuspecting visitors:

"about 2 yards off the doore of a Grotto is severall pipes in a line that with a sluce spoutts water up to wett the strangers", she wrote.

In Dorset, the travellers rode along by the sea, took a boat to an island, ate lobsters and shrimps and picked some pretty shells on the shore. Celia's spirits rose with every mile. She watched workers making green vitriol, a chemical used in dyeing and making ink, she discovered how they make cider in Somerset, though she thought it a pity that they carelessly pressed all kinds of apples instead of only the best, and in Devonshire she noticed that the lanes were so narrow that packhorses were used instead of waggons.

Asking the way

"All this knowledge so diverts me," she remarked to
her mother, "that I intend to keep a journal throughout all our travels."

This was the first of many journeys that carried
Celia all over England. Sometimes, she rode with her
mother and, after her death, with one or both of the
Filmer girls, daughters of her cousin who lived in
Hertfordshire. Often, she travelled by herself, with
only a servant and a dog for company.

It was an adventure to travel about England in
the 17th century. There were no maps, and signposts
were only just coming in. Many parts of the country
were practically unknown to anyone outside the
district, so that guides had to be hired, almost as if
the traveller were in Mexico or the Alps. Even so, it
was easy to get lost and Celia became quite cross in
Derbyshire where "the common people know not
above 2 or 3 mile from their home".

The early journeys were made through the southern and western counties. This was pretty easy country for travelling, though in Gloucestershire and Devon the roads were narrow and bad. Hertfordshire clay was almost impassable in wet weather and near Leicester, "I was near 11 hours going but 25 miles". Worst of all was the liquid mud of Sussex, "which is much in deep blind lanes and up and down steep hills".

But once she had caught the fever for travelling Celia could not stop. As soon as winter was over, preparations were made, horses newly shod, saddlebags packed and she was away down the road.

Bath, where she bathed and drank the waters, Stonehenge, where she counted the stones and got the number wrong, Oxford, "very cleane and pretty broade", Winchester, whose college was founded by an ancestor of the Fiennes, the Isle of Wight, the New Forest, Portsmouth and Southampton, "almost forsooke and neglected"—all these and a hundred other places were visited and described during the twelve summers since Mary's wedding.

So far, they had been "little" journeys of perhaps

two hundred or three hundred miles—holidays passed
in pleasant, familiar country, a few days with one
relative, a week with another, with rides of twenty or
thirty miles and many a stop to look at interesting
buildings and curious occupations. Longing to go
farther afield, Celia set out in May 1697 on her
Northern Journey.

With her young cousins, Susannah and Mary, and
two reliable servants, she left Amwell in Hertfordshire and rode to Cambridge, passing Audley End,
the Earl of Suffolk's house that was so vast that it
took a running footman all day to open and shut the
windows. Cambridge, she thought, was "mostly old
and indifferent" but King's College Chapel "the
finest building I have ever heard of". Thence to
Peterborough and "fenny" Lincolnshire, pausing to
visit Burghley House, near Stamford.

Wealthy men were building new houses on a
magnificent scale and Miss Fiennes came through a
noble park, past smooth lawns, statues, fountains
and a vineyard. She found that "my Lord's bed-
chamber is furnished very rich, the tapestry all blue
silk and rich gold thread . . . there was a blue velvet
bed with gold fringes and very richly embroidered".
But, although she admired the splendid rooms with
their marble floors, painted ceilings and walls, she
did not approve of the goddesses and nymphs with
no clothes on!

Celia liked things to be clean and modern. Old
buildings and picturesque towns bored her and she
much preferred stone buildings in the latest "London
mode", paved streets, sash windows, and prosperous
industries.

Thus Nottingham was always her favourite town—
"the neatest I have seen, built of Stone and delicate,
large and long Streetes, much like London . . . but
buildings finer". The people were busy and prosperous. They drank fine strong ale, cultivated good
farmland and had many manufactures. Celia noted
brick-making and the weaving of stockings, "a very
ingenious art", and, at a glass-blower's, "I spunn
some of the glass and saw him maake a Swann
presently with coloured glass, he makes Buttons
which are very strong and will not breake".

Their inn here was very good, but when they
reached Yorkshire, they were charged high prices,
though food was cheap enough in the markets—a
huge codfish over a yard long cost eightpence and a
shoulder of veal ninepence. York itself had "but
a meane appearance, the Streets narrow, the houses
very low". Only the Minster was a noble building
and Celia and her cousins clambered up 262 steps
to the top of the tower to see the countryside for
thirty miles round with the people below like
pygmies.

There was a Mint in York and, with her usual
enthusiasm, Celia asked if she could make a coin.
She stamped out one half-crown but the men would
not tell her the secret of milling the edges of the
coins.

The spa at Harrogate was worth a visit for it had
four different springs of medicinal waters, one being
the Sulphur or Stinking Spa whose smell was so
horrid that Celia could not force her horse near the
well. Even so, she drank a quart of the stinking
water, holding her nose as she did so.

Near Harrogate was St. Mungo's Well, a cold spring much favoured by Roman Catholics. Being a devout Nonconformist did not prevent Celia from plunging in: "you cannot bear the coldness above 2 or 3 minutes, then you come out and walk round the pavement and in again . . . I used my Bath garments and put on flannel when I came out to go into the Bed which is best . . . but some will keep on the wet Garments and let them drye to them and say its more beneficial . . . I dipp'd my head quite under every time and found it eased a great pain I used to have in my head and I was not so apt to catch Cold as much as before."

Continuing to Hull, the ladies failed to find an inn suitable for gentlefolk, there being only two or three "sorry alehouses". Fortunately, as it was getting dark, a Quaker took them in and provided them with good beds, stabling and bread, cheese, bacon and eggs for supper.

From Scarborough, where they saw seventy ships going down the coast with coal for London, they made right across country to Derbyshire, passing through Pontefract that supplied all England with liquorice.

The way became more difficult and the northern miles seemed very long because the old British mile of 2428 yards was still in use in those parts. Derbyshire was "full of steep hills and you see neither hedge nor tree but only low drye stone walls" and when they came to a town, the descent seemed so dangerous that they were obliged to employ guides, one of whom lost Celia's bag containing her nightclothes!

The Duke of Devonshire's bath

But it was fascinating country. There were pot-holes to explore and caves to crawl into on hands and knees until they could stand up in a vast echoing cavern dripping with moisture. In these wilds, they came across Chatsworth, the incredibly lavish home of the Duke of Devonshire where, amid its glories, they saw a modern marvel—"a batheing-room, the walls all blew and white marble and you went down steps into the bath big enough for two people; at the upper end are two Taps to let in one hott, the other cold water . . . the windows are all private glass".

339

At Buxton, Miss Fiennes was highly indignant to find that the landlady intended them to sleep three in a bed and to put strangers in the same room. However, they came to no harm and were given a warm welcome in the Staffordshire home of Sir Charles Wolseley, an old Cromwell-man married to Celia's aunt. At last, through Warwickshire and the "fine town" of Coventry, to Woburn and St. Albans, the ladies came safely home:

"I returned," wrote Celia, "and all our Company, Blessed be to God, very well without any disaster or trouble in 7 weeks time about 685 miles that we went together." After a tour of Kent, in the autumn, she was able to say with pride, "This year, my journeys have totalled 1045 miles, of which not more than 100 miles were in a coach".

Next year, in 1698, Celia made on horseback a journey that would be remarkable if it were done in a modern motor-car. She rode from London to Norwich, across the Midlands to the Welsh border, through Lancashire and the Lake District into Scotland, eastward to Newcastle and then right through the entire length of England to Land's End and back to London. She called it 'My Great Journey'.

She was now thirty-six, and although she never bothers to describe herself, we may picture her riding side-saddle in a full skirt of hard-wearing serge and a demure, high-necked bodice. Over all, wet or fine, she wore her "dust-coat", a huge dun-coloured cloak that kept out rain and wind, and on her head she wore a big-brimmed hat with a scarf tied over the top and knotted under her chin. There was nothing fashionable about her attire. She was a seasoned traveller and she knew the sensible things to wear that would last for weeks in all weathers and still allow her to appear to be a lady of gentle birth when she arrived at a lordly inn or at some country mansion where she dined at his Lordship's table.

Undoubtedly, she was a bit of a tartar—prim, bossy and sharp-tongued, especially to a landlady who tried to cheat her or to a villager who scratched his head and mumbled he didn't rightly know the way. But she was cheerful and fearless, out to enjoy herself and to discover the facts about her own country. Despite her concern to drink the waters of every spa and healing spring she came to, she was really as strong and sensible as one of her own horses!

This time, her companions were a greyhound and two trustworthy servants. Once, in Cheshire, a couple of suspicious characters followed them and jostled her horse but they made off when some other travellers appeared. Near Scotland it was necessary to hire a guide for protection against robbers, but the heyday of highwaymen had not yet arrived and the greatest danger to travellers was the state of the roads.

Celia might have been drowned when her horse stumbled on a flooded causeway near Ely and her "horse's feete could scarce stand" as she crossed the Sands of Dee. In Norfolk, "the roade lay under water which is very unsafe for strangers to pass, by reason of the holes and quicksands" and her horse fell on the slippery cobbles of Lancaster and threw her when falling into a hole in Cornwall.

On this journey Miss Fiennes showed more interest in the ordinary people. She liked to watch them at work, boiling sea-water for salt, mining coal, tin and lead, making cups and saucers in Staffordshire, spinning outside their houses and "knitting 4 and 5 in a company under the hedges". Her sharp eyes noticed the way they patted up butter at Ipswich into the shape and size of a pint-pot and the method of making soap from the ash of burnt ferns "which they make fine and rowle up in balls and so sell them or use them all the year for washing and scouring and send much up to London".

She could not stand people who were lazy. Ipswich folk, she thought, could prosper if they did not suffer from "pride and sloth"; in North Wales, "the inhabitants go barefoote and barelegg'd, a nasty sort of people", but the Scots were far worse: "I tooke them for people who were sick, seeing 2 or 3 great wenches as tall and bigg as any woman sat hovering between their bed and the chimney-corner, all idle and doing nothing . . . tho' it was nine of the clock!" Prim Miss Fiennes had already ridden seven long miles that morning!

Fortunately, there was plenty to enjoy. She liked the oat clap-bread of Westmorland—"they mix the flour with water, so soft as to rowle it in their hands into a ball and then they have a board made round and something hollow in the middle", the dough was clapped on to this and pressed "as thinn as a paper, placed on an iron plate and baked on the coals just to make it looke yellow and be as crisp and pleasant to eate as anything you can imagine".

In Cornwall, where she celebrated reaching Land's

End by drinking a bottle of beer, she noticed that they had no fuel except furze bushes, not even any wood, but they made the most delicious apple-pie with "clouted cream" on top, though she did not care for the local habit of men, women and children sitting round smoking pipes while she ate.

All kinds of things caught her eye as she rode along: oranges and lemons almost ripe in Derbyshire, the way country-folk in East Anglia hung cakes of cow-dung on the walls to dry for fuel, the custom of yoking oxen with horses to pull carts in the Northeast, the inland method of keeping live fish in baskets tied to the river-bank so they could be taken out when needed and cooked fresh.

She saw Holy Thursday processions, coach races at Epsom; she drank an amazing variety of healing waters, and was a keen judge of ale which she preferred to the coffee and chocolate that were becoming fashionable. She liked wine but found that it could only be obtained when she was near to the coast.

Mistress Fiennes made some later journeys, mostly short ones in the home counties, but the peak of her achievements as a traveller was in that fine summer of 1697, "in which I had but 3 dayes of wet, except some refreshing showers sometymes and it was all above 1551 miles—and many of them long miles".

No man of her time, not even Defoe, travelled as far or as thoroughly in England as she. As far as we know, she ceased her journeying when she was about forty. Perhaps she thought it was time to settle down, for she went to live in London, near to her nieces, Mary's daughters. She died at Hackney in 1741 and, judging by her will, made when she was seventy-six, she remained a tough, resolute old lady to the end.

After arranging for her own funeral at Newton Toney, she apologized for the fact that she was not as well-off as formerly and so could not leave very much to her dear nieces. However, there was enough money to carry on a charitable gift of food for poor prisoners, to make gifts to her servants, her doctor and a nephew, and to share out her jewellery, silver, furniture and books.

Strangely enough, although the manuscript of her Journal still exists in the Fiennes' home in Oxfordshire, Celia did not mention it in her will—a coffee-pot, a tea kettle and a nutmeg-box but not the journal of our first woman-explorer.

More about the people in part 3

JOHN CABOT (*c.* 1450–99) failed to find the North-West Passage but his discoveries were genuine and he made the first notable voyage in an English ship. His son, SEBASTIAN CABOT (*c.* 1476–1557) seems to have been a map-maker who used his father's name and his own charm to gain credit for voyages that he had never made. His evidence in a case brought by Columbus' relatives showed that he had little real knowledge of North America. However, in his old age he helped to awaken maritime interest in England.

LADY JANE GREY (1537–54) was the daughter of Henry Grey, Marquess of Dorset, later Duke of Suffolk, and of Lady Frances Brandon, whose mother was Henry VIII's sister. Thus Jane's misfortunes arose from her nearness to the throne. Had Northumberland's plot succeeded, she might well have proved to be as tough a character as her cousin Elizabeth, for Jane was highly intelligent, as obstinate as the rest of the Tudors and an enthusiastic Protestant.

The HAWKINS of Plymouth were a remarkable family. John's father made voyages to West Africa and Brazil in Henry VIII's reign, sat in Parliament, founded the business of merchants and ship-builders. His elder son, William, was at sea from time to time but mostly he looked after affairs in Plymouth; his grandson (William III) served with Drake, a cousin. John (1532–95) had one son, Richard, who commanded a ship against the Armada and sailed the *Dainty* into the Pacific in 1593 where he was captured by the Spaniards. After several years in prison, he came home in 1602, was knighted, served in Parliament and as Vice-Admiral of Devon. The *Minion* men who volunteered to be put ashore after the disaster at San Juan were killed by Indians or captured by the Spanish. Some were prisoners in Spain at the time when Hawkins (with Burghley's approval) pretended to turn traitor in order to learn King Philip's plan. His price included the release of his old comrades, and a few survivors did reach their homes at last.

The fame of SIR PHILIP SIDNEY (1554–86) rests upon his gallantry in one small action at Zutphen and upon the extraordinary effect he had upon everyone who knew him. His character was so lovable and his gifts so brilliant that it seemed certain that he would be one of the great figures of the age. The Queen's favour hampered, instead of helping his career. Besides *Arcadia*, he wrote a short book, *Defence of Poesie*, and some marvellous love poems (*Astrophel and Stella*) to Penelope Devereux who married someone else.

WILLIAM HARVEY (1578–1657) is honoured throughout the world as the founder of modern medicine, and a lecture in his honour is still given every year at the Royal College of Physicians. He left his money and an estate to the College. His famous discovery was complete in everything except that he did not realize that blood passes from arteries to veins in tiny channels called capillaries. The microscope was not invented until about the time of his death, and Harvey's simple lens (magnifying glass) did not show the capillaries. In his day there were only three hospitals in England, his own St. Bartholomew's at Smithfield, "Bedlam" for the insane and St. Bartholomew's at Rochester.

JOHN SMITH (1580–1631) was the real founder of Virginia, for the earlier attempts to start a colony by Raleigh and Grenville and by John White failed. Pocahontas went to live in James Town, became a Christian and married John Rolfe, a settler of good family, who brought her to England in 1616. To her delight, she met and conversed with her hero Captain Smith and she was made much of in genteel circles. The climate affected her health and she was about to embark when she died at Gravesend in 1617. She left a son, and several Virginia families claim descent from Princess Pocahontas.

PRINCE RUPERT (1619–82) is often called "Rupert of the Rhine" because his father was a German Prince—the Elector Palatine Frederick V. His mother was Elizabeth, the beautiful daughter of James I, called "The Winter Queen" because she and her husband were King and Queen of Bohemia for only one year. Driven out by the Austrians, they had to bring up a large family in poverty-stricken exile, though Elizabeth was gay enough. Frederick died and, after many years, Rupert's unlovable brother Charles-Louis regained some of the family domains. Rupert's sister, Sophia, was the mother of George I—thus, if Rupert had married and had had children, there would have been no Hanoverian Kings of England!

WILLIAM DAMPIER (1652–1715) was a buccaneer rather than a pirate in his younger days. Buccaneers believed that they were carrying on lawful warfare against Spain, and the better commanders would have been indignant to be called pirates, since pirates were outlaws who attacked ships of any nation. Some, of course, were both. In time of war, governments often supported the buccaneers and favoured the fitting-out of private expeditions like that of Captain Woodes Rogers. He was a privateer captain, never a pirate. Daniel Defoe actually met and talked to Alexander Selkirk, so that "Robinson Crusoe" is based on what he learned

from the castaway and from various books, including
Dampier's.

CELIA FIENNES (1662–1741) left no account of herself
apart from the journals which were probably written only
for her own amusement. The original diaries are kept at
Broughton Castle with portraits of her father and mother, but
little more is known about her. After the Restoration the
"tour" became quite popular and a number of travellers,
including John Evelyn and Defoe, wrote accounts of their
journeys but none of them equalled Celia's.

Part 4

Great Leaders

Robert Owen

MR. THICKNESS, schoolmaster of Newtown in mid-Wales, stepped briskly into the saddler's shop.

"Mr. Owen," he said, "I am here to speak of your son, Robert."

"Robert? I hope the boy has done nothing ill?" replied Mr. Owen anxiously.

"Nothing, nothing ill whatsoever. Indeed, all that he does is so exceptional that I propose, with your permission, to employ him to teach the younger children. In return, he shall have the rest of his schooling for nothing."

"But Robert is only seven!" cried Mrs. Owen, coming in from the kitchen.

"So he may be, ma'am," replied the schoolmaster solemnly, "yet I declare that boy to be a little marvel!"

At that moment, the "little marvel" himself ran into the shop.

"Robert," said his father, "do you think you could help Mr. Thickness to teach the other children?"

"I can beat them all at running and jumping, Father. Can I teach them dancing as well as reading?"

The boy spoke so eagerly that his words hardly sounded boastful. It seemed quite natural to him, as to everyone else, that he should be the best at lessons and sports.

So, at the age of seven, Robert Owen became a teacher. His group of children sat in front of him learning the alphabet and he was so patient and good-tempered that they tried extra hard to please him. Mr. Thickness noticed that the boy had a rare gift for making people listen to him.

But, at nine, Robert left school and went to work in a shop that sold drapery and grocery and, in his spare time, he read every book that he could borrow.

"At this time, I was reading a book a day," he said later. "I read *Pilgrim's Progress, Robinson Crusoe, Cook's Voyages* and all the lives of Great Men I could meet with."

He had already made up his mind to be a Great Man. He was ten and it was high time to set off to London where his brother William was already in business as a saddler.

With a bundle of clean clothes and forty shillings in his pocket, Robert was put on the London coach:

"Farewell, Father!" he cried. "Do not worry—I shall maintain myself and make my fortune presently!"

He spent a few weeks with his brother before receiving the offer of a job with Mr. McGuffog, linen-draper of Stamford. The offer was for three years with free food and lodging, no pay the first year, £8 the second and £10 the third.

Mr. McGuffog had built up such a high-class trade that every day six or seven carriages stood in line outside his shop. For these genteel customers, the shop-hours were from ten until four and the whole business was conducted in a most leisurely, refined manner.

Young Owen became a favourite with his employer who taught him a great deal about best-quality fabrics and, after four years, he recommended him to Flint and Palmer, haberdashers, who kept a shop on Old London Bridge.

This was a very different business from Mr. McGuffog's. From eight in the morning till ten at night the shop was crowded with people turning over the huge stock of cottons and muslins in search of bargains. Business was brisk and the assistants were expected to be brisker.

"Don't waste time seeing that customers are satisfied!" cried Mr. Flint. "Wrap up the goods, take the cash and serve the next lady!"

Robert had no regular meal-times; he just snatched a bite when he could and, after the shop closed, he had to sweep and tidy up before crawling into his attic bed.

He stayed there a year before applying for a job with Mr. Satterfield, a Manchester draper, who offered him the fine salary of £40 a year. He was now fifteen and had been keeping himself for five years.

In Lancashire, the great, booming industry was cotton-spinning. Robert saw factories for the first time. He went about and looked at new machines making new materials and he heard on every side that fortunes were being made. He also noticed that most of the workers lived in miserable poverty.

In this hard, go-ahead world, he kept his eyes open for the chance to become something more than a shop-assistant. He was eighteen when he met Mr. Jones.

Jones was a mechanic who supplied Satterfield's with wire-frames for ladies' bonnets, and when he called at the shop he would tell Robert about the spinning-machine he had made at home.

"Ah, Mr. Owen", he said one day, "you're a sharp young man. If only you and I had a little capital, we could set up in business together making machines."

"I think my brother William would lend me £100," replied Robert eagerly.

"Shake hands!" cried Jones. "The firm of Jones and Owen is launched!"

With the borrowed money, they put up a workshop and engaged forty men to construct Jones's machines but Robert soon found he had made a poor bargain.

Jones had no notion of business and left everything to his partner who, in fact, knew very little about machinery. Owen did his best.

"I looked carefully at the men in their different jobs," he said, "although I really knew nothing. By observing everything with the closest attention, I kept the business going."

Even so, the venture failed and Jones went off, leaving his partner nothing but five machines.

Undaunted, Owen rented a big factory, and let off all the floor except one corner where he set up his machines. Then he hired three spinners and began to make yarn for the muslin trade. At twenty, he was an employer and he worked so hard that, within a year, he was making £6 a week for himself.

One morning, the men were talking about an advertisement in the paper. A Mr. Drinkwater was seeking a manager for a new mill, so Owen put on his hat and went round to Drinkwater's to ask for the job.

"You are too young," said Mr. Drinkwater.

Robert knew that his fresh complexion made him look even younger than he was but he managed to brush this objection aside.

"What salary do you ask?"

"£300 a year."

"What? Several men want this post and all their askings put together would not come to £300."

"I cannot help what others ask, for I cannot take less. I am making that sum in my own business."

"Can you prove that?"

"Yes, I will show you my business and my books."

Mr. Drinkwater was so impressed by what he saw that he offered him the post at the salary asked. Robert was to take complete charge of everything, including the 500 workers.

Astonished by his own boldness, he went along to the mill and walked round as though making a thorough inspection. He said not a word, apart from "Yes" and "No". Years later, he confessed, "After six weeks of watching and studying the workings of the machines, I felt so much master of my position that I was ready to give orders".

Owen was so successful that Mr. Drinkwater raised his salary and promised to make him a partner after three years. But, when the time was up, he had to explain that because of company changes, he could not grant the partnership:

"I am anxious however to retain you as my manager at any salary you care to ask," he added hastily.

Owen looked him straight in the face and answered:

"I have your agreement here. Look, I put it into the fire. But I will not stay as your manager!"

When word went round Manchester that the brilliant young Welshman had left Drinkwater, two wealthy firms offered to help him form a new company to manufacture yarn.

"But we will not compete against Mr. Drinkwater," he told them, "he was always good to me and I do not wish to injure him."

As his business grew, Robert had to travel to various towns and sometimes to Scotland. One morning in Glasgow, he happened to meet two young ladies in the street and, although extremely bashful in the company of ladies, he felt obliged to raise his hat, since one was Miss Spear, daughter of a rich cotton-broker whom he knew. Miss Spear introduced her companion as Miss Caroline Dale, daughter of David Dale, the owner of New Lanark spinning-mills. Caroline liked the shy young man so much that she afterwards said to her friend:

"If ever I marry, there is my husband!"

But, for the moment, she invited Robert to visit her father's mills. This he did, not merely to see one of the biggest factories in the country, but because

his mind was busy with plans that almost every other
business-man would have considered crazy.

Ever since he had come to Lancashire, he had been
troubled by the wretched condition of the workers.
Many families lived in one room or in a corner of a
cellar. They worked long hours yet their pay was so
low that they took their children at five years old to
earn a few pence mending broken threads or creeping
under the machines to clean the wheels. No wonder
that these mites were whipped to keep them awake.
No wonder they died young or grew up mis-shapen,
brutish and ignorant. Unlike other employers, Owen
did not believe that workpeople were naturally dirty
and lazy.

"I would change them into good citizens if only I could run a factory in my own way," he said to himself.

The mills at New Lanark seemed to be exactly right for his plans. In his enthusiasm, he forgot his shyness and asked Caroline to marry him. She agreed, but he had still to persuade Mr. Dale to sell him the mills and to allow him to marry his daughter.

"I am by no means sure that I approve of that pushing young man from Manchester," declared Mr. Dale.

But when Owen really wanted something, he could be the most charming, persuasive talker in the world. In the end, Mr. Dale gave in. He sold the mills to Owen and his partners and he permitted Caroline to marry the man she loved. On New Year's Day, 1800, Robert and his bride arrived at New Lanark.

The mills employed well over a thousand people but so many were needed that batches of orphans and foundlings were sent north from English workhouses. These tiny children had to work thirteen and fourteen hours a day, six days a week and for part of Sundays, in the hot, damp atmosphere of cotton-mills.

Mr. Dale employed 500 children and, although he treated them better than most masters, the situation filled Robert Owen with horror.

"Children so young should not be working from six in the morning until seven at night," he cried indignantly. "Many are dwarfs in body and mind. Some are deformed. Numbers continually run away and what can then become of them? Caroline, what can become of these poor children?"

As for the grown-up workers, they lived, he said, in wickedness and misery. And, for their part, they hated the prying Welshman who had come to live in the village, doubtless to squeeze more profit out of their labours. Owen was determined to turn these sullen people into good citizens. His first reform was to build an upper storey to their one-room hovels. He had piles of filth cleared away; the streets were paved and new homes were started. Finding that the wives were being cheated by rascally shopkeepers, he opened a company store that sold goods at fair prices and he bought coal by the truckload in order to re-sell it cheap.

Although the men did not like being punished for drunkenness and their wives were furious when Owen's "Bug-Hunters" came to see that they kept their houses clean, they found that all the fines for misbehaviour went into a sick-fund and that Owen himself paid the doctors' bills.

In the factory itself, he put a stop to thieving and, to shame the slackers, he invented a device that he called "The Silent Monitor". A four-sided piece of wood was hung over each workplace. The sides were painted black, blue, yellow and white. Black denoted bad conduct, blue meant poor, yellow good and white excellent and the superintendent changed the tablets daily so that everyone could see who had worked well or badly. This childish scheme was a success because Owen realized that most of his workers, old and young, were no more than children.

The mills prospered. Owen's partners were delighted with the profits and the workers were better-off than ever before. Yet, because mill-owners were

normally so hard, the men still distrusted their Boss.
In 1806, a dispute between Britain and America
stopped the arrival of raw cotton and, for four
months, cotton-mills were closed and many workers
were dismissed without pay. At New Lanark, Owen
called a mass-meeting:

"Lads," he said, "there's no work for you until
this trouble blows over. But it's none of your doing
and, until the machines start up again, you shall all
have your wages!"

It cost him well over £7000 but, from that time on,
the workers trusted and adored him.

At heart, Owen was always a teacher and, after
various set-backs, he was able to begin educating the
children of New Lanark. He erected a large building
that he called The Institute for the Formation of
Character, and he insisted that every child in the

village should attend from the age of one until at least ten, though he liked them to stay longer.

His ideas were amazingly modern. There was no cane and no timetable, for he believed that children ought to be happy and active in school. Lessons were often out-of-doors and he had paths cut through the woods to encourage the children to ramble and to learn nature study in the fresh air. There was singing and a kind of "drill" with marching to fife-and-drum bands and, of course, dancing, in which Robert himself joined with the utmost gusto.

Above all, there was kindness. In his earnest, patient way he said to a young teacher:

"These children must never hear from their teacher an angry word. From the moment they arrive, you must tell them that the first aim of school is to try to make each other happy."

His cherished plans were threatened when his partners refused to pay out any more money for the school.

"I shall buy you out. How much do you want?" Owen said.

"Well, Mr. Owen, we can rely on you to name a fair price."

"Eighty-four thousand pounds!" he snapped and the offer was gratefully accepted.

But, although he was growing rich, Owen did not have £84,000 and he had to find some new partners who, he believed, would allow him to run the business in his own way.

Unfortunately, they proved to be greedy and spiteful. They complained that he was too generous to the workers, that the school was a piece of high-flown nonsense, that they were in business for profit not for charity.

As before, Owen offered to buy them out.

"No, the mills must be sold," they said. Secretly, they meant to buy New Lanark for themselves at a low price. Owen resigned and went away to London.

For a year, the struggle dragged on. Owen's enemies imagined that he was ruined, not realizing that he had found six wealthy admirers to support him. On the day of the sale, while Owen and his friends stayed in the background, their solicitor kept raising the price £100 above every bid until, at £110,000, the old partners could go no higher and the property was knocked down to Owen's supporters.

Straightaway, they set off by carriage to New Lanark but, about a mile from the mills, the London gentlemen were alarmed to see a huge crowd running towards them, shouting and hallooing. The horses were taken from the shafts and, heedless of the gentry's protests, the crowd seized the carriage and dragged it uphill to the village where the street was lined with cheering crowds.

"The mills are saved!" they shouted. "Mr. Owen has come back!"

Robert Owen was to become world-famous, to travel all over Europe and America, explaining his ideas and founding new towns, schools and trade unions. Thousands of visitors were to come to New Lanark and he was to meet most of the distinguished men of his time. But in all the triumphs and disappointments of his long career, there was no happier day than when the people dragged his carriage into New Lanark and the children cried:

"Mr. Owen has come back!"

Wellington

"THERE he goes, that long-nosed beggar that beats the French," remarked Private White of the 43rd, jerking his wine-bottle towards a spare, grey-coated figure who rode along the lines of resting soldiers.

"Aye, the Peer don't dress much like a general compared with them Spaniards and Froggies covered with blooming gold lace and medals," replied Private Kemp, between mouthfuls of bread and meat.

"No, Kempy, but up and down this 'eart-break country, his long nose among us has been worth ten thousand men. He's beat all of Boney's marshals and he'll beat Boney himself one of these days."

A bugle sounded. Orders to fall in were repeated down the line and Lord Wellington's soldiers, cursing as they eased on their 60-pound packs, resumed their march across the parched, biscuit-coloured land. Behind them creaked the bullock-waggons that carried food and ammunition for the army that was driving the French back to their own frontier.

As he rode with a single staff-officer, Wellington's mind was busy with tents, camp-kettles, blankets, wine and cloth. The muleteers and a Spanish guide had to be paid and compensation must be offered to a farmer whose barn had been accidentally set on fire.

The Commander-in-Chief saw to everything. He looked after his troops like a stern parent. He scolded

and punished them, hanged a few for looting Spanish homes, called them the scum of the earth and occasionally praised them as "fine fellows".

Today, he was in good spirits.

"Ned, I am going to hustle the French out of Spain," he remarked to a staff-officer, pausing to scan the hills with his telescope. A distant movement caught his attention and he drew out one of the pieces of paper that he kept tucked in his waistcoat. He wrote rapidly and handed the note to a trooper:

"General Picton, on the right. Sharp!"

In his abrupt way, he gave orders:

"Light Division cross the river and get possession of the ridge."

"Support the Light Infantry by Cavalry and Heavy Infantry."

"3rd Division cross the road and take up such posts as you think proper."

After four years, he had the French on the run and he was not going to let them escape. Marshal Jourdan and King Joseph, Napoleon's own brother, decided to stand at Vitoria among the foothills of the Pyrenees and, as usual, Wellington left nothing to chance. He rode over the ground, studied maps and talked to local goatherds. Then he brought up his guns and troops to the exact positions that he desired, knowing that the one-time rabble of convicts and runaways would not fail him:

"I could have done *anything* with that army," he said proudly, "it was in such splendid order."

At Vitoria, the French fought hard but in the end they reeled back, groping for a way through the mountains, and Wellington followed them into France.

While the armies of Austria, Russia and Germany were massing against Napoleon, Wellington beat the French again, this time on French soil, and he was in the market-place of Toulouse when a colonel rode up from Bordeaux.

"I have extraordinary news, sir," he said, saluting.

Wellington raised two fingers to his hat:

"Aye, I knew we should have peace. I have long expected it."

"No, sir," said the colonel. "Napoleon has abdicated."

"How, abdicated?" cried the Peer. "You don't say so, upon my honour! Abdicated! Hurrah!"

To the astonishment of his staff, their ice-cold general spun round and round, snapping his fingers with delight as he performed a victory jig on the spot.

*   *   *

Arthur Wellesley, now Lord Wellington, had not always been the cool masterful hero. Sixth of nine children, he was regarded as the dunce of the family, and at Eton he made so little progress that his widowed mother Lady Mornington exclaimed crossly:

"I vow to God I do not know what to do with my awkward son Arthur. He wins no prizes at all. Really, he is fit only for gunpowder!"

She took him away from school to Brussels where the lonely unloved boy occupied himself learning French and playing the violin. Since the only place for a dull boy was the Army, he was sent to a French military college.

"If soldiering is to be my profession, I had better try to understand it," he remarked drily.

Away from his mother and his brilliant brothers, he began to enjoy himself and to take an interest in military books and French ideas about war. His older brother Richard bought him a commission in the infantry, and at eighteen Arthur was an ensign in the Seventy-third.

For a time he served on the Staff of the Lord Lieutenant in Ireland where, during the round of parades, parties and balls, he fell in love with Lady Kitty Pakenham, an Irish peer's daughter. But it was hopeless to think of marriage on a junior officer's pay. Perhaps Kitty would wait for him.

"I will give up parties and music and devote myself to being a soldier," he said as he broke his violin in half and put it on the fire. He never played again.

Arthur's prospects brightened when his brother bought him command of an Irish regiment.

His ill-kempt troops and dandified officers soon nicknamed him "Nosey" on account of his large nose and his habit of enquiring into their laziness and dishonesty. Now that war had broken out with revolutionary France, "Nosey" wanted to lead an efficient and well-trained regiment against the enemy.

His chance came when the 33rd was sent to the Low Countries. Unfortunately, the campaign was no more than a continuous retreat across icy plains and Wellesley could only try to preserve his shivering troops.

"I am so disgusted with my senior commanders that I shall leave the Army," he angrily told his brother.

But before he could do so, the regiment was posted to India and in 1797 the Colonel landed at Calcutta to find that India was suffering from famine, banditry and ceaseless wars between rival princes. One of the most powerful rulers was Tippoo Sahib, Sultan of Mysore, who hated the British and was offering to assist the French.

In hard fighting through jungles and across rocky plains, Wellesley defeated Tippoo, stormed his capital and became the real ruler of Mysore. He put down the robber-chieftains and had established order when his borders were threatened by a vast army of the warlike Mahrattas.

By now Wellesley had learnt that the art of making war in a huge parched country lay in organizing supplies for his soldiers:

"If I had bullocks and rice, I had men," he said, "and if I had men, I knew I could beat the enemy."

The defeat of Tippoo at Mysore

In a series of battles, sieges and long slogging marches, he broke the power of the Mahrattas and returned to England as Major-General Sir Arthur Wellesley.

Presently he crossed to Dublin and married Lady Kitty who had waited ten years for her hero. He was now rich and famous and he naturally expected to be given a high command against Napoleon and the all-conquering French. But the old generals pooh-poohed his Indian victories and sent him to take charge of a mere brigade on the south coast.

Suddenly, there was news from Spain. Napoleon had put his brother on the throne and the Spaniards were up in arms. So were the Portuguese whose king had been driven into exile.

"Here is our chance to take a crack at the French!" cried Wellesley to his friend Lord Castlereagh and Sir Arthur was sent to Spain with a small army.

In the years of waiting, he had thought how to beat the French. They fought in dense columns—very well, he would meet them in a double line, having trained his men to hold their fire and to finish the work with the bayonet. The French had splendid artillery—he would post his men in trenches and behind ridges for protection. The French had the best cavalry in the world—he would form his infantry into squares to stand rock-like against the fiercest charges. French armies moved fast, living on food collected on the march but he would set up supply points and follow slowly with store-waggons, as in India.

For Spain reminded him of India. In this vast, hungry land, a small army might be beaten but a big one would certainly starve and Wellesley, the master of feeding his troops, was certain he could beat the French.

His arrival brought the enemy out of Lisbon like a swarm of angry bees and they met him at Vimiero, moving in columns of attack.

"I received them in line which they are not accustomed to," said Sir Arthur. "Volleys halted their columns and the bayonets broke them."

His cavalry charged and the French were defeated. At that moment, a senior general arrived from England to take over command. He ordered a halt.

"But, Sir Harry, we must advance! In three days, we shall be in Lisbon," cried Wellesley indignantly.

But Sir Harry was old and cautious. His delay was supported by an even more senior general who made a truce with the defeated foe and actually agreed to carry them back to France in English ships!

In disgust, Wellesley demanded to be sent home and, since the public shared his disgust, the two elderly generals were brought back to face a Court of Enquiry. Meanwhile, the French crushed the Spaniards and flooded back into Portugal.

When the Court of Enquiry praised Wellesley's conduct, the Government ordered him to resume the struggle. With only 25,000 British soldiers, his task was to clear the Peninsula of 250,000 Frenchmen who hardly knew the meaning of the word defeat.

Wellesley had to go warily. His own troops were poor, the Portuguese were brave but undisciplined and he found the Spaniards useless except as guerrilla fighters.

"But I *am* at the head of the only army in Europe that is capable and willing to fight the French," he said. "And I do not intend to lose my army."

Portugal was to be his base. The Royal Navy would bring supplies; mule-trains and bullock-carts would carry them to his army in the field. He was a plain man in a plain grey coat and a low cocked hat covered with oilskin. There were no valets, cooks, musicians or actresses on his Staff. If the men had bread, meat and sixty rounds of ammunition apiece, he was content.

He drove Marshal Soult out of the north and advanced into Spain, grumbling a bit about his troops:

"They are a rabble—I am endeavouring to tame them. But," he added cheerfully, "the ball is now at my foot and I hope I shall have the strength to kick it".

At Talavera, "after two days of the hardest fighting I have ever been a party to", he beat the French and promptly retreated because his army was half-starved in that barren country and the enemy was massing four huge armies against him. Napoleon sent his best general, "the old fox" Massena, to drive the British into the sea.

That winter, Wellesley waited for the French, drilling his redcoats and his Portuguese "fighting cocks". Aided by thousands of civilians, he built the Lines of Torres Vedras, a series of mounds, ditches and ravines that protected Lisbon.

"Every calf, hen and sack of corn must be brought inside my lines," ordered Wellesley, and when Massena advanced he did so through a bare countryside. After weeks of battering, he was forced to withdraw his starving army and Wellesley followed him into Spain.

In August 1812, now Lord Wellington, he rode into Madrid. High-nosed, looking straight ahead, he took no notice of the frenzied inhabitants who strewed the road with silken shawls, cheered, wept and ran alongside to kiss his sword, his stirrups and even his horse's flanks.

But he lacked the strength to hold Madrid. In driving rain, he led his army back to Portugal and prepared for the final spring. In May 1813 his redcoats, guns, waggons and bridging-teams were ready and, as they crossed the frontier, Wellington flourished his hat and cried, "Farewell, Portugal! I shall never see you again". He never did.

This time he drove the enemy clean out of Spain until, having beaten them all the way, he learned in the market-place of Toulouse that Napoleon had abdicated. "Hurrah!" he cried as he snapped his fingers, "Europe is free!"

In March 1815 the Duke was in Vienna when a servant brought a letter to his room. It stated that Napoleon had escaped from Elba and was on his way to Paris.

As the assembly of princes and statesmen broke up in alarm and the generals scurried away to raise their armies, Wellington calmly ordered a carriage to take him to Brussels.

"It is there or thereabouts that I shall have to meet the Tyrant," he remarked.

As he rattled along, he reflected that it was a pity that his Peninsular veterans were mostly in America or on the high seas.

"Well," he said to himself. "I must make do with whatever troops the Allies can scrape up. At least Blucher, that stout old Prussian, will fight like a man."

Brussels was buzzing with rumours and alarms. Mr. Creevey, an English politician staying in the city, met the Duke in a park and asked him what he thought of his chances. Wellington looked down his long nose at the self-important little man:

"By Heaven!" he snapped. "I think Blucher and myself can do the thing!"

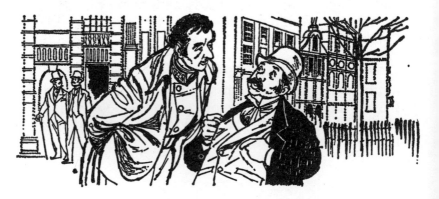

Napoleon, even more confident, defeated Blucher before he could join forces with Wellington. Then he hurled his matchless cavalry against the British and their allies at Quatre Bras. The Duke was at full-stretch to rally his unsteady troops and once, almost surrounded and ahead of his own line, he had to put his horse at a ditch lined with Highlanders.

"Lie still and keep your heads down!" he cried as his horse leapt the obstacle. Then, as cool as ever, his deep voice was heard calling out:

"92nd, don't fire until I tell you."

When he heard of the Prussian defeat, he remarked grimly:

"Old Blucher has had a good hiding and has gone eighteen miles to the rear. We must do the same. I suppose they'll say in England that we were licked. Well, I can't help that."

He shepherded his army back towards Brussels and took up a position along a ridge near the village of Waterloo. The weather was cold and wet but as one of his veterans said to a shivering recruit:

"It's nothing to what we had in Spain with old Nosey."

It was still raining at dawn and Napoleon delayed his attack to allow the ground to dry. There was no need to hurry for he was certain of victory now that Blucher was in full retreat. He was wrong. The tough old Prussian was already urging his troops across the marshes in order to keep his promise to Wellington.

At noon the French attacked. As in Spain, Wellington waited behind the ridge, his men holding their fire until the word of command.

The Battle of Waterloo

"The Emperor did not manoeuvre at all," said the Duke. "He just moved forward in the old style in columns and was driven off in the old style."

Ahead of the line there was desperate fighting round the outposts but the Guards held out all day amid the broken walls of a chateau. Farther back, the infantry formed squares and withstood thunderous cavalry charges as though they were rooted to the ground. Artillerymen blazed away and worked like demons to haul their guns back to safety. The Duke was everywhere. Astride his horse "Copenhagen", he was scribbling orders, galloping to reform a broken line, chiding and encouraging the troops:

"There, my lads, in with you!"

"Ah, that's the way I like to see horse-artillery move!"

"Hard pounding, gentlemen. We shall have to see who can pound the longest."

He ordered the Life Guards to charge and as the
survivors rode back, he was there to meet them, his
hat raised:

"Life Guards, I thank you!"

Towards the end of that awful day, the British
were still holding the ridge when the Prussians were
seen approaching. In a last bid for victory, Napoleon
ordered the invincible Imperial Guard to break the
British line.

To the tap of the drum, they advanced up the slope,
6000 of them in perfect order, Marshal Ney and their
officers walking in front with drawn swords. At sixty
paces, a deep voice called:

"Now, Maitland. Now's your time!"

The British stood up and crashed out their terrible
volley. As the smoke cleared and the Imperial Guard
was seen to waver, a figure on a chestnut horse
pointed with a cocked hat. The line sprang forward.

That night the vengeful Prussians kept up the pursuit, but back at Waterloo Wellington waited at his headquarters, watching the door for the men who would not come back. In the morning, they brought him the lists of the dead and the Iron Duke wept.

He returned grim-faced to Brussels where busy Mr. Creevey came to ask him how the battle went.

"It has been a dam' serious business," he replied. "Blucher and I have lost 30,000 men. It was the nearest run thing you ever saw in your life."

He walked up and down, praising the courage of his men, courage that astonished even him.

"Yes, a close-run thing," he said, adding almost to himself, "By Heaven! I don't think it would have done if I had not been there!"

Elizabeth Garrett Anderson

EVEN before *Lucy* had nosed alongside the rickety timbers of Slaughden Quay, Mr. Garrett was bawling orders to the men ashore.

"Harry, bring the cart nearer! Lambert, don't drive forward. Back the mare, you fool! Albert, you come aboard for the boxes!"

A landing-plank was heaved into place. Boxes, chairs, tables and trunks were trundled on to the quay and hoisted into the waiting carts. Having seen to everything, Mr. Garrett turned jovially to his wife and two little girls who were clutching their mother's skirts in a fever of excitement.

"Now, my dear," he boomed. "You take Louie's hand and I'll have Lizzie. Upsadaisy, my pigeon."

With Lizzie on his shoulder, he handed Mrs. Garrett ashore and soon they were rattling along the High Street to their new home on Church Hill.

It was 1840 and the Garretts had come from London to settle at Aldeburgh on the Suffolk coast. The town consisted of three rows of forlorn cottages straggling for half a mile between the shingle beach and the marshes. There were no industries, apart from fishing, and it seemed a strange place for an energetic young man to choose to set up in business.

However, within a few years, Newson Garrett had made a comfortable fortune and for his growing family—there were to be ten children altogether—he built himself the biggest house in the town.

The Garrett children loved Aldeburgh. All summer, they swam, picnicked and ran wild. Led by Lizzie, they explored the marshes, fished, sailed and rode their ponies across the windy heathlands.

In all their games they had the boisterous support of their father. Newson Garrett was a character. He quarrelled with the parson, the town councillors and his own workmen; he had a voice like a bull and a heart as soft as butter. Everyone knew that the master's bark was worse than his bite and his children adored him but, like their father, they stood in awe of their pretty mother.

Mrs. Garrett was absolute mistress of Alde House and when she remarked one day:

"Newson, it's time those girls had a governess," Mr. Garrett did not argue. Within a week, Miss Edgeworth arrived from London.

Poor Miss Edgeworth, in her shabby bonnet, was a typical Victorian governess. Prim and ill-educated, her one aim was to please her employer, but she had no idea how to teach lively children like the Garretts.

She owned three books—Mangnall's *Questions*, Slater's *Book of Dates* and a volume of French verbs. These and a set of rules for "ladylike behaviour" were her sole equipment for teaching. Mornings in the schoolroom were torture but the afternoon walks were worse. Miss Edgeworth did not let up for one minute:

"No talking, if you please! Elizabeth, hold up your head! Milly, do not lag behind and put down that flower at once! Louie, repeat to me your list of verbs."

There was no escape from "the enemy" until the older girls discovered a way to confuse Miss Edgeworth. Secretly, they studied her horrid books until they knew them better than she did and then they would trap her with difficult questions. "Oo, Miss Edgeworth, yesterday you said the opposite to that," they would shrill gleefully.

Mrs. Garrett was distressed by their naughtiness.

"I am afraid that Miss Edgeworth cannot manage our girls," she sighed.

"The woman's a fool!" snorted Mr. Garrett. "Better send 'em away to school."

At Blackheath, in south London, there was a genteel finishing school for young ladies run by the two Miss Brownings. After their experience of a governess, Lizzie and Louie loved it. They made many friends and they liked the gentle Miss Brownings with their passion for fresh air and French conversation. After two years, the girls were considered "finished" and they came home to Aldeburgh.

In Victorian days, young ladies helped to teach their small brothers and sisters, visited the poor and attended tea-parties until they married. At twenty-two, Louie married the brother of a school friend and went away to live in London but Elizabeth showed no sign of following her sister's example.

One day, she went into her father's study and said, "Father, Jane and Annie Crowe have written to ask if I may pay them a visit."

"So you shall, my dear. Your mother can spare you, now that Alice manages the little ones so nicely."

"And, Father, while I am away, I want to think what I shall do with my life."

Mr. Garrett was puzzled. Girls got married. Why should Lizzie think about anything else? With her fine eyes and determined chin, she was his favourite daughter. Didn't Mother say, "Dear Lizzie takes after Father"?

"Are you not happy at home?" he asked gently.

"Oh yes, but I want to *do* something, to use the mind that God gave me."

During her holiday, Elizabeth met Emily Davies, the vicar's daughter, a fiery little person with some very strange ideas about the position of women.

"What are we fitted for in life?" she demanded. "For marriage and nothing else! Men make us into the dear dull creatures they admire. They won't let us use our brains!"

Elizabeth and Emily became close friends. They talked about things that would have shocked Mrs. Garrett and wrote long letters about their hopes of having a career. In London, they stayed with Louie and were thrilled to meet some ladies who talked about jobs for women. They went to hear a lady from America who had actually qualified as a doctor.

When Elizabeth heard this slight pale woman say, "I never thought about failure", she vowed that she too would never admit defeat. After the lecture, Elizabeth was introduced to the speaker who looked at her keenly and said:

"I noticed you in the audience. You have more strength than I had and I know you will succeed as a doctor."

A woman doctor! The idea was absurd in England. "I felt," said Elizabeth, "as if I were thrust into something too big for me." But, as the weeks passed, the idea would not leave her.

She wrote to Emily. They discussed the difficulties —examinations, Latin, chemistry and other subjects that girls were never taught. And she would have to tell her parents. It was not too difficult to speak to Father but to tell Mother was another matter.

Mrs. Garrett was horrified. She retired to her room and made herself ill with weeping. Lizzie set her obstinate mouth and went to the local schoolmaster for Latin lessons.

Mr. Garrett was too fond of his daughter to let her battle alone. In June 1860, the two of them went to London to call upon the leading doctors for advice.

"Women would make bad doctors," said a famous surgeon coldly. "Moreover, it would be extremely improper for them to work alongside gentlemen-students. I bid you Good-day, ma'am."

As the day wore on, Mr. Garrett's fatherly pride was wounded by these sneering fellows in frock-coats and in the cab on the way to Louie's, he burst out:

"Drat me, Lizzie, if we don't beat the pack of them!"

From that day, it was his struggle as well as Elizabeth's and he never failed to support her with money and encouragement. Through friends, he arranged an introduction to Mr. Hawes who was on the Board of the Middlesex Hospital.

"I do not think that a young lady will be able to stand the sights and smells of a hospital ward," said Mr. Hawes earnestly. "But you seem determined to try so I can arrange for you to spend six months as a nurse."

Armed with a linen apron and notebook, Elizabeth

384

presented herself to the Matron and was taken to meet the nurses. Believing her to be a rich lady with an interest in the sick, they offered to cook for her and to do her laundry during her stay.

"No, thank you," smiled Elizabeth. "I would like to do all the work of a nurse, just as it is."

Mr. Nunn, Dean of the Medical School, Dr. Willis, the senior surgeon, and Mr. Plaskitt, the apothecary, were charming and polite. Like the nurses, they had no idea what was in Elizabeth's mind.

Presently, she followed her new friends into the surgical ward. A sickening smell unnerved her for a moment but she went forward to look at the festering stump of a leg amputated below the knee.

At this time, very little was known about germs and a surgeon would put on his oldest and filthiest frock-coat for an operation and would wash his hands after but not before an amputation. As a result, surgery was desperately risky and many patients were certain to die from simple operations.

But, after the first shocks, Elizabeth found the work fascinating. Soon, she was writing to Emily:

"I begin my day by preparing lint, lotion, poultices, bandages and various ointments. While I am doing this, the sister goes round examining all the wounds. The simpler cases she now leaves to me entirely. The doctors are uncommonly civil to me . . ."

They remained civil until their visitor applied to become a medical student.

"My dear young lady, how on earth can I admit you as a student?" said the College Treasurer with amused contempt.

"By allowing me to pay the usual fees," replied Elizabeth.

"You may certainly make a donation to the Hospital and continue as an observer, but a student, oh dear me no!"

Elizabeth said no more but, one morning, she slipped into the chemistry laboratory with the men-students. Apart from a few whistles and raised eyebrows, they said nothing and if the lecturer saw her, he gave no sign.

Emboldened by this success, Elizabeth asked the Dean if she could enter the dissecting-room.

"Well, I suppose we might give it a trial," mused Mr. Nunn.

Elizabeth could have kissed him. She felt that she was now accepted as a real student and she worked so hard that she gained honours in every class examination.

"I beg you to keep your marks a secret," warned one of the examiners but when a physician asked a difficult question that reduced the class to silence,

Elizabeth could not help blurting out the correct answer.

Next day, her friend Mr. Plaskitt took her aside:

"Miss Garrett, I implore you not to go into lectures today. The students have signed a petition to have you dismissed."

"But why? What harm have I done them?"

"None, but they say they are being made to look silly by a lady who has no right to be here. The College is considering the matter this morning."

At lunchtime, Elizabeth's friends avoided her. The Dean and even Mr. Plaskitt were absent but she spied Dr. Thompson, a kindly physician. He would tell her what the Council had decided.

The doctor looked upset. He coughed and took out his watch as if in a hurry.

"My dear young lady," he mumbled. "Most distressing affair . . . presence of female students considered unsuitable . . . great regret . . ."

He pressed her hand, gave her a little pat of sympathy and hurried away. Elizabeth understood his meaning. After a year, the most exciting year of her life, she must go, and with her head held high to keep back the tears, she walked out of the Hospital.

At Alde House, there were thirteen cousins staying for the holidays so, between picnics and parties, it was as much as Elizabeth could do to slip away to an attic with her books. At all costs, she must keep up her studies in the hope that a college somewhere would accept her.

She wrote letter after letter and the replies were always the same. Oxford, Cambridge, London, Edinburgh, Glasgow and Dundee universities all refused to admit a woman student. The College of Surgeons would not even allow her to take its diploma for midwifery.

Fuming with indignation, Mr. Garrett took a hand. He and Elizabeth discovered that the Society of Apothecaries was bound to examine anyone who completed a five years' apprenticeship:

"Right," cried Mr. Garrett, "we'll creep through that loophole, Lizzie, my love."

When Mr. Plaskitt agreed to accept Elizabeth as his "apprentice", it seemed certain that she would qualify as a doctor but it was not what she really wanted.

"A medical degree, even a foreign one, would win more respect than an apothecary's licence," she said.

There was just a chance that St. Andrews University might accept her, so she travelled to Scotland, where "a dear old buffer actually wrote my name in the register and gave me a card with the magic words STUDENT OF ST. ANDREWS UNIVERSITY beneath my name."

Alas, the authorities demanded the card back and she had to take private lessons both in Scotland and in London.

"What I need most of all is surgical knowledge," she lamented. "There are no dissecting-rooms open to me and Dr. H. has written me the rudest letter when I asked him for lessons in anatomy."

"I will pay for you to study in America," replied her father.

"No," she answered. "For the sake of women in England, I must qualify in England, just to prove that it can be done."

Her obstinacy was rewarded for, in 1864, she won permission to visit the London Hospital where she gained her first experience of midwifery in the slums of Stepney.

"I worked all night on a difficult case," she told Emily, "and my kind doctor allowed me to carry out the operation. He let me do everything apart from giving the chloroform. It wasn't easy but I enjoyed it immensely."

By autumn, she had completed the course for the Society of Apothecaries and she applied to take the examination.

Forgetting their own rules, the examiners refused to accept a woman candidate but they had Mr. Garrett to deal with.

"I will sue you in every Court in the kingdom!" he thundered and the Society yielded. Elizabeth passed so high that the examiners declared it was a mercy they did not have to publish the list in order of merit for, in that case, they must have given first place to Miss Garrett.

She had done it! At long, long last, she was a doctor, the first woman to qualify in England.

As proud and happy as if he himself had qualified, Mr. Garrett took a house for Elizabeth in Upper Berkeley Street, London.

"We must put your name on the door, Lizzie," he said. "I have ordered a brass-plate with 'Doctor Garrett' on it."

"Oh, Father, do you not think that the title will put some strangers off. I want poor people, especially women, to know that a woman doctor lives here."

"Then 'Miss Garrett' will do very well."

"That sounds like a dress-maker. Let us put, quite simply, 'Elizabeth Garrett, L.S.A.' "

Robert Baden-Powell

HE was a boy of medium-size, with freckles and red curly hair. At thirteen, he was not very good at games or lessons and his school-mates regarded Baden-Powell as an amusing card who could draw funny pictures with either hand and make them laugh with his comic songs and imitations.

Unknown to most of them, B-P had invented a secret game. Near the school was a stretch of wood-land known as The Copse. It was out-of-bounds but this did not prevent B-P and two or three of his closest friends from going there on half-holidays. Years later, he confessed:

"In the Copse, I learned to snare rabbits and to cook them over the tiny fire of the bushman. I learned to use an axe and to move through the bush. I knew how to hide my tracks, to climb a tree and 'freeze' there while the authorities passed below."

Holidays were even more exciting than school for, besides enjoying tramping expeditions in Wales, Robert was cabin-boy aboard his brother's 5-ton yacht when they sailed her round Scotland to Norway.

At nineteen he had not made up his mind about a career. Half-heartedly, he sat for an Army examina-tion, and to everyone's surprise he passed so high that he was excused the usual officer-training at Sandhurst. Instead, he was gazetted a sub-lieutenant in the 13th Hussars stationed in India.

In the eighteen-seventies, most officers were wealthy young men who enjoyed sport and the gay life of British India with little thought for the soldiers in the ranks. B-P however had to live on his pay and he showed an unusual enthusiasm for soldiering and for looking after his men. At camp concerts he became enormously popular as a comic turn, though some of the officers looked down their noses at his foolery.

Some years later, a young officer named Churchill was laughing loudly at a brilliantly funny performance in a regimental concert:

"That's Baden-Powell," whispered his companion. "An amazing chap. Has seen no end of active service, is a marvellous polo player and is a coming man. But fancy a senior officer kicking up his legs on the stage like that!"

Along the North-West Frontier the army was constantly in action against the fierce tribesmen, and in this barren mountainous land it was dangerous to move troops without knowledge of the enemy's whereabouts. Young Baden-Powell made a name for his ability to scout ahead of the main force with small patrols that he trained himself. He taught them the skills he had begun to learn in The Copse—how to move silently, to observe the tiniest evidence of enemy movement, to remember landmarks and patches of cover.

He had been promoted Captain when the regiment returned to England for a spell of home duty. This was too quiet for B-P and he obtained permission to go to Russia with his younger brother, an officer in the Scots Guards.

In order to find out about some secret search-lights and observation-balloons, the brothers each bought a Russian civilian hat and coolly walked into a fort and examined the equipment as though they were Russian military experts. With similar impudence, they were watching some important manoeuvres when B-P was arrested as a spy. However, he managed to warn his brother and, on the way to prison, he gave his guards the slip and escaped to a ship that carried him safely home.

M.W.4—4 393

After another Secret Service trip, B-P was sent to South Africa where the Zulus had rebelled against the rule of white men. It was during this campaign that he first heard the Een-Gonyama chorus that he was later to introduce to the Boy Scouts. In honour of their chief, the Zulu warriors chanted:

"Een-Gonyama! Gonyama! Invooboo!
Yabo! Yabo! Invooboo!"

meaning:

"He is a lion, a lion! He is a hippopotamus!
Yes, sir! Yes, sir! He is a hippopotamus!"

During the Ashanti campaign in West Africa, B-P commanded native troops whose duty was to scout ahead of the army through dense jungle criss-crossed by swift streams. For this work he found it best to divide the men into small companies, each under a patrol-leader. He himself took to wearing a wide-brimmed "cowboy" hat to protect his face from low branches and, in the open, from the fierce African sun. He also found it useful to carry a long pole marked in feet and inches for this helped him to cross streams, to test swampy ground and to make quick measurements.

For his good work in West Africa, B-P was promoted Lieutenant-Colonel and, soon afterwards, he took part in the Matabele War, "my best adventure", as he called it.

In wild, hilly country, small British forces were trying to subdue a brave wily enemy and it was B-P's job to track down the tribesmen and discover their strongholds. By day he organized operations and at night he went out alone or with a single companion into the Matoppo Hills.

A war correspondent wrote this about him:

"Wearing soft rubber-soled shoes, B-P used to spend nights prowling about, spying on the rebels, calculating their numbers and locating their camping-grounds. One night he took me with him. Walking with an easy swing, he stepped into the darkness amidst the giant boulders of the Matoppos where he seemed completely at home. He led me by a rough path on to a kop. Peering over, we could see, not 500 yards away, the fires of an impi (native force). Signing me to be silent, we watched for a few minutes and presently moved off by another path. 'Never return by the same road,' he whispered. It was with a sigh of relief that I found myself back in camp. I never asked to be taken again."

The Matabele warriors gained so great a respect for the Colonel who harried them that they named him "Impeesa"—"the wolf that never sleeps".

In 1899 B-P was sent to Rhodesia with orders to train two mounted regiments and he had just taken up his headquarters in the town of Mafeking when the Boers declared war on Britain.

Mafeking, an outpost town in the veldt, contained stores of food and railway equipment but it had no defences. B-P immediately set to work to build a 7-mile ring of forts and earthworks connected to his H.Q. by trenches and telephone lines. Wells were dug and shelters prepared for the civilian population since the town contained about 250 white persons and 8000 natives of the Baralong tribe.

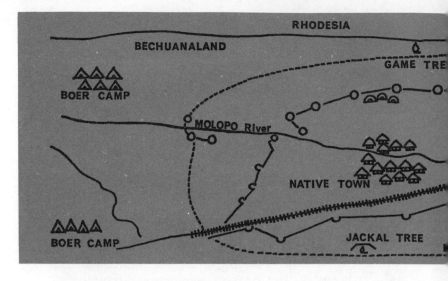

To hold this outpost B-P had only 1250 soldiers
and no artillery apart from seven small guns that
were old and almost useless. However, his slender
force had manned the forts and the Colonel was up
in his look-out post when the Boer army was seen
approaching.

General Cronje surrounded Mafeking with 10,000
men and began a bombardment. After several hours,
he sent a messenger under flag of truce demanding
surrender "to prevent further bloodshed".

"What bloodshed?" enquired B-P. "Tell your
general that I shall be obliged to know when it starts.
So far, the only blood shed has been one chicken's!"

During the siege that followed, B-P kept up the
townsfolk's spirits by posting up copies of his impudent replies to the Boer commander. He started a
newspaper, the *Mafeking Mail*, that was issued daily,
"shells permitting", and he devised all kinds of tricks
to deceive the enemy.

Bogus orders were blared through camp mega-

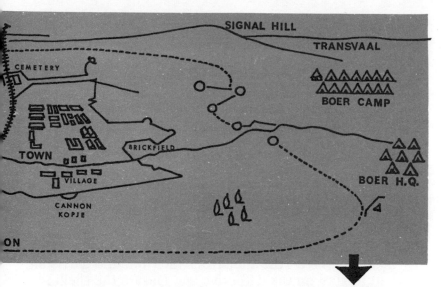

SIGNAL HILL

TRANSVAAL

CEMETERY

BOER CAMP

TOWN

BRICKFIELD

VILLAGE

BOER H.Q.

CANNON
KOPJE

ON

SOUTH

phones, dummy figures were placed in the
forts and false information was allowed to fall into the
hands of spies inside the town. To discourage night-
attacks, B-P pretended that he was well supplied with
search-lights—actually he had only one, made out of a
biscuit-tin nailed to a pole, but at night it was rushed
round from one fort to another, giving out a few
flashes at each to make it seem as if a whole series
of searchlights was being tested.

Not content merely to sit still and await relief,
B-P soon went on the attack and pushed back the
Boer lines by night charges and by using a train that
puffed up and down, its crew firing at the enemy
until the lines were destroyed. The lack of artillery
was partly overcome when the railwaymen made a
howitzer called "The Wolf" out of a steam-pipe
reinforced with iron railings and they provided iron
cannon-balls for an old 18th century gun-barrel
that someone discovered was being used as a gate-
post!

397

"It was all a game of bluff from start to finish," said B-P but as the weeks turned into months he knew that the position was serious. To keep boredom at bay, he organized games, competitions, concerts and even a baby-show but the greatest worry was food. Horses, dogs and mules were killed to eke out the rations. Nothing was wasted and when the skins and bones had been boiled for brawn and soup, even the manes and tails were used to stuff mattresses in the hospital.

Fifty men were killed in an attack on a Boer post at Game Tree Hill and, from then on, the garrison had to stay on the defensive and endure the shelling.

After seven months, news began to filter into the town that the British were advancing. At this, the Boers redoubled their efforts and they succeeded in breaking in at one point until B-P, watching from his tower, regrouped his forces and drove them out.

At last the Boers could be seen withdrawing and from distant hills General Plumer flashed a message, "How are you getting on?" B-P replied in one word, "Welcome!"

At seven that evening, the British force entered Mafeking. The siege was over. "We all tried to speak at once," said an engineer. "But we could only gaze at each other and say senseless things like 'By Jove!' and 'Well, I'm hanged!' One man tried to cheer, buried his face in his hands and sobbed. It had been 217 days."

The joy of the Mafeking garrison was nothing compared with the outburst in Britain. On "Mafeking Night", people went mad, lit bonfires and danced in the streets. Baden-Powell was a public hero.

His picture was everywhere, the Queen sent her personal congratulations and he was promoted to the rank of General, the youngest general in the British Army.

It was several years before B-P reached England, where he found himself famous, not only because of Mafeking but because of a little book he had written called *Aids to Scouting*. In it, to help young soldiers, he had described what he had learned in India and Africa about tracking, observation, map-work and even spying.

The book turned out to be a best-seller. Thousands of copies were supplied to soldiers embarking for the war and, more surprisingly, schoolmasters, Boys' Brigade officers and club leaders bought it because the book was full of ideas that appealed to boys.

B-P found so much enthusiasm for the kind of woodcraft and outdoor activities that he described, that he decided to hold an experimental camp. Twenty boys were invited to Brownsea Island where they were divided into four "patrols" called Wolves, Curlews, Bulls and Ravens. There was no uniform but each was asked to bring "shorts", a most unusual garment in those days.

Each morning, the camp was roused at 6 a.m. by a Koodoo horn that B-P had captured in Africa and the day was given over to tracking, stalking, life-saving and boating. The boys also had the usual chores of camping. There were games, night patrols and expeditions to allow the boys to cook and fend for themselves and the day usually ended with camp-fire yarns and the Een-Gonyama chorus.

This camp at Brownsea Island was the start of the Boy Scout Movement. Having seen the boys' terrific enthusiasm, B-P re-wrote his soldiers' handbook and called it *Scouting for Boys*. In 1908 the book appeared in fortnightly parts and almost at once thousands of boys began to form their own scout troops.

Within a year B-P was faced with the problem of 60,000 scouts with no rules, uniforms or leaders. He never meant this to happen.

"I did not intend to have a separate organization of Boy Scouts," he said. "I hoped the Boys' Brigade and the Y.M.C.A. would use the idea. But the movement grew up of itself."

Some alarming stories reached him. One boy read the book and went off and organized a gang of his own. They set fire to some property while trying to light a camp-fire, got marooned on top of a church tower and, having been rescued, put out to sea on a home-made raft and were brought back by life-boat! Enthusiastic youngsters like these clearly needed B-P's help. But he was a senior Army officer. Should he not devote himself to his real career rather than to a boys' movement that might fizzle out as quickly as it had begun?

The War Office solved his problem by suddenly placing him on the retired list. It is still a mystery why this able soldier was put on one side at the age of fifty but, as Sir Winston Churchill said, "How lucky for him and how lucky for us all".

At once B-P threw himself heart and soul into the new work. He toured the country, explaining the idea of Scouting, appealing for funds and help from anyone who was interested. He was a humorous speaker with dozens of stories from his adventures and the public soon realized that a new Movement had arrived. What kind of movement was it?

Some people expected that a retired General would turn boys into little soldiers. They wanted drill and Army discipline. Others felt that scouting ought to be linked to their Church. Some wanted B-P to forbid drink, smoking, Sunday games or some other pet dislike.

M.W.—26

B-P was firm with these well-meaning people.

"Scouting is merely a step to help develop a boy into a capable and happy man," he said. "Scouting is fun."

He wanted as few rules as possible, merely a simple law or promise so that boys of every kind and religion could come in. Friendly with everyone, he still followed his own ideals. The Scout Headquarters was set up to train scoutmasters and to obtain funds and camping-sites. There was a weekly magazine in which B-P wrote articles illustrated by his own comical sketches and he devised a uniform based upon what his men wore in the South African Constabulary—the wide-brimmed hat, the shorts and tough shirt, the scarf that could be used as a sling or bandage and the staff marked in feet and inches.

When a system of badges was started, B-P fought hard to prevent badges becoming another kind of examination:

"Scouting is a GAME!" he cried. "If a boy is a *trier*, no matter how clumsy, his examiner can award him the badge and this will inspire him to go on trying."

As early as 1909 the scouts made their first big public appearance when 10,000 Boy Scouts gathered at the Crystal Palace. B-P was going round to see various activities when he came across a small band of girls wearing scout hats and scarves. He stopped, looked them up and down and his eyes twinkled as he asked who they were.

"Please, we are Girl Scouts and we want to do scouting like the boys."

Thus the Girl Guide Movement came into being. Wolf Cubs, Brownies, Sea Scouts and Rovers were founded for the same reason—simply because boys and girls wanted to take part in the movement that B-P had started.

He devoted the rest of his life to scouting, travelling all over the world to encourage new associations that were springing up. Always he was lecturing, writing and sketching because his books and articles paid for his journeys and did not cost the scout movement a penny. Yet he never seemed to be harassed or overworked. Scouting was fun and the Chief Scout enjoyed it all.

There were huge Jamborees when thousands of Scouts from dozens of nations travelled to London, Denmark, Australia, Hungary and Holland. On these occasions, no man was more hero-worshipped than B-P but he remained as humorous and modest as ever. Over and over again, scouts found themselves chatting to a friendly scoutmaster who asked them questions, teased them a bit and got them to talk about their homes and interests. Only later did they discover that he was Chief Scout of the world.

At Pax Hill in Hampshire scouts were always welcome to camp in his grounds and if they woke early enough, they might see the Chief (who slept out of doors winter and summer) up and about at five o'clock, walking with his dogs, gardening or writing some of those innumerable letters and articles before most people had breakfasted. But he had time to joke with the smallest scout and to put him at ease—"A scout is a brother to every other scout", he would say.

He was over eighty when he went to South Africa to see how the scouts were faring in the country he loved. His health failed and he settled in Kenya where he continued to write and to draw the wild animals that came almost to his door.

B-P died there in 1941 and among his papers were found messages to Boy Scouts and Girl Guides. The last words he wrote were these:

"The most worthwhile thing is to try and put a bit of happiness into the lives of others."

Lord
Nuffield

THE bicycle stood ready. It had been mended and was almost as good as new.

"How much, boy?" asked the undergraduate.

"Front fork straightened, new spokes, brake blocks—four shillings," replied the boy. He took the money, wrote the amount in a small notebook and turned to get on with another repair job.

William Richard Morris was fifteen, a wiry little chap with a thatch of dark hair and a determined jaw. As he worked he was adding up in his mind the value of the repairs he had done that week. Already it came to several times the five-shillings wage that he would receive on Saturday.

Presently, the boy's employer came into the shop.

"If you please, I wish to ask for a rise of a shilling a week," said William abruptly.

"Five shillings is a very good wage, Morris, and it's all you'll get from me!"

William wiped his hands on a piece of rag and took his cap from a nail.

"It's all you'll ever pay me," he said. "Good morning."

When he reached his home in James Street, Oxford, William's mother was alarmed to learn that her son had given himself the sack.

"What will you do now? Whom will you work for?" she asked.

"I have decided that no-one will pay me such good wages as W. R. Morris, so I am going to work for him!" he replied loftily.

William's father was a mild, easy-going man who had never earned much money and, when he came home for dinner, he raised no objection to his son's plan.

"Why not start in our garden shed?" he said. "It only wants sweeping out but we'll have to buy a bench and a few tools."

Thus, in 1892, Will Morris set up in business as a cycle repairer. Nearly everyone in Oxford went to work or to college by bicycle and there were plenty of repairs for a willing lad who would work until midnight to get a job finished.

One day Mr. Pilcher, the rector, called in at James Street. He was a very tall man and he needed an exceptionally large bicycle. Could William make one for him?

Young Morris made up a bicycle with a 27-inch frame to which he added 28-inch wheels and best-quality fittings. Mr. Pilcher was delighted and there could have been no better advertisement than the sight of the rector's outsize bicycle in the streets of Oxford.

Having made one machine, William began to make others and it was not long before he was using his mother's front parlour as a showroom. Larger premises were needed so he decided to rent a shop in the High Street and to advertise himself as:

"W. R. Morris, Practical Cycle Maker and Repairer. Sole maker of the celebrated Morris cycles."

In order to prove his bicycles, Morris took up cycle-racing with the same determination as he did everything else. Having made a light-weight machine, he started training late at night, and since he was strong and had no thought of being anywhere but first, he soon won several cups and medals. By 1900 he was champion of three counties and had held the one-mile and the fifteen-mile championship cups for two years. One more win would make the cups his own property but, for some reason, the races were not held for a couple of seasons. Then a letter arrived asking for the return of the cups since the organizers assumed that Morris had retired from racing.

"That's where they're wrong," snorted W. R. "Alfred, get my racer out, I'm starting training tonight. Those cups are not leaving our shop window!"

There was only a fortnight and his shoulders and leg-muscles ached abominably for the first few days but he trained hard and in the mile race, he got away fast to discourage the others. Only one rider was able to keep with him but, with 400 yards to go, he was almost exhausted.

"I was desperately tired," he said, "but I thought to myself that the other fellow must be tired too. It was a question of who could hang on longest and I did."

He won by a length and, in the fifteen-mile race, he again set such a pace that the rest of the field dropped out and he finished alone. Morris kept the cups.

Business was so good that a disused stable had to be rented as a workshop and the staff of W. R. Morris, Cycle Maker, grew to five men and two boys, one of them Alfred Keen, a tiny little chap, a brilliant mechanic, who stayed with the "Boss" for fifty years. Like the rest of the staff, Alfred wore a white jersey embroidered back and front with the words: "Ride Morris Cycles."

Bicycles brought in good money but it was the new motor-cars that really interested W. R. and whenever a car broke down in the High Street, he was quickly on the spot. Engines fascinated him and he missed no opportunity to find out how they worked and why they went wrong.

"I never had a lesson on an engine," he boasted, "but once I saw a thing done, I could do it myself."

After various experiments, Morris fitted a $2\frac{3}{4}$ h.p. de Dion engine to one of his cycle frames. The frame was specially strengthened and the driving-chain was enclosed in a metal casing in order to keep out dirt and rain.

"Alfred, we'll build two models for the Cycle Show," he cried triumphantly.

The parts were ordered but, with only a few days to go, they had not arrived. Morris took off his jacket:

"I'll have to make them myself," he said.

For four days and nights, he worked without stopping, except for an occasional nap in a chair.

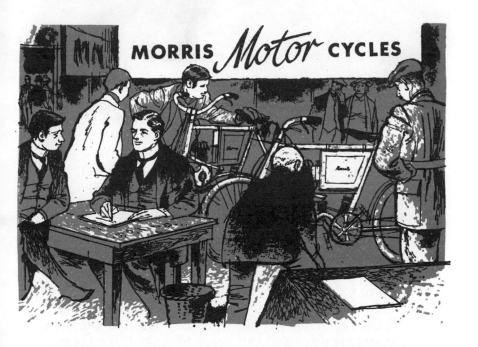

MORRIS *Motor* CYCLES

When the machines were finished, he decided to take
them himself to London and he arrived at the
Exhibition Hall just in time to put his cycles on their
stand. Presently he was taking orders for the first
Morris motor-vehicle and this success enabled him
to open a garage for motor-car repairs.

One day a wealthy undergraduate walked in and
asked to speak to him. He and a friend were keen to
go into the motor-business if they could find a partner
with the necessary knowledge of engines. Would he
care to join them?

Thus, *The Oxford Automobile and Cycle Agency*
was born. Workshops and a showroom were opened
but while Morris worked day and night, his partners
spent money like water. Not surprisingly, the business
collapsed, and in 1904 Morris had nothing left but
his own kit of tools.

"I'll have to start again from the floor," he said grimly. "And I've learnt one or two things. Never spend an unnecessary penny. Put every ha'penny into production and never trust those educated college gentlemen!"

He went back to the shed in James Street. It was a hard year, for he now had a young wife to support, but his name was good and he still made the best bicycles in Oxford.

By now all kinds of motor-cars were coming on to the road and most of them gave trouble. Morris carried out repairs and, one night, working late, he said to his wife when she came to call him for supper:

"Look at this thing! Much too complicated and expensive. What people want is a reliable car at a reasonable price and I'm going to make it for them!"

Meanwhile, he drove round the country, demonstrating new cars, testing and delivering them. It was lowly work for a man with big ideas but as soon as he reached home, his spirits rose. He would hurry to his workshop for there, at the far end, was the car that he was building. Canvas hood, wooden running-board, brass-rimmed headlamps and bull-nosed radiator had been assembled by his own hands and because he made it in his own city, he called it the Morris-Oxford.

The new car appeared in the 1912 Motor Show and was praised by the experts. It was "a two-seated flush torpedo, painted pearl-grey, upholstered in leather and brass-mounted". Under the snub-nosed bonnet was a 10 h.p. water-cooled engine and the car "complete and ready for the road" was priced at £175.

Several dealers ordered the new Morris-Oxford, so William found a backer and moved to a disused school next to Cowley Church. The main school-room became the assembly space and above, in a loft, was the paint-shop staffed by Bill Anstey and a boy. William's father became clerk to the firm that numbered twelve workers including the Boss. He himself took the headmaster's study for his office where he placed above the mantel-piece a glass-case containing his cycling medals.

On the school-room floor were laid out the parts for each car—chassis, axle, transmission-set, engine, gear-box etc. While the parts were hammered and bolted together, Bill Anstey and the boy painted the wheels grey or blue and let them down on a rope from the loft. The wheels were fitted, a box was tied on the chassis and a lad named George Lucas jumped on and drove the car out of the works, up a hill and back again. Having been tested, it was ready for the finishing touches—body, mudguard, hood, lamps.

Sometimes the works turned out as many as thirty cars in a week and still the orders came in for more. Morris, known as "Uncle" to the men, was salesman, buyer, engineer, designer and inspector. His pale blue eyes were as sharp as gimlets and his tongue was merciless to anyone who scamped a job. He drove the men hard but he filled them with his own enthusiasm whether it was for work or for football.

The greatest problem was to find suppliers who could deliver the parts that Morris needed, for the British motor-trade was not used to being hustled. A Birmingham manufacturer once telephoned White and Poppe who made the Morris-Oxford engines.

The new assembly-line layout

"Mr. Poppe, there's a crazy young fellow here from Oxford. His name is Morris and he wants us to supply him with 3000 transmission-sets. Is he all right? Has he got the money?"

Mr. Poppe answered briefly:

"Morris is all right. At least, I hope he is—I've just agreed to make him 3000 engines!"

But W. R. was never satisfied. In 1914, determined to find out how Henry Ford turned out such vast numbers of cars, he sailed to New York, taking with him a brilliant Norwegian designer named "Pop" Landstad. In America he went to see manufacturers who could supply parts more cheaply than in England, and as he went round their factories he kept a sharp look-out for ideas that would be useful. Then he would rush back to his hotel where Landstad put the ideas on to his drawing-board.

Having placed some big orders, Morris returned to Oxford eager to bring out a bigger car called the Morris Cowley. But the Great War started.

For four years weapons were more important than cars and the Morris works turned out hand-grenades, shell-cases and special parts for sea-mines required by the Navy. A few models of the Morris Cowley were made in a corner of the factory but when the

war ended there was only a small stock of parts and the American firms could supply no more.

"We can make a start with what's left of the stock," said Morris to Landstad, "but we must get engines from somewhere."

In Coventry he found a firm named Hotchkiss that was short of work and he took along Landstad's drawings of the American engine.

"Can you make this for £50?" he asked.

The chief engineer looked doubtful.

"It's a very keen price," he said, "but we will do it."

Thus the excellent Morris-Hotchkiss 11·9 h.p. engine came to be used in the new Morris cars. A radiator firm was in difficulties, so W. R. bought it and when the firm that supplied car-bodies could not keep up with his orders, he bought that too. But most parts were made for him by independent firms.

"I only buy a concern when they can't produce enough for my programme," he remarked.

The Cowley works were enlarged and laid out in a new way. Instead of the men moving about from one job to another, W. R. put them into sections that dealt with only one part—the wheels were fitted to the chassis and the car was pushed to the next section that fitted the engine and so on until the car reached the paint-shop. A man did the same job all day long and if his work was less interesting than in the old days, his pay was good and the cars rolled out in ever-increasing numbers.

Morris was still the Boss who worked longer and harder than anyone else and he collected a team of brilliant men to carry out his ideas.

"All of us worshipped the ground W. R. Morris walked on," said Miles Thomas. "His wish was our command. He was a lonely man for the reason that he strongly preferred to think alone."

He inspired everyone who worked for him yet he could be strangely touchy and mean.

For years he was on bad terms with the heads of Oxford University and suspicious of anyone with a "college education". In the early days, a wealthy friend who had put £35,000 into his business once found Morris busy at a bench testing some carburettors.

"What are you doing?" he said jokingly. "Why don't you leave that job to experts who understand it?" Morris's face darkened. He was proud of his engineering skill and had made a special study of carburettors. He said nothing but next day he called on his bank manager. Was his account strong enough to write a big cheque? It was? Good. He sent a cheque for £35,000 to his friend and never spoke to him again.

Yet this lonely, ruthless man would take the closest interest in a workman who was seriously ill and would have him treated at his own expense. A tramp at his door was certain of a meal and tobacco and on more than one occasion the owner of an ancient Morris-

Oxford was astonished to have it completely over-hauled for nothing.

After the war, business was booming for a time and then came the slump.

"People simply can't afford to buy cars," said one of Morris's directors.

"Then we'll make 'em cheaper!" snapped W. R. "Bring me the cost-sheets."

He peered at every item. A pound could be saved here, ten pounds there and the company's profit could be cut to the bone.

"Tell the Press, £100 off the price of the Morris Cowley!" he said.

"The man's mad. He'll ruin himself," cried his rivals.

"No, I won't," grinned W. R. "Any profit is better than a loss. At least I shall still be selling motor-cars!"

When other firms had to close down, the Morris works were going at full pressure. From 60 cars a week, production rose until one Morris car was finished every five minutes of the day and still W. R. studied the costs.

"People say I'm mean. I know they do. I'm always round the works cutting down and saving expense," he said. "But the one object of my life has been to make cars that people can buy."

He lived in a small house, drove an old car and was never known to waste a penny or take a holiday. He always wore a cheap suit and one evening, early on in his career as a successful employer, he called on Dr. Girdlestone, a surgeon who had founded a hospital for crippled children in some old Army huts

near Oxford. The doctor's house-keeper told him that a workman was at the door.

"What can I do for you?" enquired Girdlestone.

"I understand your hospital is very hard up."

"That is so. We need money badly," replied the surgeon, won-dering what this had to do with his shabby caller.

"I know something of your work. Perhaps you'll accept this," said the man holding out an envelope. When he had gone, Girdlestone opened the envelope. Inside was a cheque for £1000 signed "W. R. Morris." It was his first gift to a hospital.

A stream of new cars continued to leave the Cowley works—the Morris Oxford, Morris Cowley, the little Morris Minor that did "a 100 m.p.h. and 100 miles to the gallon", the big Isis, the MG sports, the Morris Eight and various vans and lorries. In addition, there were cars produced by firms that Morris took over, such as Wolseley Motors and Rileys, and as his riches grew so did his gifts.

He always believed that he suf-fered from ill-health, though apart

416

from indigestion and sleeplessness, he was as hard as
nails. However, his horror of illness made him determined to do something to relieve pain and disease.

From 1927 onwards he began to make gifts to
hospitals. There was £140,000 for the Radcliffe
Infirmary at Oxford, £104,000 to St. Thomas's and
£70,000 to rebuild Dr. Girdlestone's hospital for
children. By the thirties, he had practically adopted
Guy's Hospital and he ended his long feud with
Oxford University by making one enormous gift
after another.

In recognition of his generosity, W. R. became Sir
William Morris, Oxford gave him an honorary degree

and in 1936, taking his title from a pretty village
near Cowley, he became Lord Nuffield.

The gifts continued—extensions to hospitals,
nurses' homes, a new church, a college for priests,
help for the blind and for areas where there was bad
unemployment. He sold some shares in his company
for £5,000,000 in order to give it all away.

"I was getting tired of working for myself," he

M.W.—27

said. "I could just as easily go back to where I started. In fact, I might be happier if I did."

He offered £1,250,000 for a Medical School at Oxford and when he learned that even this vast sum was not enough, he said quietly "I would like to increase my donation to two million pounds".

A year later, he gave another million to found Nuffield College and there were gifts to other universities, as well as grants for cancer research, "iron lungs" and the development of penicillin, for Boy Scouts, the Y.W.C.A., the Red Cross and for men in the Forces.

Not everyone admired the millionaire. Some people seemed to feel enraged by the size of his fortune.

"It's an advertisement for Morris cars," they said. "He only gives away his money instead of paying income-tax."

This was untrue, for Nuffield was giving away his capital, not his income. When he sold great blocks of shares, he was parting with the business that he had started in a garden-shed, but he made sure that the money was put into the hands of trustworthy persons. Begging letters went into the waste-paper basket:

"I don't give money to individuals," he would say. "It's too risky. Giving money away is a serious business. You have to make sure that it's going to do more good than harm."

While the Second World War was still being fought, he made the greatest of all his gifts—ten million pounds to set up the Nuffield Foundation, a fund that was to advance the health and well-being of people of all ages. To obtain this enormous sum, he sold the last of his shares:

"I myself no longer own a single share in Morris Motors," he announced and, to the chorus of thanks, he replied:

"I don't do it for thanks but because it needs doing."

Gradually, he gave up control of his vast business and settled into old age. His wife died, he had no children, so he busied himself in his workshop, mending watches, tinkering with bits of machinery. In 1963 Nuffield died at the age of eighty-five.

Throughout his life, W. R. gave the impression that he was a ruthless man of business. He rarely smiled and could never play the part of the beaming, warm-hearted donor, yet all his happiness came from building up a vast fortune in order to help those in need.

"With the strong, he was very hard," said one of his friends, "but with the old, young and sick, he was full of compassion."

Amy Johnson

A SLIM fair-haired girl stood in the corridor out-side the Headmistress's door. On her head she wore a white Panama hat and there were giggles as each class went by on the way to Assembly.

"Amy Johnson in trouble again," whispered one of the girls.

"What's she done this time?"

"Ringleader of a revolt against our beastly straw hats. She persuaded all the Third Form not to wear them but they let her down and she was the only one to turn up in a Panama. She's got to stand there all day wearing the thing!"

At the Boulevard School, Hull, the staff regarded Amy as a harum-scarum rebel. She was clever but her behaviour was shocking. She played all the boys' games, was the only girl who could bowl overarm and was the most daring gymnast in the school. Often she would play truant and go off alone all day on bicycle rides with a pocketful of biscuits stolen from the larder.

There was adventure in the family, for Amy's grandfather, a Dane, had run away to sea and her father had taken part in the Klondyke goldrush of 1898 before settling down in Hull.

"Had I been a man, I might have explored the Poles or climbed Mount Everest," said Amy. "But, as it was, my spirit found its outlet in the air. Everything in my life has spelt adventure."

From school, Amy went to Sheffield University, where she was gay and restless. She danced, played games, changed her "digs" dozens of times and got so much into debt that she had to borrow £50 from a friend. By last-minute swotting, she passed her degree and decided to leave.

"I don't want to teach," she told her parents. "I think I shall go into business."

After three months of trying to learn typing and shorthand, she got a job in Hull at £1 a week and hated it. Her shorthand was so bad that she could not read it back, but the secret of that £50 worried her into finding another job at thirty shillings a week. She gave her mother five shillings, kept five shillings for herself and paid off the debt at £1 a week. On the day the last pound was paid, she walked out of the office.

"What are your plans now?" enquired her father. "Would you like me to pay your fare to Canada where Uncle Edward will find you a job?"

"No thank you, father. I'm going to try my luck in London," replied Amy.

With enough money from her father to last a month, she arrived in the capital to look for work. Jobs were scarce and her money was running short when, in desperation, she accepted a month's trial as an assistant on the ribbons counter of a big store. At the end of her first week, a note in her pay-envelope said, "Your services have been valued at 4s. 7½d."

It looked as if she would have to go back home to tell her father that she had failed again when she met an old family friend who offered her a post in his solicitor's office. Her salary would be three pounds a week.

At last she was independent and able to afford to share a flat with a girl from college. The flat was not far from Stag Lane aerodrome, and at weekends, when the girls played tennis, the sky was full of aeroplanes. They fascinated Amy.

"Often, I would stop and gaze wistfully skywards," she wrote. "I envied those pilots. . . . I had always wanted freedom and adventure and I felt that flying could give these to me."

One Saturday, hardly realizing where she was going, she took a bus to Stag Lane. The planes were almost overhead as they glided in to land. Breathless with excitement, she ran past a notice saying "London Aeroplane Club: Private" and found herself on the grass of the aerodrome.

People were watching the planes landing and taking off and no-one took any notice as Amy sat herself down in a deckchair outside a club-house. For an hour, she watched enthralled. She knew what she was going to do. She *must* learn to fly.

Summoning up her courage, she spoke to an instructor:

"Excuse me, how much does it cost to learn?"

· "Two pounds an hour, miss, for instruction. Thirty shillings an hour solo."

Amy did some quick mental arithmetic. At a pinch, she could just afford it.

"Can I start now?" she asked innocently.

"Not quite, miss. You have to apply to the secretary to join the Club. I warn you, there's a waiting-list."

It was several months before she took her first lesson and it was not a success. The flying helmet that Amy borrowed was so enormous that the earphones almost met under her chin and she could not understand a word that the instructor was saying.

"Hopeless," he said when they came down. "You'll never learn to fly and you're simply wasting your money and my time!"

Instead of bursting into tears, Amy set her jaw. Never learn to fly? She would show him!

Next week, she went up with a different helmet and a different instructor, who found her quick to learn and extraordinarily cool-headed.

Within a few weeks, she was ready to make her first solo flight. She taxied her little yellow plane across the grass, and waited for the take-off signal.

The De Havilland Moth gathered speed until, exactly as she had been taught, she pulled the stick gently back. She was airborne—alone!

In July 1929, after fifteen hours' instruction, Amy obtained her pilot's licence. Her greatest ambition had come true.

From now on, all her spare time was spent at Stag Lane. Since she could not afford to fly every day, she took to nosing about in the workshops. As she watched the mechanics, she became so interested in engines that she asked if she could study for the ground engineer's licence. Mr. Humphreys the chief engineer scratched his chin and said:

"Well, I suppose there's a first time for everything, Miss Johnson. I've never heard of a woman mechanic but if you can get up early, we'll see how you go along."

For two years Amy worked on engines from six o'clock in the morning until eight. Then she rushed to the office for her day's work and hurried back in the evening to return to the workshops. At weekends she was there all day. Armed with oil-can, grease-gun and spanner, she learned to clean petrol filters, to check plugs, to strip an engine and to re-assemble it perfectly. The men accepted her as one of themselves when they found that she never tried to dodge the dirtiest and heaviest jobs. She had a sense of fun and a real knack with engines so they felt proud when "Johnnie" became the first woman ever to hold a ground engineer's certificate.

"If ever anyone lives for flying, it's that girl," declared Mr. Humphreys.

Her employers obviously thought the same, for they told her that she must choose between her hobby and her office work. Amy chose flying.

"But who will employ a woman pilot?" asked Mr. Johnson.

"If I can prove that I'm as good a pilot as a man, I'll find plenty of work. I mean to make a big flight—not as a stunt but to get the money to make flying my real career."

"And where will you go on this 'big flight'?"

Amy flicked over the pages of an atlas and put her finger-tip on the map of Australia.

"I shall go *there*," she said.

What a mad idea! thought her father. Never would he agree to such folly but, to enable her to obtain a commercial licence, he agreed to give her £150.

Amy returned to London intent on finding someone to support her plans. A newspaper editor showed no more faith in her talk of flying to Australia than if she had said she was going to ride up Mount Everest on a bicycle. In any case, the flight had been done by a crew of four in a *Vimy* bomber and quite recently that brilliant pilot, Bert Hinkler, had reached Australia in the incredible time of 15½ days.

Flying experts advised Amy to abandon the idea. A girl who had never even flown across the Channel must be out of her mind to think of flying 12,000 miles on her own.

But Amy persevered. After calling on all kinds of important people and writing hundreds of letters, she was sent to Lord Wakefield, a most generous supporter of civil aviation.

"I admire your pluck, young lady, but isn't flying to Australia too big a task for a girl?" asked Lord Wakefield. "Have you a plane?"

"Not yet, but I know one that is absolutely ideal," replied Amy eagerly. "It's Captain Hope's D.H. Moth, the one he used to photograph the Prince of Wales' route over Africa. It's not new but it already has extra fuel tanks and I am planning to put another one in the passenger-seat."

"What's the price?"

"£600—a perfect bargain!"

"Hm, if you were a man, Miss Johnson, I'd give

you a job as a salesman. If you can get £300 yourself, I'll put up the other half and pay for your petrol into the bargain."

Joyfully, Amy went home and persuaded her father to give her the £300 that she needed. The plane was hers and, in gratitude to her father, she christened it *Jason* after his business trademark.

On May 5th 1930 she was ready. *Jason*, painted green and with a spare propeller tied to its side, was taxied on to the field of Croydon Aerodrome and, having waved to her father and the two or three friends who came to see her off, Amy took off and headed away to the south-east.

As she crossed the Channel, Amy's mind went over the route she had carefully planned. First stop, Vienna, then Constantinople. After Europe had been left behind, she must use the landing-fields that the R.A.F. had set up for the route to India. The Dutch had some airfields in the East Indies and the last stage would be across the lonely Timor Sea to Port Darwin. She looked proudly along the wings of her plane. The D.H. Moth was a tiny aircraft, no longer than two parked cars, but it behaved beautifully and would cruise all day at 80 m.p.h. Normally, it carried two persons but the passenger space was filled with the extra petrol tank and Amy, wearing a parachute, was strapped into the rear seat of the open cockpit.

From time to time, she checked her position . . . Belgium . . . the Rhine . . . that big town must be Frankfurt. Late in the afternoon, she picked up the Danube and, after ten hours' flying, she landed at Aspern aerodrome, Vienna. She had covered 800 miles.

No fuss was made of the pilot who booked in for a room in the airport building and took off after breakfast. She followed the Danube across Hungary and turned south over Bulgaria to reach Constantinople after twelve long hours in the cockpit.

Her departure next morning was noted by a newspaperman who sent word to London that a girl flying a Moth G-AAAH had taken off for Aleppo, 500 miles away. This report in the evening papers caused some mild interest and, next day, readers learned that the solitary flyer was past Aleppo and still going well. Who was she? A typist from Hull? Funny thing for a girl to do all by herself.

From Aleppo the way was across 500 miles of desert. Amy had been warned of the danger of sandstorms, but throughout the morning she was more concerned about the terrific heat that made the metal parts of her aircraft impossible to touch. Ahead she noticed a dark haze.

With terrifying suddenness a storm hit the little plane, whirling it about as though it were a leaf caught by the wind. Amy's eyes and nostrils filled with sand that almost choked her and she sensed that *Jason*'s engine was not firing properly. The plane plunged down to within a few feet of the ground and it was only by fighting with all her strength that she managed to make a landing. Jumping down, she hung on to the tail to prevent *Jason* from being blown over and smashed. During a lull, she took all her luggage out of the cockpit and piled it against the wheels as a makeshift anchor.

As the wind slackened, rather than risk a night in the desert, she took off and landed at Baghdad when

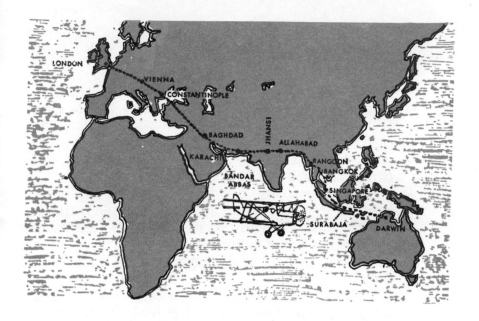

it was almost dark. Here, for the first time, she found some interest in herself but she was too busy checking *Jason*'s engine to bother about reporters and, early next morning, she was heading down the valley of the Euphrates towards the Persian Gulf.

From Bandar Abbas, where she worked until midnight on her plane, she set off at dawn to cover the last lap to Karachi. This was the sixth day. She had beaten the solo record from London to India by two days and she was already famous.

To her astonishment, she was taken to Government House where she spent the night as guest of honour. A cable arrived from her parents:

"Good Luck. Keep it up. You are doing splendidly. Great interest here in your flight."

By this time, newspapers were vying with each other to produce front-page photographs of Amy in flying kit, in overalls and as a little girl.

"Next stop, Allahabad!" announced the headlines but, owing to shortage of petrol, Amy had to land at Jhansi in Central India and it was not until the eighth day that she reached Allahabad. After a short stay, she went on to Calcutta where she was still two days ahead of Hinkler's record.

Over Burma, she ran into the monsoon and it seemed impossible that an aircraft could survive. But the little Moth battled its way up to 12,000 feet to cross the Yoma mountains.

"It was like flying through Niagara Falls in a hurricane," said Amy.

Visibility was so bad when she came down to look for the railway line that, at 150 feet, she could see nothing. Not daring to go lower, she flew blindly to and fro until the steamy mist cleared for an instant to reveal an open space flanked by buildings. It must be Rangoon race-course and, gratefully, she went in to land. *Jason* bumped across a ditch, breaking the propeller and damaging the right wing before coming to rest between a pair of goal-posts. Amy had landed, not at Rangoon, but on a football field ten miles from the city.

Luckily the field was next to a Technical College and willing helpers came out to change the propeller and to fit a new section to the wing. This work took more than a day and then *Jason* had to be taken on a lorry to Rangoon race-course since the field was useless for a take-off.

The next stopping-place was Bangkok, only 350 miles away, or about four hours' flying in good weather. The monsoon closed in and, for seven hours in dense cloud, Amy fought a murderous wind that constantly threatened to dash *Jason* against the mountain slopes.

At half-past six, too exhausted to speak, she came down on an airfield of the Siamese Air Force. After a night's sleep, she was away to Singapore where two Moths came up to escort her into the landing-ground.

This was the fourteenth day and the delays had put an end to her hopes of beating Hinkler's record. However, she was still smiling when the R.A.F. drove her to the Officers' Mess for dinner, for *Jason* was being fitted with a new wing for the last lap to Australia.

On the following day, after nine hours' flying, Amy found her petrol so low that she was forced to land in a sugar plantation where the wing fabric was badly torn by some sharp sticks. Although the local people worked furiously to repair the holes, this meant more delay, all the worse because it was going to be very difficult to fly the plane out of a small muddy field.

"There's a much bigger field two miles away," said the plantation manager.

"If you will have all my luggage taken out of the plane," she replied, "I'll have a go."

The lightened machine just skimmed the trees and came safely down on the new field. Grinning porters soon arrived with the luggage and Amy was off to Surabaja.

By now, millions of people were following the flight almost mile by mile, and when a day and a night passed without news of her progress they imagined that she had crashed.

The Dutch authorities sent out wireless messages to the islands and to ships at sea and two flying-boats were about to take off when a message came in that Amy had landed at an isolated place far from a telephone. A crowd of natives had rushed towards her waving spears but they led her over the hills to a mission church where the Dutch pastor gave her a meal and a room for the night.

After this, the flight across the Timor Sea was easy. Halfway across, she sighted an oil tanker and as she swooped joyously down over its deck, the men waved and the wireless operator was already tapping out the news to Port Darwin.

Aircraft came out to lead her in and, as *Jason* touched down and the Australians came surging towards her, Amy could only say:

"I've done it! I've done it!"

All over the world, newspaper placards bore two words:

"SHE'S THERE."

The flight had taken nineteen days, nearly four more than Hinkler's but a week less than the *Vimy* bomber. It was a wonderful achievement and the whole of Australia acclaimed the girl from Hull.

432

There were banquets, speeches and public welcomes. From tiredness or from a misunderstanding with her escort, Amy crashed at Brisbane and, although she was unhurt, *Jason* was wrecked and she had to be taken on by another plane to Sidney where she was to attend the State Ball. Her pilot was a handsome young man named Jim Mollison and, during the flight, he passed Amy a note asking if he might dance with her at the Ball. She agreed but, on the evening, she was surrounded by so many people that she did not catch sight of her pilot. Two years later, when he too was famous, they met again in South Africa and not long afterwards they were married.

By ship and plane, Amy returned to England where two hundred thousand people came to Croydon to welcome her home. From the air-liner steps, she looked across this vast crowd and there, to her delight, beside the platform where a group of distinguished persons was waiting, stood *Jason* repaired and splendid in a fresh coat of green and white paint!

Through streets lined with cheering crowds, she drove to the Savoy Hotel to receive the *Daily Mail's* cheque for £10,000 and on to Buckingham Palace to be decorated by King George V.

Amy did not rest on one success. She made a flight to Tokyo, and after her marriage she beat Jim Mollison's record flight from London to the Cape and back, and was the first woman to fly the Atlantic. On this trip, she and her husband were lucky not to be killed when they crashed at night a few miles from New York.

There were many other flights, records and mishaps in her adventurous career. The end came in 1941 when, as a war-time pilot in the Air Transport Auxiliary, her plane broke up in mid-air as she was crossing the Thames estuary. The wreckage fell into the river mud but no trace was ever found of Amy Johnson. As she said herself, her spirit found its outlet in the air. Everything in her life spelt adventure.

Winston Churchill

"IF you have any money in your possession, you may hand it over," said the Headmaster.

He was a large man with an imposing moustache and his manner showed that he expected obedience. The small, freckled boy dug unwillingly into his pockets and produced three halfcrowns that his mother had just given him.

"The School shop is open once a week," snapped the Headmaster as he placed the money in a drawer.

The boy eyed him with hostility. This was his first day at school; he was only seven and the halfcrowns were a last link with home and his toy-filled nursery. Now they had vanished like the Headmaster's smile when Mother departed.

Presently the boy found himself seated at a battered desk in an empty form-room. A master came in.

"So you're Churchill? Have you done any Latin?"

"No, sir."

"Here is a Latin grammar. You will learn the first page. I shall come back in half an hour."

A strange collection of words stared back at the boy:

Mensa—a table.   *Mensa*—O table.
Mensam—a table   *Mensae*—of a table.
Mensae—to or for a table.
Mensa—by, with or from a table.

435

It made no sense but the boy had a good memory and when the master returned he gabbled it off correctly.

"That is satisfactory, Churchill."

"Please, sir, what does it mean?"

"It means what it says. *Mensa,* the Latin word for a table."

"But what does "O table" mean."

"That is the vocative case. You would use it when speaking to a table."

"But I never do!" blurted out the boy.

"If you are impertinent, Churchill, you will be punished—and punished very severely," replied the master. He was quite right. Punishment was frequent and severe at this expensive school. Two or three times a month, the Headmaster summoned the entire school to listen to the screams of an offender being thrashed until he bled.

Winston Churchill decided that he hated school. He was obstinate and no amount of beating would make him learn things that did not interest him.

"In all the twelve years I was at school, no one ever succeeded in making me write a Latin verse," he said.

After a time his father, Lord Randolph Churchill, noticed that his son was making no progress.

"Winston's reports are very bad," he remarked to his wife. "We had better find another school."

They did so at Brighton. It was a smaller, kindlier place where Winston enjoyed French, History, lots of poetry and, above all, swimming and riding, but his behaviour was far from perfect.

"A small red-headed pupil, the naughtiest boy in the class," reported one of his teachers.

At the age of twelve, Winston had to take the Entrance Examination for Harrow. His father was a successful politician and his mother was one of the most fascinating women in England. The Churchills knew or were related to nearly everyone of importance and it was naturally expected that their eldest son would be as brilliant as his parents.

Yet, faced with the Latin paper at Harrow, Winston could do no more than write his name at the top of the page. There was not a single question that he could answer.

However, the Headmaster admitted him and placed him in the lowest form. Since Latin, Greek and Mathematics were the most prized subjects at Harrow and Winston loathed all three, he stayed at the bottom of the school for a very long time.

"But I *was* taught English," he said cheerfully. "We were considered such dunces that we could only learn English!"

At least he won a prize. This was for reciting over a thousand lines of poetry without a mistake and he also won the Public Schools' Championship for fencing. But, to most people and to his father, he was a merry, truculent little chap, the dunce of a famous family.

One day, in the holidays, Lord Randolph found Winston and his brother Jack in the old nursery. Winston had fifteen hundred toy-soldiers, besides forts, artillery and transports and the game was being played with such skill that Lord Randolph watched for twenty minutes. Then he said:

"Would you like to go into the Army, Winston?"

The boy looked up eagerly. He would do anything to please this great man, to prove that he was not really a dunderhead.

"Yes, father," he answered.

"We'll have to see if you can get into Sandhurst," said his father, adding under his breath, "You'll never make a lawyer as I had hoped."

At the third attempt, Winston entered Sandhurst as a cavalry-cadet. Even this did not please his father.

"I hoped you would pass high enough for the infantry," he snorted. "The cavalry is expensive. Horses, grooms and uniforms are most costly and, from what I can see, there is every prospect of you turning into a waster!"

Poor Winston! He never managed to impress his father, for within a short while Lord Randolph died at the early age of forty-five.

At Sandhurst, Winston took subjects that interested him—tactics, map-making, gymnastics and riding. For the first time he worked hard, and by the end of his year he passed out eighth of his batch of 150 cadets. He was gazetted to the 4th Hussars.

It was a glorious thing to be a cavalry officer in 1895 and Winston was thrilled by the hard training,

the glittering jingle of men and horses, the excitement of manoeuvring at a gallop. In addition, because of his name and his mother's position in Society, he was able to enjoy himself as a dashing young man-about-town.

The only disappointment was the lack of adventure. The British Army had not fought a serious war for almost forty years and the one place in the world where shots were being fired in anger was Cuba. A guerrilla war was going on between the local rebels and their Spanish rulers, so, through family influence, Winston obtained permission to go to Cuba as an observer.

On his 21st birthday, in the Cuban forest, he heard for the first time the crack of gunfire and the whistle of bullets. It was immensely exciting and, to his surprise, rather less dangerous than he had thought.

Home from this first taste of adventure, Winston found that his regiment was posted to India where the cavalry settled down to the usual routine of parades and polo.

Winston was bored. He loved polo but his mind was too active to enjoy idleness and he almost began to wish that he had not wasted his time at Harrow.

"It's not too late," he said to himself. "I always liked history at school. I will start with history."

He wrote to ask his mother to send out some books. Box upon box of thick heavy volumes arrived at his bungalow. He had no idea there was so much learning in the world and he began to read.

"All through the long glistening middle hours of the Indian day, from when we quitted stables to the hour of Polo, I devoured Gibbon," he wrote. "I enjoyed it all. I went on to Macaulay . . . I read for four or five hours every day—history, philosophy and a great deal more."

After two years of this "curious education", Churchill heard that a rebellion had broken out on the Indian frontier. He was off like a shot. Having wangled leave from his regiment, he made north and joined the Malakand Field Force as correspondent to an English newspaper. This would help his expenses since, even with £500 a year from his mother, he was finding it impossible to live on his pay.

Lieutenant Churchill was soon toiling up the side of a rocky valley with a small party that was to capture a village of mud huts. The resistance was so fierce that they were ordered to retire. Several men were hit and, since it was a point of honour never to leave wounded men to be tortured to death, Churchill, the Adjutant and several soldiers went back to rescue them.

"We were not half-way across the open space when thirty or forty furious figures appeared firing frantically and waving their swords . . . I looked to my left . . . the Adjutant had been shot . . . the leading tribesman rushed upon his prostrate body and slashed it three or four times with his sword. I forgot everything except a desire to kill this man . . . I

pulled out my revolver and fired. No result. I fired
again. No result. I fired again. Whether I hit him or
not, I cannot tell. At any rate, he ran back and
plumped down behind a rock. I looked round. I
was alone with the enemy."

In a rain of bullets, he reached his friends behind a knoll. Just when it seemed certain that they would be wiped out, the Buffs arrived and the tribesmen were driven off.

Churchill saw some more action before being recalled to his regiment and, by this time, he had decided to write a book about the campaign. Called *The Story of the Malakand Field Force*, it was praised in the Press and by the Prime Minister and the Prince of Wales. There were other opinions.

"Who the devil does this conceited whipper-snapper think he is?" exploded one colonel. "How dare he criticize Her Majesty's senior officers!"

Thus, when Churchill tried to join General Kitchener's Staff in the Sudan, Kitchener refused to have him at any price. Nothing daunted, Churchill got himself attached to the 21st Lancers without pay. He cheerfully agreed that if he got killed in the forthcoming campaign, there must be no claim on Army funds!

The 21st Lancers joined Kitchener's army just before the battle of Omdurman and were ordered to head off the enemy's right flank.

"Talk about fun!" wrote Churchill. "On horseback, at daybreak, within shot of an advancing army . . ."

The trumpet sounded "Right wheel into line" and 300 lancers swung round and broke into a gallop.

Because of a dislocated shoulder, Churchill sheathed his sword and drew his pistol. The lancers swept through the Dervish riflemen and plunged unexpectedly into a dry water-course among 3000 of the enemy. They were instantly engulfed by a mass of tribesmen who fearlessly slashed at horses and men. Churchill fired, straightened himself in the saddle and rode so hard at a figure with an uplifted sword that his pistol struck the man's chest. He aimed at an Arab horseman in a steel helmet and suddenly was through and clear. He reined his horse and looked for his troop. He found them re-forming, the enemy made off and one of the last cavalry charges in history was over.

Soon after Omdurman, Churchill went home. He had made three decisions. Since he could not live on his pay, he would leave the Army. He would earn his living as a writer. He would enter Parliament.

Thus, in 1899, brimful of confidence and energy, he was writing a book about the recent campaign and was standing as Conservative candidate at Oldham. To his astonishment, the electors did not choose him but actually preferred Mr. Runciman, a Liberal.

"Never mind," said Mr. Runciman to his disappointed rival, "I don't suppose the world has heard the last of either of us!"

A number of influential people already knew that "the little square-headed fellow" had dash and a ready wit, but he was not yet known to the general public. He became a hero through a series of accidents.

The Boer War broke out soon after the Oldham election and Churchill went to South Africa as a newspaper correspondent. He arrived to find that the Boers were beseiging Mafeking, Kimberley and Ladysmith. From Durban, he could get no further along the railway than the little town of Estcourt.

Here he met Captain Haldane, an old friend who offered to take him in an armoured-train that patrolled a stretch of line towards besieged Ladysmith.

"Nothing looks more impressive than an armoured-train," wrote Churchill, "but nothing is more vulnerable and helpless. It was only necessary to blow up a bridge to leave the monster stranded, far from home and at the mercy of the enemy."

The train, carrying 120 soldiers armed with rifles, consisted of an engine and six trucks, three in front and three behind. This moving fort had puffed along for fourteen miles when a party of Boers was sighted near the line. The order was given to return home. As bullets and shrapnel tanged against the steel-sided trucks, the driver put on speed, rounded a bend and crashed into a huge boulder placed on the line. The three trucks, now in front, were overturned, two falling clear but the third lay half on, half off the track.

Many of the soldiers were badly injured but those in the rear trucks under Captain Haldane returned the Boers' fire while Churchill went along the track to survey the damage and to get the injured under cover. After an hour's work, he realized that the best hope was to uncouple the rear trucks and to

direct the engine-driver to butt and pull the obstruction. At last, with a rasping screech, the engine scraped by. The way home was clear if he could recouple the rear trucks.

Haldane was engaged so hotly that it was impossible to spare men to move the trucks.

"Get the wounded on to the engine, Churchill," he shouted. "I'll bring my men along on foot."

Crammed with wounded men, the engine moved slowly forward while the rest of the soldiers marched alongside, sheltering from the shells and bullets as best they could. On a slope, the engine began to get ahead of the soldiers who became fully exposed to the enemy fire. Churchill jumped down and ran back to bring along Haldane at a faster pace.

In a cutting, he saw two men with rifles. They were Boers. He turned and scrambled up the bank as their bullets hissed past him. He was over and making for shelter when he found himself covered by the rifle of a seated horseman. He put his hand to his belt but his revolver was gone. When clearing the line, he had put it down in the engine-cab. The Boer looked along the sights of his rifle and Churchill ruefully surrendered. He was taken to where Haldane and his men had been captured and, with sixty others, he was soon on his way to Pretoria.

Formerly a school, the prisoner-of-war camp was surrounded by a wall patrolled by sentries, and at night the entire area was brightly lit by electric lamps. While he was considering various ways of escape, Churchill noticed that one part of the wall was in shadow and that it might just be reached from a lavatory built alongside.

One evening he strolled across the yard and hid himself in the lavatory. Through a chink he watched two sentries some fifteen yards away until, after an age, they turned their backs and began to talk.

"Now or never!" he said to himself. Jumping up, he gripped the top of the wall and heaved himself over. For one horrible moment, his waistcoat became caught in some ironwork, he freed it and dropped down into a shrubbery.

There was still a sentry to pass outside but, jamming a civilian hat on his head, Churchill strolled past him, whistling a tune and deliberately walking in the middle of the road.

The streets were full of people but no-one took any notice of a short figure in a brown suit who sat down by a bridge to consider his next move. He was in the heart of the enemy country, without a map or a compass. All he knew was that Delagoa Bay in Portuguese East Africa lay about 300 miles to the east so he had better find the railway and follow that.

Presently, he struck the railway and began to walk briskly along the track. After two hours, he came to a station and hid himself in a ditch. A train drew in, waited a few minutes and began to pull out, gathering speed faster than he expected. He hurled himself forward, missed, clutched again and hung on until he pulled himself on to the coupling of a truck.

Just before dawn, he jumped off the train, quenched his thirst in a pool of water and lay up in a wood to await another train that night. The day crawled by and when darkness fell, he returned to the line in high hopes. Hours passed but no train came along so he set off on foot.

Dozens of detours were necessary to avoid guards at bridges and stations. He fell into swamps, waded across streams and was becoming exhausted when he sighted what seemed to be the fires of a native village. The Kaffirs, he understood, hated the Boers and might be willing to help an Englishman so he stumbled on towards the lights. They proved to be the fires not of a village but of some furnaces. He had come to a coal mine.

All through his life, in critical situations that called for a sudden decision, Churchill put his faith in Providence and his own courage. Taking a deep breath, he knocked on the door of the colliery house.

An upper window opened and a voice called out.

"I want help," answered Churchill. "I have had an accident. I have fallen off a train."

A man came to the door. He was holding a revolver.

"Well, come in," he said suspiciously.

Indoors, the man lit a lamp and surveyed his grimy exhausted visitor. "I think I'd like to know a bit more about this accident," he said slowly.

"I think I'd better tell you the truth," replied Churchill.

When he had finished, the man got up and locked the door. Then he held out his hand.

"This is the only house for twenty miles where you would not be handed over. We're British here and we'll see you through."

He was John Howard, manager of the Transvaal Colliery and, with a few others, the Boers had let him stay on to keep the mine in working order. But it was dangerous for him to offer help, especially as there were Dutch servant-girls sleeping in the house.

"It must be done. We'll manage it somehow," he muttered as he fetched bread and meat for his famished guest.

Before daylight, he lowered Churchill into the mine where two Scots led him to a disused shaft.

There, with only rats for company, he spent the next few days while the Boers scoured the district, offering a reward for Churchill's capture, dead or alive.

Meanwhile, Mr. Howard was making plans to smuggle the fugitive on to a train leaving for Delagoa Bay. In a narrow space between huge bales of wool covered by a tarpaulin, Churchill jolted eastwards for three days. At last, through a crack, he saw the uniforms of Portuguese officials. He waited until the train moved on and then, unable to restrain his joy, he stuck his head out of the tarpaulin, sang and crowed at the top of his voice and fired Mr. Howard's pistol into the air!

At Delagoa Bay, the British Consul put him on a steamer to Durban where he was greeted by a big crowd and a brass band. After a series of defeats, Churchill's escape gave the British something to cheer about and although he said himself that the whole affair was exaggerated, it brought him fame and he was not the man to waste his good fortune.

Within a month he was an unpaid officer in the South African Light Horse and had taken part in a sharp fight at Spion Kop. After this he entered Ladysmith when the town was relieved, marched 500 miles with Lord Roberts' army and cycled into Johannesburg while it was still in Boer hands.

In October 1900, exactly one year after he had set off to South Africa, he was elected to Parliament for Oldham, defeating the same Mr. Runciman by 230 votes. The world had heard of him sooner than even he had expected!

For the next sixty years Churchill's career was more brilliant and stormy than his father's had been. He left the Conservatives to join the Liberals, served under Lloyd George and, as First Lord of the Admiralty, he had the Fleet ready and at sea when the Great War broke out in 1914.

A year later, his plan to shorten the war by attacking Turkey was a failure and he left the Government to become a serving-officer in France. After the war, the Conservatives would not forgive him for deserting them and all through the thirties he was out of office and out of favour. His career seemed to be over.

In adversity, Churchill never lost his courage and sense of fun. He devoted himself to writing history and, having picked up a child's box of paints by chance, he became such a colourful painter that several of his pictures were hung in the Royal Academy. Visitors to his home in Kent often found him in the gardens that he had laid out and, chuckling with pride, he would show them the garden wall he had built himself.

In Parliament and in the newspapers, he was never silent. Year in and year out, he warned the country of Germany's rising strength and Hitler's violent ambition. People scoffed at his constant talk of danger. "A brilliant failure. An old war-monger," they said.

But in 1939, when Germany attacked Poland, he was given his old post at the Admiralty and a message went round the Fleet, "Winston's back!" In 1940 he became Prime Minister.

France fell. The Germans crushed western Europe and although the British army escaped from Dunkirk, all its arms and equipment were lost. The country was on the brink of complete defeat. Was it not sensible to ask for peace, to make terms even with Hitler?

The country asked for leadership and Churchill spoke:

"I have nothing to offer but blood, toil, tears and sweat . . . You ask what is our policy? I will tell you, it is to wage war, by sea, by land and air, with all our might and with all the strength that God can give us. You ask what is our aim? I can answer in one word: Victory."

But what if Britain was invaded? The Germans were massing their armies on the French coast and the British had not enough rifles to go round.

Churchill gave the answer:

"We shall defend our island, whatever the cost may be, we shall fight on the beaches, we shall fight on the landing-grounds, we shall fight in the fields and in the streets, we shall fight in the hills, we shall never surrender."

The words of one "little square-headed fellow" rallied the nation. But more than words were needed in the years of bombing at home and of disasters overseas.

By his courage, hard work and unflagging confidence in victory, Churchill inspired his people and heartened his allies. At an age when most men are growing old, he showed superhuman ability to do without sleep, to see into every part of the war effort, to travel thousands of miles to meet allied leaders and to see the troops in the field. Only the king's protest stopped him from joining the landings at Normandy! Always he seemed to be the voice of his own people, expressing their anger and pity, their stubborn will to go on to the end.

Once, during the bombing of London, he was interviewed by an American as he stood among the ruins of homes of ordinary people:

"They deserve victory," he growled, "and by God they shall have it!"

Victory came at last and he was in Germany conferring with Stalin and the American President when he learnt that he was no longer Prime Minister. The people had voted for a Labour government and Mr. Attlee took his place.

Churchill was over seventy but he returned to lead the Conservatives and to write a magnificent six-volume history of the war. In 1951 he was Prime Minister again until, at the age of eighty, he decided to retire, but not to rest. He went on writing, painting and travelling all over the world.

In his long adventurous career, Winston Churchill suffered defeats and disappointments. He was rash, he made mistakes and sometimes he was unfair to his opponents. But, if he had faults, he had the gift of leadership. He was the greatest Englishman of our time.

He died in 1965 and was given a State Funeral. The only other commoner to receive this honour was Wellington in 1852.

Leonard Cheshire, V.C.

"EVERYTHING'S O.K., Captain, except Taffy's inter-com."

"Where are we, Desmond?"

"Between Wesseling and Cologne."

"We'll go for Cologne. Tell Taffy to aim for the marshalling-yards."

The captain remembered that Davidson, the wireless operator was making his first trip.

"You all right, Davey?"

"Fine, thank you, sir."

"Good lad. We'll want your flares in five minutes."

"I think there's a fighter behind us, Captain."

"O.K., Revs, keep an eye on him. We're almost up to Cologne now. Taffy ready?"

"Bombs fused! Bomb doors open!"

"Left, left, about 20 degrees."

"Look out! Turn quick! Over . . .!"

A violent explosion rocked the aircraft and caused it to plunge downwards. Blinded by the brilliant flash, half-choked by smoke, the pilot fought for control. His mind raced over the things he must do; he wondered how the crew was behind, cursed himself for not having put on his oxygen mask, for forgetting where he had thrown his parachute.

Pull the stick back. Steady, steady. That's better, smoke clearing, can see the instruments. All haywire but the altimeter says 5000 feet. Not bad. Level out.

454

Behind him, a voice cried:

"Fire! The tank's on fire!"

"Well put it out!" he snapped.

The Whitley wallowed and flopped. The port wing dropped but the pilot stopped her spinning as more shells came up from the German guns. A searchlight caught the damaged bomber, then another, but he dared not take violent evasive action so he flew straight and level, hoping for the best.

His back felt hot and, half-turning, he could see red streaks of fire. There was an awful smell of rubber burning and sounds of slapping and cursing. The second pilot appeared alongside him.

"Hello, Desmond. How's the fire?"

"Taffy's got it under control. There's a blooming great hole in our side. Can you keep her going?"

"Of course. Have we still got the bombs?"

"Yes, we have."

"Well we'd better find Cologne and drop 'em."

Another figure appeared on the step. His face was a blackened burnt mask with blood-filled circles where his eyes had been. It was Davey. When the shell hit the Whitley, it had ignited the flare he was about to drop. On fire, he had pushed it out and also the second flare that would have exploded and destroyed the plane. The others had beaten out the flames before tackling the fire under a petrol tank.

"You'll want a fix, sir. I won't let you down, I must get back to the wireless, but I can't see, sir, I can't see."

Revs took him back to his set. Freezing air through the hole in the Whitley's side was agonizing to the burnt boy but he talked only about his wireless set.

Unable to see, he told Revs how to set the dials, got him to guide his hands to the key and refused to give up until he collapsed. Revs wrapped him in his own flying jacket and held him like a child, while the others fixed up a parachute for him. There was no parachute for Revs.

The damaged Whitley flew doggedly on and crossed the English coast at Cromer. It was growing light when they touched down at Base where the waiting ground-crew gazed at the smashed fuselage.

"Blimey!" said an awed voice, "it's only half a kite!"

The captain was last out.

"Steady with Davey," he said to the stretcher-bearers as he saw his wireless-op. into the ambulance.

The official account of that episode in 1940 announced the award of the Distinguished Flying Medal to Sergeant Davidson and the D.S.O. to Pilot Officer Cheshire. To his indignation he learned that for Desmond, Taffy and Revs, there was nothing.

456

Leonard Cheshire was twenty-three when he became captain of the Whitley bomber. A slight, oval-faced young man, he had joined Oxford University Air Squadron just before the war when, as a wild law-student, he was looking for thrills more amusing than racing his red sports-car through the Oxfordshire lanes. War came and Cheshire was trained for bombers.

"I was never what you would call a good pilot," he said. "My cockpit drill was terrible . . . always hated it . . . And if I left off flying for more than a day, then I flew shockingly. But I was lucky. Everyone knew I was lucky."

To survive, a pilot had to be lucky, no matter how good he was. Every single one of the friends with whom he flew in those days was killed or missing— Lofty, his first captain, Desmond, Willy, Jimmy, Christopher, his brother, Taffy, Revs—but Cheshire stayed alive. Night after night, he went out into the darkness towards Germany—to Cologne, Essen, Duisberg, Berlin, and Berlin again—and he always came back.

From Whitleys he moved to four-engined Halifaxes and had to master new equipment. So, on non-flying days, he would blindfold himself and move around inside his plane teaching himself to find every knob and panel by touch. He would talk to his ground-crew and ask their advice about engines and gun-turrets before taking them out for a drink.

"He gave us all the feeling that we were important and could be trusted and I'll never forget what that trust meant," said Aircraftman Laurie Scott.

At the end of his first operational tour Cheshire was awarded the D.F.C. and was sent by sea to the United States on special duty. The Americans, not yet in the war, gave a terrific welcome to British airmen and "Chesh" basked in the bright light of fame and gay parties before flying a Hudson back to England.

By 1943 he was Wing-Commander Cheshire com-manding 76 Squadron and, besides his other missions, he had taken part in seven raids on Berlin. The strain told on his health and beneath his jaunty charm he was moody and irritable. Awarded a second D.S.O., he was taken off flying and promoted Group Captain, at twenty-five, the youngest who had yet reached that rank.

He soon became bored with the duties of a Station Commander. To him, war meant flying against the enemy, not training other people to do so or sitting in an office signing papers. But it was far from easy to get back into the air when some of his senior officers considered him an odd character, too much of a showman for their liking. In any case, it seemed as if his nerves had cracked up.

Intelligence picked up information about a new German weapon, a long-range rocket bomb known as the V2 that was intended to wipe out London. When Mr. Churchill gave orders that Bomber Command must attack the launching-sites, Cheshire managed to persuade his superiors to give him the chance he had been longing for.

Dropping to the rank of Wing-Commander, he took over the famous Dam-buster Squadron 617, whose Lancasters were specially equipped for attacking the heavily-guarded sites. The Germans had built rocket-shelters covered by thirty feet of concrete and it was difficult to hit, let alone to penetrate, such targets. An "earthquake bomb" weighing 12,000 pounds was produced that needed to be dropped so expertly that it would sink into the earth alongside the shelters and explode under the foundations. From a great height this was impossible, so Cheshire practised low-flying in a fast Mosquito in order to place a marker bomb for the Lancasters, 20,000 feet above.

He gave the credit for this success to Mick Martin, a brilliant Australian pilot:

"I learned all I know of this low-flying game from Mick. I never saw him make a mistake."

Rocket-sites, explosive factories, E-boat pens were successfully attacked. After a time Cheshire asked for an American Mustang, a single-engined fighter that was faster than the Mosquito. Acting as his own navigator, bomb-aimer and wireless operator, he would dive the Mustang through a hail of shrapnel to drop his marker at the last second and flatten out just above the guns.

Altogether, Cheshire led 617 Squadron on forty raids and he had made exactly one hundred trips when he was called to Group Headquarters.

"I see that you've done a hundred trips," said Air Vice-Marshal Cochrane. "That's enough. It's time you had a rest."

Cheshire began to protest. The A.V.M. looked at him keenly, noticing his thinness and the fact that one eye twitched all the time.

"It's no good arguing," he said quietly. "A hundred's a good number to stop at."

For leadership and courage, Cheshire was awarded the Victoria Cross and as he left Buckingham Palace he was surrounded by the Press reporters:

"My V.C. was given me not for anything I did but for all of 617 Squadron," he snapped. "Lots of other chaps deserved them more than I did."

When the Allies were able to turn all their strength against Japan, Group-Captain Cheshire was sent to America where an explosive of fantastic power had been produced. Since President Truman had decided to use this atomic bomb against Japan, the British Government insisted on British observers being present. Two only could go, a scientist, Dr. Penny and an R.A.F. officer, Group-Captain Cheshire.

Thus, on 9th August 1945, Cheshire was seated in the nose of an American B.29 Super-Fortress bomber, flying at 39,000 feet towards the city of Nagasaki. Seated comfortably in a warm pressurized atmosphere, he could not help smiling a little at the tremendous excitement of the American crew. Of course, he knew that it was a very important bomb they were carrying but this was armchair stuff compared with those freezing nights over Germany.

461

He grinned across at Dr. Penny. These scientist-chaps had been talking about millions of degrees of heat—well, he had seen a few explosions in his time and figures didn't mean much when people talked in millions. They must be over Japan now. No gunfire, not a sign of fighters anywhere.

"Glasses on, everyone!"

Cheshire put on his pair of thick dark glasses and, at that instant, the bomber was lit by a searing flash fiercer than the very heart of the sun. Appalled by its brightness, Cheshire looked back and saw a gigantic ball of fire soaring upwards drawing with it a trail of smoke that rose in a colossal pillar and spread slowly into a mushroom-shaped cloud.

Although he did not yet know that this single bomb had ripped a city away from the surface of the earth, destroying 40,000 people in a split second,

Cheshire sensed that he had witnessed one of the most disastrous events in history. He realized that man had made a bomb that could destroy not a city or a country but life itself. Somehow, he had had a share in this. From now on, the world was changed and Cheshire was a changed man.

After the war, life in England seemed very dull and Cheshire, who had left the R.A.F., longed for the fun and excitement of Service life.

Why shouldn't ex-service men and women form groups to work together for the good of all? He asked the question through a newspaper and 200 enthusiasts joined his scheme.

"We'll take over a disused aerodrome or a big estate," he told them. "Everyone will contribute a sum of money to get started and then we'll farm the land and follow our trades to make ourselves self-supporting. Everyone will have an equal share."

The first colony started with enthusiasm and it failed because people were selfish and argumentative. Cheshire did not give up easily. He opened another colony at Le Court in Hampshire, an estate that he bought cheaply from an aunt. Its chances of success seemed to be quite bright and he went off to raise funds in Canada but, in his absence, the colony fell to pieces. To pay its debts, he had to sell the land and he was about to close down the big, shabby house when he heard about Arthur Dykes.

Arthur, an ex-airman, had been one of the early colonists but he was now in hospital suffering from cancer. The matron told Cheshire that his case was hopeless. He was alone, with no relatives or money and his hospital bed was urgently wanted.

"I'll take you back to Le Court, if you'll risk it," said Cheshire.

The big house was empty for everything had been sold but Cheshire borrowed a bed and blankets and carried Arthur into a room that he had cleaned and decorated himself. At least he had found himself a job.

"Life became pretty full," he said. "When I wasn't looking after Arthur and cooking meals, I was scything grass and tidying the place up. It was at night we used to talk. Arthur was a Roman Catholic and he used to talk about religion. Then, before he went to sleep, he would read for a bit—always the same book."

As Arthur grew weaker, Cheshire had to do everything for him. At first, he knew little about nursing but he would ring up the hospital and charm the matron and nurses into telling him what to do:

"You see, I must look after this chap," he would say. "There's no-one else."

464

Nor was there anyone else to look after the old Cockney woman of ninety, bedridden and deaf, whom he took into Le Court. She was his second patient and he became very fond of her, even if he had to do battle to get her bedsocks off every time he washed her!

Arthur died quietly, still holding his book. Cheshire took it gently from him and looked at its title, *One Lord, One Faith.* He started to read.

He had been trying to live a Christian life, to do some good through the colonies and Le Court and, ever since Nagasaki, he had thought a lot about God. Now it seemed as if Arthur had left him the answer to so many of his questions; he spoke to the priest who used to visit Arthur and, after months of instruction, he was received into the Roman Catholic Church.

At Le Court the work went on. By 1949 there were over thirty patients, many suffering from incurable illnesses. Some were old, some were crippled and all of them needed help. In the "family" that Cheshire created, they learned that most could do something for themselves and for the others.

"He just took in anyone who knocked at the door," said one of his helpers, for by now there was a band of friends who scrubbed floors, peeled vegetables and nursed the sick.

Cheshire became ill simply because he would not stop working, and with difficulty his friends persuaded him to leave the Home in their care while he took up some other occupation for a time.

He went back to flying as a civilian pilot and he was testing secret equipment in Cornwall when, from the air he noticed a group of old R.A.F. huts.

"Just the place for another Home," he declared. At the aerodrome people scoffed at the idea:

"There's no heating or sanitation. The huts have been used as cowsheds and the whole place is derelict. The fellow's crazy."

"I'll tell you something I've just found out," remarked a test-pilot thoughtfully. "You remember Hilda, the little grey-haired woman who works in the canteen? Well, she fell ill some weeks ago and was dying in some wretched cottage with no-one to look after her. Cheshire went along and, against all regulations, smuggled her into his own quarters and nursed her until she was better. They say she worships the ground he walks on."

There was silence. Then an engineer spoke.

"Crazy or not, I reckon the bloke's a saint. If he wants to mend those huts, let's give him a hand."

With the cheerful assistance of men from a nearby naval air-station, they laid floors, mended roofs and put in stoves and window-panes. When the first patient arrived, an ex-Frogman suffering from T.B.,

the second "Cheshire Home", St. Teresa's, was ready.

"My son is mentally ill and I can no longer manage him. As he was a bomber pilot, I think that he might listen to you. Please will you help me?"

Cheshire read this anguished letter and wrote immediately:

"I will take him into St. Teresa's."

When the man proved to be so difficult that he upset the other patients, Cheshire decided that he must open another home for men whose minds and nerves were broken. Called Holy Cross, it stands near to St. Teresa's.

Ceaseless work and several bouts of influenza made him so tired that his priest advised him to rest. Cheshire's reply was to work harder than ever until, quite suddenly, he collapsed.

Examination showed that he was suffering from tuberculosis of the lungs and, from hospital in Cornwall, he was taken to a sanatorium in Sussex where he had several severe operations.

Two years in bed gave him time to think and to deluge his friends with new ideas. Before his illness, he had meant to start a crusade to take religion to people who never went to church. He obtained some second-hand buses and, since he could not leave his bed, his supporters drove the buses round the streets and played recordings of his voice to attract people to listen and to enter his "churches on wheels".

Another of his ideas was to charter planes to take sick people to the Shrine at Lourdes in France where many miraculous cures have taken place and on his first weekend from the sanatorium he himself went there with a drainage tube in his chest.

Meanwhile, the Cheshire Homes still filled his mind. Le Court was rebuilt by the Carnegie Trust to become a place for the care of young people who are ill or crippled. St. Teresa's was enlarged; a new Home, St. Cecilia's, opened in Kent and there are now more than a score of others in various parts of Britain, India, Malaya and Africa. They are there to relieve suffering. Cheshire's work goes on.

More about the people in part 4

ROBERT OWEN (1771–1858) is often called "the father of British Socialism" because he put forward so many ideas to improve the lives of working people. After he left New Lanark to found new communities in America and elsewhere, people came to look on him as a crank. Most of his projects failed; he spent his fortune and died almost poor at Newtown but he was never bitter and the workers continued to revere his name. He was a pioneer ahead of his time and most of his ideas—nursery schools, state education, decent housing, national insurance, trade unions and planned towns—are accepted today without argument.

ARTHUR, DUKE OF WELLINGTON (1769–1852) was only forty-six at the time of the Battle of Waterloo. He lived to be eighty-three, to play a leading part in politics and to become Prime Minister. His opposition to the Reform Bill of 1832 made him very unpopular and his windows were broken by the London mob. He despised public opinion, danger, show and extravagance, but as he grew old he came to be regarded with enormous respect. Although there was a gay side to his nature, he was a lonely man and his marriage was not happy. Unlike Napoleon and Nelson, he was always modest about his own career and said that he would die to prevent the people suffering the horrors of war. He died at Walmer Castle where his bare, plain room may be seen unchanged.

ELIZABETH GARRETT ANDERSON (1836–1917) built up a large practice among the London poor for whom she opened St. Mary's Dispensary, and she helped to found the New Hospital for Women and the London School of

Medicine for Women. She found time to study for a doctor's degree of Paris University and passed its examination in the French language! While she was physician to a children's hospital she met James Anderson, a ship-owner, and they were married in 1871. When nearly seventy, Elizabeth went back to live in Aldeburgh and became its Mayor, the first woman mayor in Britain.

ROBERT STEPHENSON SMYTH BADEN-POWELL (1857–1941) was born in London, the sixth son of Professor Baden Powell, an Oxford mathematician who died when Robert was three. Known to his family as "Ste", B-P was educated at Charterhouse and he entered the Army in 1876. During his life he wrote over thirty books, mostly for soldiers and Boy Scouts, besides innumerable articles and stories. He could have been a journalist, actor or artist but he succeeded in giving more happiness and idealism to young people than perhaps anyone who has lived in modern times. In 1929 he became Lord Baden-Powell of Gilwell and in 1937 he was awarded the Order of Merit.

WILLIAM RICHARD MORRIS, later LORD NUFFIELD (1877–1963) was the eldest son of Frederick Morris who had various jobs in farming and offices; he was asthmatic and William, who wanted to be a surgeon, realized that he would have to be the family's main support. He was not an inventor but a born engineer with a flair for business and his fortune came from mass-production of cheap reliable cars. Always a difficult man to work for, irritable, touchy and often petty, he had the gifts of a leader who could win loyalty and high endeavour from those who served him. By the time of his death, his gifts totalled about £30 million and the work of the Nuffield Foundation will go on for generations.

AMY JOHNSON (1905–1941) was one of the small band
of pilots whose exploits led to the founding of regular air
services throughout the world. Besides Alan Cobham,
Byrd, Lindbergh, Kingsford-Smith and Bert Hinkler, there
were a few well-known women flyers including Lady Bailey,
Amelia Earhart of America and Jean Batten of New Zealand.
Amy's greatest achievement was in 1936 when she beat the
outward and homeward records to the Cape. Her marriage
to Jim Mollison ended in 1938 and she resumed her maiden
name and took up gliding and motor-racing before becoming
a ferry pilot. After her death the Amy Johnson Scholarship
was founded to assist girls to train for careers in aviation.

WINSTON LEONARD SPENCER CHURCHILL (1874–
1965) was born at Blenheim Palace, built in honour of his
ancestor, John Churchill, Duke of Marlborough. His boyhood was not happy for he felt neglected by his parents both
of whom he adored. He was devoted to Mrs. Everard, his
nurse, and continued to visit her after he was grown-up.
During his long and stormy career, Churchill held almost
every important office in the Government but his fame rests
chiefly upon his leadership of Britain during the Second
World War. However, if he had done nothing else in his
life, he would have made a name as a writer, a historian
and perhaps as a painter.

LEONARD CHESHIRE (1917–   ) was born at Chester,
the elder son of an Oxford professor. From Stowe School
he went to Oxford to read law. His liking for fast cars,
betting and night-clubs got him into various scrapes but he
took his degree and entered the R.A.F. in 1939. He became
the most celebrated airman of the war not only because of
his heroic record as a bomber pilot but because he was a

favourite with the Press. Like T. E. Lawrence, he courted publicity yet despised it; he was a man of immense courage with a deeply spiritual nature. In 1959 he married Susan Ryder who had worked in refugee camps, and together, they set up the Ryder-Cheshire Foundation to continue their work for the relief of suffering.

OTHER PEOPLE AND EVENTS OF THE TIMES

PYTHEAS c. 310 B.C.	Ancient World in turmoil after Alexander's conquests	Aristotle
JULIUS CAESAR 102–44 B.C.	Expansion of Roman Empire; century of internal strife	Pompey Virgil
HADRIAN 76–138	Roman Empire at its peak Pompeii destroyed Pantheon built	Plutarch Tacitus
ETHELBURGA and PAULINUS c. 597–647	Conversion of Britain to Christianity	Augustine Aidan
CUTHBERT 635–687	Mohammedan conquests checked in Frankland	Caedmon Theodore
BEDE 673–735		Wilfrid
ALCUIN 735–804	Rise of Mercia and Wessex Charlemagne founded Holy Roman Empire	Charlemagne Offa

473

ETHELFLEDA c. 878–919	Viking invasions Resistance by Wessex	Alfred Edward the Elder Athelstan Dunstan
EDMUND IRONSIDE 980–1016	Danish invasions; submission of English	Ethelred Canute
MATILDA 1102–1167	War in England Second Crusade	Stephen Alexander I and David I of Scotland
HUGH OF LINCOLN 1135–1209	England part of Angevin "empire" Third and Fourth Crusades	Henry II Saladin Richard I
JOHN 1167–1216	Normandy lost Magna Carta; civil war	Langton William the Lion
ROGER BACON 1214–1292	Barons' wars Conquest of Wales	de Montfort Llewelyn Edward I
EDWARD, THE BLACK PRINCE 1330–1376	Hundred Years' War Black Death	Edward III Wycliffe Chaucer
OWEN GLEN- DOWER 1350–1416	Peasants' Revolt Agincourt	Hotspur Henry V

JAME I OF SCOTLAND 1394–1437	Loss of English lands in France	Joan of Arc Henry VI
WARWICK, THE KING-MAKER 1428–1471 MARGARET PASTON c. 1424–1484	Wars of the Roses	Margaret of Anjou Edward IV Caxton
JOHN CABOT c. 1450–1499 SEBASTIAN CABOT 1476–1557	Discovery of America; sea-route to India	Columbus da Gama Henry VIII
LADY JANE GREY 1537–1554	Reformation; religious intolerance in Europe	Luther Knox Edward VI Mary
JOHN HAWKINS 1532–1595 SIR PHILIP SIDNEY 1554–1586	African slave trade Enmity with Spain Armada France weakened by religious wars Dutch struggle for survival	Elizabeth I Philip II Raleigh Leicester William the Silent Shakespeare

JOHN SMITH 1580–1631	First American colonies; Pilgrim Fathers	James I and VI
	France revived	Henri IV Richelieu
WILLIAM HARVEY 1578–1657	Civil War	Charles I Cromwell
	Rise of the Dutch Republic	Rembrandt
PRINCE RUPERT 1619–1682	France predominant Fire of London	Louis XIV Wren
WILLIAM DAMPIER 1652–1715	"Glorious Revolution" Wars with France; Blenheim	William III Marlborough
CELIA FIENNES 1662–1741	Growth of trade and overseas rivalry Union with Scotland	Walpole Newton Wesley
ROBERT OWEN 1771–1858	French Revolution Napoleonic wars Industrialization of	Pitt Watt Stephenson
WELLINGTON 1769–1852	Britain	Peel Grey Victoria

ELIZABETH GARRETT ANDERSON 1836–1917	British supremacy in world affairs	Disraeli Nightingale
	Advance in public health, education, trade unions	Gladstone Lister
	Rise of Germany	Bismarck
BADEN-POWELL 1857–1941	Boer War	Smuts Kitchener
	Motor-cars, aeroplanes	Wright brothers
NUFFIELD 1877–1963	Great War	Lloyd George
	Russian Revolution	Lenin
	League of Nations	
AMY JOHNSON 1905–1941	Mass unemployment	
CHURCHILL 1874–1965	Second World War	Hitler
	United Nations	Stalin
		Eisenhower
	End of the Empire	Nehru
		Attlee
LEONARD CHESHIRE 1917–	Cold War	Krushchev
	African independence	Nkrumah
	Vietnam war	Nasser
		Mao

INDEX

The principal figure in each story is shown in capitals, thus —ALCUIN. Other important people in the stories are shown in small type, thus—Edwin, 36–43.

478